Progressing Students' Language Day by Day

*To all children who ever learned an additional language
and every teacher who taught them*

Progressing Students' Language Day by Day

Alison L. Bailey

Margaret Heritage

Foreword by Paola Uccelli

CORWIN

A SAGE Publishing Company

FOR INFORMATION:

Corwin

A SAGE Company

2455 Teller Road

Thousand Oaks, California 91320

(800) 233-9936

www.corwin.com

SAGE Publications Ltd.

1 Oliver's Yard

55 City Road

London EC1Y 1SP

United Kingdom

SAGE Publications India Pvt. Ltd.

B 1/I 1 Mohan Cooperative Industrial Area

Mathura Road, New Delhi 110 044

India

SAGE Publications Asia-Pacific Pte. Ltd.

3 Church Street

#10-04 Samsung Hub

Singapore 049483

Program Director and Publisher: Dan Alpert

Associate Editor: Lucas Schleicher

Editorial Assistant: Mia Rodriguez

Production Editor: Melanie Birdsall

Copy Editor: Meg Granger

Typesetter: C&M Digitals (P) Ltd.

Proofreader: Ellen Brink

Indexer: Kathy Paparchontis

Cover Designer: Anupama Krishnan

Marketing Manager: Maura Sullivan

Library of Congress Cataloging-in-Publication Data

Names: Bailey, Alison L., author. | Heritage, Margaret, author.

Title: Progressing students' language day by day / Alison L. Bailey, Margaret Heritage.

Description: Thousand Oaks, California : Corwin, 2018. | Includes bibliographical references and index.

Identifiers: LCCN 2018000795 | ISBN 9781506358833 (pbk. : alk. paper)

Subjects: LCSH: Language arts (Elementary) | Language arts—Correlation with content subjects. | English language—Study and teaching—Foreign speakers.

Classification: LCC LB1576 .B244 2018 | DDC 372.6—dc23

LC record available at https://lccn.loc.gov/2018000795

This book is printed on acid-free paper.

18 19 20 21 22 10 9 8 7 6 5 4 3 2 1

Contents

PART III   LEADING LANGUAGE AND CONTENT LEARNING   187

Foreword

One of the most pressing educational challenges of our times is to better support all students with the increasing oral and written language demands of today's world. Recent reports by international educational experts, economists, and civics scholars identify the ability to work with new information and complex communication skills as essential to successfully navigate our 21st century global and information-based society. The world is changing more rapidly than ever. It is almost impossible to anticipate the job opportunities and societal needs that today's learners will face in the near future. Scientific knowledge and health and civics news are updated at a much faster rate than ever before. In this state of affairs, schools need to prepare students to be independent, lifelong learners. Diversity is another defining feature of our digital age of global intercommunication and mobility. Students and teachers interact more than ever before with people from diverse backgrounds. In this context, the languages students bring from home constitute assets to be leveraged and expanded for learners to flexibly communicate with ever more diverse communities at school, at work, and in their neighborhoods. To prepare students to be lifelong independent learners and skillful communicators, attention to language is essential.

Students need to learn how to participate successfully in the advanced language practices that open the doors to educational, professional, and civic engagement opportunities. New information is mostly shared via written or oral language practices (for example, paper or digital texts, face-to-face or Internet conferences). Even if supported by videos, graphs, or other visuals, it is through language that abstract ideas, multiple perspectives, and complex relations are taught, learned, and communicated to others. We already know from prior research that large proportions of students struggle with the language of reading, learning, and discussing ideas at school. Yet how to properly address these needs in the classroom remains a formidable challenge for educators and researchers alike.

Educational research and practice in this area is most likely to lead to significant advances only through a collaborative methodology such as the one proposed in this book: through teams of teachers and researchers tracking and reflecting together on individual students' language produced in situated and authentic content-area learning activities. Language proficiency is a vast construct; language learning is highly variable from child to child, and language use varies considerably from context to context. Hardworking, engaged, caring teachers can benefit from the support of research-based tools to identify which language skills deserve pedagogical attention and how to go about scaffolding those skills. Conversely, researchers need teachers' help to integrate practitioners' pedagogical expertise and to understand what is feasible and most effective in the classroom. While summative assessments make educational needs visible, research-based formative assessment is particularly well suited to inform the day-to-day classroom practices that can better address the urgent and challenging pending task of scaffolding students' language learning.

Alison Bailey and Margaret Heritage have led a program of research dedicated for years to understanding the development and the scaffolding of school-relevant language proficiency. Their extensive expertise and insightful collaborative work with teachers and administrators position their research as highly promising to achieve the urgently needed improvement in students' simultaneous language and content-area learning. Here, I highlight only three aspects of their innovative Dynamic Language Learning Progression (DLLP) approach. First, based on their analysis of an extensive corpus of students' oral language productions, their DLLP approach provides the missing stepping-stones to guide teachers on what to do to achieve English-language development standards. Second, their DLLP approach illustrates how language scaffolding needs to happen in the context of situated authentic content-learning activities. Their data reveal that as students learn new knowledge, they also need to learn new words, sentence structures, and ways of organizing discourse. Even in a content area, such as mathematics, that is often perceived as far removed from language, students also need help with language to understand word problems, mathematics instructions, and technical concepts. Third, by attending flexibly to the situated language needs of individual students as they perform specific learning activities, Bailey and Heritage move away from the teaching of discrete and decontextualized lists of language skills to offer instead an approach that flexibly attends to the multiple language skills and practices needed for a variety of school learning activities. This approach is aligned with the most current research that shows that language varies by context and that schools cannot wait for English learners to achieve English proficiency before they join content-area classes; it is only by participating in the language of mathematics, social studies, and science that students will learn the language of mathematics, social studies, and science.

Addressing the challenges in understanding or producing the language of a content area is not pertinent only to language development but lies at the core of content-area achievement. Attention to students' language during authentic content-area practices, as proposed in this book, will improve not only students' language proficiencies but also their content learning and deep understanding. After all, isn't it only once we can explain a newly learned concept in our own words that we have truly learned it? In paying more attention to an individual student's language in the context of the real demands of content-area learning, teachers will become more adept at addressing the needs of English learners. And in doing so, they will become more attuned to the language needs of all their students, bilingual or monolingual. After all, all students are learners of the language of school. The DLLP approach opens our eyes to the often invisible and context-specific language demands embedded in content learning. Understanding the ubiquitous and highly influential role of language in learning takes time and effort but leads to transformative practice. The DLLP approach offers an insightful and concrete framework to begin this transformation.

Paola Uccelli
Professor of Education
Harvard University

Preface

This book presents a research-based approach to assist K–6 teachers in understanding the progression of *explanation*, a core language function that cuts across the college- and career-ready standards in use in U.S. schools. The approach requires assessing English learner (EL) students' development of their explanation skills with reference to progressions of key language and discourse features, and determining immediate next steps to support their language development in the context of day-to-day language and content learning. This approach, the use of Dynamic Language Learning Progressions (DLLPs), is novel and comes about as a result of the national effort to create next-generation assessment systems for EL students.

The DLLP approach represents an extension of our prior work on formative assessment with EL students published by Corwin (Bailey & Heritage, 2008). To capitalize on this work, WIDA (a 36-state consortium for standards and assessment for EL students) invited us to develop the formative assessment component to complement the assessment work funded by the U.S. Department of Education. WIDA's interest in this work stemmed from a recognition of the absence of robust approaches to formative assessment with EL students and addresses issues of equity for EL students in their access to rigorous, high-quality instruction in core academic content areas, such as mathematics, science, social studies, and English language arts.

Purpose of the Book

New content standards integrate content and language in ways prior standards have never done. The increased emphasis on communication and collaboration in new standards compared with prior standards requires teachers to understand relationships between content learning and the nature of the language that students will need in order to understand content and display their understanding to others (Bailey, 2017; Bailey, Blackstock-Bernstein & Heritage, 2015; Bailey & Heritage, 2014, 2017). As a consequence, teachers of all students must attend to both language and content development simultaneously. This may well represent a challenge for content-area teachers lacking sufficient knowledge of language development and for English-as-a-second-language (ESL) teachers without sufficient content knowledge to engage students in language learning that supports content-knowledge acquisition. A further challenge for teachers is that new content standards describe learning goals at the end of each grade level rather than identify the detailed intra-grade development of underlying or relevant language skills necessary for meeting these goals. The DLLP approach is designed to address these collective challenges and support opportunities for EL students to learn English and access the content areas.

Recent English language development (ELD) standards and frameworks created by states and consortia taking account of the new content standards have primarily focused on the scholastic *contexts* (i.e., mathematics, English language arts, literacy uses in science and history) in which English language knowledge is necessary. As such, the ELD standards are useful for explicitly articulating the language used in service of disciplinary practices or routines.

Lately, however, less attention has been paid to the linguistic *content* of the ELD standards—for example, how students' extended talk is coherent and cohesive or expresses sophisticated relationships between ideas using sophisticated vocabulary and sentence structures and how their language might progress over time as a result of learning and development. Teachers need the level of detailed knowledge that the DLLP approach provides to understand development and act on that understanding to continuously move language and content learning forward. The book represents a unique contribution to the fields of both general education and second-language acquisition.

Hallmarks of the DLLP Approach

The DLLP approach captures the development of several high-leverage language and discourse features that students need to acquire as they engage in a range of contexts of explanation language use, including core disciplinary ideas in school. The DLLP approach is dynamic because (1) it is designed to capture multiple pathways to the development of English language proficiency and (2) the progressions are designed to take account of multiple facets that influence the pathways of development, for example, contexts of language use and students' backgrounds.

The DLLP approach places a strong emphasis on the pedagogical advantages of using language corpora for teaching. Indeed, the DLLP approach is conceived of as a tool that helps teachers become aware of the language features used by their students in order to implement formative assessment practices (Bailey, Blackstock-Bernstein, Ryan, & Pitsoulakis, 2016). The DLLP project used new longitudinal corpus data from K–6 students to provide a data-driven model of how language learning progresses, which can help educators refine their teaching and assessment practices. In addition, the DLLP approach can be used as a tool by students as part of self-assessment routines to track the progression of their own language learning.

Research Basis of the DLLP Approach

The DLLP team analyzed students' oral explanations for a personal routine (teeth cleaning) and a mathematics activity (finding the number of cubes with the choice of counting, repeated addition, or multiplying groups of cubes). The increasing sophistication of language and discourse features that the project identified can be arrayed on progressions intended to assist teachers in gauging the characteristics of language that students from diverse language backgrounds and experiences produce at the word, sentence, and discourse levels.

We invite you to take a second look at the photograph on the cover of this book. The image of the backlit leaves was chosen deliberately to bring home some key aspects of what progresses when we talk about language progressions. Notice that the main vein in each leaf is oriented to represent an upward line or positively increasing slope as on a growth chart or graph. But more than just being represented by increase or growth over time, language can develop in ways other than sheer amount or quantity. Language can become more sophisticated, and this is represented in the cover image by the complexity found in the interconnected smaller veins that create a web or dense network within each leaf. The DLLP approach is designed to unearth the nature of these complex "veins" or, in reality, the key language features of students' language development.

While the emphasis of the DLLP project has been on EL students, the project includes native speakers who can also be challenged by the communicative demands of college- and career-ready standards. We describe how teachers can determine the "best fit" of the students' explanations for the language features on the language progressions at one of four phases: *Not Evident, Emerging, Developing*, or *Controlled*.

The notion of formative assessment we present is one of a feedback loop in which both teachers and students play distinctive yet complementary roles in support of learning. In the course of instruction, teachers intentionally elicit responses from students during the ongoing flow of activity and interactions in the classroom (Heritage, 2010, 2013). Evidence gathering is planned and has a place in the "rhythm" of instruction, built in as part of the ongoing interaction that is essential to ensure that the teacher and the student are mutually and closely involved in a common purpose. The evidence teachers obtain provides them with the information they need to assist students' immediate or near immediate next steps in learning. Teachers also support students in assessing their own learning and in providing feedback to their peers. Our pilot implementations took place over 3 years in collaboration with several university demonstration school teachers and public elementary and middle school teachers. Together, we generated specific examples of how teachers implemented the DLLP approach and the tools they created to do this most efficiently. The teachers elicited evidence of student language learning during content instruction to inform their assessments using the progressions. We also studied student involvement in this formative assessment process.

This phase of our research was valuable for examining how the DLLP approach acts as an "interpretive framework" for teachers. We found that when teachers intentionally obtain evidence of students' language use in the classroom, they can consider the evidence in light of the progression, determine the student's "best fit" on the progression, and then make decisions about what is next in terms of the individual's language learning.

Who Should Read This Book?

K–6 teachers of both EL and proficient or native English-speaking students will find much in the book to assist them in their day-to-day instructional and formative assessment practices aimed at helping students access content and language learning. Additionally, we directly address school leaders and those who support them, such as ESL specialists and district administrators, in the final chapter with its focus on setting up and sustaining communities of practice as a means of DLLP implementation in classrooms. Finally, teacher candidates and their instructors in teacher education programs can benefit from studying and piloting the DLLP approach in their preparation for meeting the needs of diverse students in their future classrooms.

Organization of the Book

The book is divided into three parts. In Part I, three chapters provide background on learning progressions and how the DLLP approach was developed, as well as the use of DLLPs to guide formative assessment and instruction. Part II focuses on the different features of the DLLP approach at the word, sentence, and discourse levels of language—the discourse chapter coauthored with nationally recognized teacher Gabriela Cardenas. These chapters provide examples of student performances across language development status and in different contexts and content areas. These chapters also introduce a number of tools and proven teacher-friendly resources for use in implementation of the DLLP approach to formative assessment of language learning during content lessons.

In Part III, the final chapter addresses how to facilitate the implementation of the DLLP approach using communities of practice. We provide concrete tools, such as suggested meeting goals and agendas, based on our experiences with implementation in real school settings. We coauthored this chapter with professional development practitioners Nancy Gerzon and Sandy Chang and middle school vice principal Eusebio Martinez.

We include a description of the structure of the communities of practice that were, by design, across grade levels and centered on three main questions at each meeting: *How did you obtain evidence of a student's current phase of language learning? Using the DLLP approach, what did the evidence tell you about the student's language? What will you do next to move this student's language learning forward?* Again, extensive examples of the teachers' experiences are included, specifically the value of cross-grade communities of practice for illuminating the growth of language or the absence of growth over time. We also provide access to websites for teachers to listen to audio recordings of students' explanations placed at different phases on the progressions. This will be an important adjunct for developing teachers' knowledge and skills in identifying students' "best fit" along the progressions.

We conclude with the words of one of our collaborating teachers, mentioning some of the benefits of their learning: "[Using] the DLLP has helped me become a lot more reflective about language development. It's helped me meet my students' needs, especially at an individual level."

Online Resources

For more information about the DLLP project, including tools for teachers and audio and transcripts of example student explanations, visit DLLP.org.

For video excerpts on the DLLP approach from professional development institutes, visit projectexcel.net/pages/learning-resources-2.

For six learning modules developed by the Oregon Department of Education to support DLLP implementation, see the section on Language Learning Progression PLC Modules at www.oregon.gov/ode/educator-resources/assessment/Pages/Formative-Assessment-PLC-Modules.aspx.

REFERENCES

Bailey, A. L. (2017). Progressions of a new language: Characterizing explanation development for assessment with young language learners. *Annual Review of Applied Linguistics, 37,* 241–263.

Bailey, A. L., Blackstock-Bernstein, A., & Heritage, M. H. (2015). At the intersection of mathematics and language: Examining mathematical explanations of English proficient and English language learner students. *Journal of Mathematical Behavior, 40,* 6–28. http://dx.doi.org/10.1016/j.jmathb.2015.03.007

Bailey, A. L., Blackstock-Bernstein, A., Ryan, E., & Pitsoulakis, D. (2016). Data mining with natural language processing and corpus linguistics: Unlocking access to school-children's language in contexts to improve instructional and assessment practices. In S. El Atia, O. Zaiane, & D. Ipperciel (Eds.), *Data mining and learning analytics in educational research* (pp. 255–275). Malden, MA: Wiley-Blackwell.

Bailey, A. L., & Heritage, M. (2008). *Formative assessment for literacy, grades K–6: Building reading and academic language skills across the curriculum.* Thousand Oaks, CA: Corwin.

Bailey, A. L., & Heritage, M. (2014). The role of language learning progressions in improving instruction and assessment of English language learners. *TESOL Quarterly, 48*(3), 480–505.

Bailey, A. L., & Heritage, M. (2017). Imperatives for teacher education: Findings from studies of effective teaching for English language learners. In M. Peters, B. Cowie, & I. Menter (Eds.), *A companion to research in teacher education* (pp. 697–712). Berlin: Springer.

Heritage, M. (2010). *Formative assessment: Making it happen in the classroom.* Thousand Oaks, CA: Corwin.

Heritage, M. (2013). *Formative assessment: A process of inquiry and action.* Cambridge, MA: Harvard Education Press.

Acknowledgments

Above all, we thank the students, teachers, and administrators who participated in the generation of thousands of explanations to create the DLLP corpus. We also thank Anne Blackstock-Bernstein, Despina Pitsoulakis Goral, Cindy Lee, Marlen Perez Quintero, Karla Rivera-Torres, Eve Ryan, and Amy Woodbridge at UCLA; Kimberly Kelly at CSULB; and Ali Abedi, Sandy Chang, Markus Iseli, and Barbara Jones at CRESST, as well as numerous other students, visiting scholars, and colleagues for all of their feedback and assistance over the years with data collection, transcription, coding, analysis, programming, and web design. A special word of thanks to Gabriela Cardenas, Nancy Gerzon, Sandy Chang, and Eusebio Martinez for coauthoring sections with us. We also thank Tamara Lantze Lau for taking our unsightly scrawls and making them into useful graphics.

We also acknowledge Rita MacDonald, Gary Cook, Margo Gottlieb, Mariana Castro, and Tim Boals at WIDA and Laura Wright, formerly of the Center for Applied Linguistics (CAL), for their input throughout the project, and we thank numerous other ASSETS Consortium colleagues at WIDA and CAL for their feedback on the DLLP analyses and professional learning applications.

This work was funded jointly by the WIDA Consortium at the Wisconsin Center for Educational Research and the ASSETS Enhanced Assessment Grant from the U.S. Department of Education. However, the contents do not necessarily represent the policy of the U.S. Department of Education, so you should not assume endorsement by the federal government. Alison Bailey also acknowledges serving as a consultant and advisory board member for WIDA projects.

This write-up of the DLLP work would never have come to fruition without the generosity of time and the tenacity of Dan Alpert at Corwin. He and his colleagues Mia Rodriguez, Lucas Schleicher, Melanie Birdsall, and copy editor Meg Granger are gratefully acknowledged for their input and skillful guidance throughout the production of this book.

Finally, we thank our families: Frank and William Ziolkowski for living through and surviving the writing of a third book this past year and John Heritage for his continual support and endless reserves of patience.

Publisher's Acknowledgments

Corwin gratefully acknowledges the contributions of the following reviewer:

Michele R. Dean, EdD
California Lutheran University
Thousand Oaks, CA

About the Authors

Alison L. Bailey is professor of human development and psychology at the University of California, Los Angeles, working on issues germane to children's linguistic, social, and educational development. She has published widely in these areas, most recently in *Annual Review of Applied Linguistics*, *Teachers College Record*, *Educational Researcher*, and *Review of Research in Education*. Her previous books with Margaret Heritage include *Formative Assessment for Literacy, Grades K–6* (Corwin) and *Self-Regulation in Learning: The Role of Language and Formative Assessment* (Harvard Education Press). Other recent books include *Children's Multilingual Development and Education: Fostering Linguistic Resources in Home and School Contexts* (Cambridge University Press), with Anna Osipova, and *Language, Literacy and Learning in the STEM Disciplines: How Language Counts for English Learners* (Routledge Publishers), edited with Carolyn Maher and Louise Wilkinson. She serves as a member of the National Assessment of Educational Progress (NAEP) Standing Committee on Reading, the National Council on Measurement in Education (NCME) Task Force on Classroom Assessment, and the National Academy of Sciences' Consensus Committee on English Learners in the STEM Disciplines.

Margaret Heritage is an independent consultant in education. For her entire career, her work has spanned both research and practice. In addition to spending many years in her native England as a practitioner, a university teacher, and an inspector of schools, she had an extensive period at UCLA, first as principal of the laboratory school of the Graduate School of Education and Information Studies and then as an assistant director at the National Center for Research on Evaluation, Standards, and Student Testing (CRESST) UCLA. She has also taught courses in the Departments of Education at UCLA and Stanford. In addition to her two prior books with Alison Bailey, her books include *Formative Assessment: Making It Happen in the Classroom* (Corwin) and *Using Formative Assessment to Enhance Learning, Achievement, and Academic Self-Regulation* (Routledge Publishers) with Heidi Andrade.

About the Contributors

Gabriela Cardenas is a UCLA Lab School dual language demonstration teacher and the 2018 recipient of the Presidential Award for Excellence in Elementary Mathematics (National Science Foundation). Before teaching at the UCLA Lab School, she was a founding teacher at Para Los Niños Charter Elementary School in Downtown Los Angeles. Gabriela has 14 years of experience in the field of education, of which 12 have been spent working in bilingual/dual language programs. She is a graduate of the California State University of Los Angeles, where she earned her bachelor's degree in Mexican American studies with an emphasis on Latinos in education, and a master's degree in education with an emphasis on curriculum and instruction. Gabriela received her teaching credential with an emphasis in Bilingual, Cross-Cultural, Language, and Academic Development (BCLAD). Her interests involve supporting second-language learners through an interdisciplinary approach to teaching.

Nancy Gerzon is a project director at WestEd, where her work focuses on designing effective site-based professional learning, primarily in formative assessment. She currently designs online professional development for several formative assessment projects, including Formative Assessment Insights, a yearlong online course for teachers, and Student Agency in Assessment for Learning (SAAL), a foundation-funded project focused on developing student agency in the classroom. Nancy is passionate about creating site-based learning opportunities for teachers that support them in their day-to-day work. For more than 20 years she has led professional development and leadership coaching to assist schools and districts to design, implement, and support effective peer reflection and dialogue practices, including inquiry teams, communities of practice, video study groups, and school-level data teams. Nancy is coauthor, with Sonia Caus Gleason, of *Growing Into Equity: Professional Learning and Personalization in High-Achieving Schools*, which documents case studies of four high-achieving Title 1 schools and outlines principles of teacher support, leadership, and systems that contributed to significant improvements in student learning.

Sandy Chang, PhD, specializes in the learning and teaching of language and literacy, especially for English learners. She develops, writes, and provides professional development resources to guide teachers in the implementation of new standards, formative assessment, and language and literacy learning. She has been involved in research on academic language, reading comprehension, and assessment accommodations for English learners. Her work also includes reviewing research-based practices that increase state, district, and school capacity to implement college- and career-ready standards aligned with high-quality assessments. Sandy earned her PhD in human development and psychology from the University of California, Los Angeles, and her EdM in language and literacy from the Harvard Graduate School of Education. Sandy is a National Board Certified Teacher in Literacy, and she was a K–8 classroom teacher and reading specialist.

Dr. Eusebio Martinez, Jr. has worked with TK–12 English learners for over a decade as a school counselor, program coordinator, and administrator in New York City and California. His original research involved assessment frequency and impact on grades for English learners.

Dr. Martinez is currently working as an administrator in a dual immersion Spanish-language school in California's Central Coast. He is also currently serving high school students and parents as they determine their ideal postsecondary plans. Dr. Martinez's influence includes his latest book, *Degree or Not Degree: Five Ways to Know if College Is for You*, and his social media presence creating informational videos related to college/career options. Dr. Martinez can also be found on www.drmartinez.net.

When he is not helping students determine the best road to their success, Dr. Martinez enjoys spending time with his wife, Giselle, his children, and his grandchildren.

Laying the Groundwork

Part I addresses foundational aspects of the Dynamic Language Learning Progression (DLLP) approach. In three chapters, we provide basic definitions, the context of the DLLP approach and creation, the rationale for its use, and a description of formative assessment. In Chapter 1, we present our theory of action that guides the implementation of the DLLP approach. In Chapters 2 and 3, we give a detailed picture of the DLLP approach to formative assessment and how teachers can implement it to progress language learning in the content areas in their classrooms.

I didn't have this level of knowledge [about language]—definitely not. I've always been told that language development is important—I remember learning that throughout my teacher education program that I went through, but it was not explicitly taught like this. I gained a much deeper understanding of that progression and all the different elements to look at.

—Kindergarten teacher

CHAPTER 1

Definitions and Contexts

To learn is to progress. Whatever students are learning—soccer, chess, physics, piano, Jenga, history—with instruction, practice, and experience, they can progress from an emerging understanding or skill through increasing levels of expertise over time. This book is about how language progresses. Specifically, it focuses on explanation, a language function used to "convey understanding; a mutual declaration of the meaning of words spoken, actions, motives, etc., with a view to adjusting a misunderstanding or reconciling differences" (Random House, 2016). In other words, as a form of expository language, explanations convey information about how and why things happen. An explanation can be of actions, events, processes, motives, theories, or claims. Other uses of language may be embedded within explanations, or explanations may be embedded within them. These other uses of language fulfill the purpose of argument, justification, and description, among others.

The purpose of the book is captured in the quote from the kindergarten teacher on the facing page: to increase teachers' knowledge of language development—specifically, explanation skills—so they can better support language learning in their classrooms en route to college and career readiness.

Why a Focus on Explanation?

There are three main reasons for our focus. First, explanation is an important crosscutting language practice of the academic disciplines, used by students to clarify their thinking and consolidate their understanding. For example, explanation is important in students' acquisition of new content knowledge in (a) English language arts (Goldman & Wylie, 2011), specifically to promote conceptual knowledge and their English language proficiency skills; (b) in mathematics (Hill et al., 2008), to support the learning of mathematical concepts, procedures, and reasoning; (c) in science (Sandoval & Çam, 2011), to conduct scientific inquiry and procedures and to support the understanding of phenomena; and (d) in history/social studies (Leinhardt, 1997), to describe the causes of events and to support the analysis and interpretation of sources.

Second, assessments of college- and career-ready standards (CCRS), such as the Common Core State

> ### What Experts Say
>
> Arguments are essential to the process of justifying the validity of any explanation as there are often multiple explanations for any given phenomenon.
>
> —Osborne and Patterson (2011, p. 629)

Standards for reading and mathematics (National Governors Association Center for Best Practices, Council of Chief State School Officers [CCSSO], 2010) and the Next Generation Science Standards (NGSS Lead States, 2013), require students to provide explanations of their knowledge (see examples in box below). Third, student explanations can provide teachers with insights about their students' content-area understanding as it develops during a lesson, as well as about their language use.

Examples of What the Standards Say

CCSS.ELA-LITERACY.SL.5.3

Summarize the points a speaker makes and explain how each claim is supported by reasons and evidence.

CCSS.ELA-LITERACY.SL.2.1.C

Ask for clarification and further explanation as needed about the topics and texts under discussion.

CCSS.ELA-LITERACY.RI.4.2

Determine the main idea of a text and explain how it is supported by key details

CCSS Standards for Mathematical Practice

Mathematically proficient students are also able to compare the effectiveness of two plausible arguments, distinguish correct logic or reasoning from that which is flawed, and—if there is a flaw in an argument—explain what it is.

Next Generation Science Standards.
Constructing Explanations and Designing Solutions

Asking students to demonstrate their own understanding of the implications of a scientific idea by developing their own explanations of phenomena . . . engages them in an essential part of the process by which conceptual change can occur.

Sources: National Governors Association Center for Best Practices, Council of Chief State School Officers (2010); NGSS Lead States (2013).

Given the heavy reliance of the CCRS on students' explanations of their content learning, there is some concern about the pedagogical value of explanations if the content and conceptual understanding of what students are explaining are inaccurate or incomplete (Rittle-Johnson & Loehr, 2017). We believe that explanations are of value when they are given under the guidance of a teacher. For example, they can provide feedback to both the teacher and the student and an opportunity for making adjustments or modifications on the part of the student, often with teacher support.

This book is for teachers—all K–6 teachers. No matter the subject, the grade level, or the students teachers teach, explanation will be part of their students' learning and part of their teaching. The book is primarily about oral language, although we do include references to written language along the way to illustrate how students were able to transfer their oral language skills into their writing and how teachers intentionally capitalized on this to reinforce language learning in both oral and written areas. In this chapter, we address how students can develop explanation skills, the importance of integrating language and content learning, and implications for students who are acquiring English as an additional language. We will elaborate on these ideas in subsequent chapters.

Explanation Skills Can Be Learned

Most students do not arrive in school with fully formed explanation skills. But they certainly should not leave school without them! We know from studies of child development that explanations are important for revealing "underlying causal relations and properties" to young children (Legare, 2012, p. 183). Explanatory talk between parents and their children has been linked to the development of cognition, literacy, and later discourse skills (e.g., Snow, 1991).

Students need to develop the vocabulary, sentence structures, and organization of language that can "convey understanding" and must work with other students to create a "mutual declaration," for example, of the new knowledge they may be building together.

Figure 1.1 The DLLP Approach to Language and Content Learning

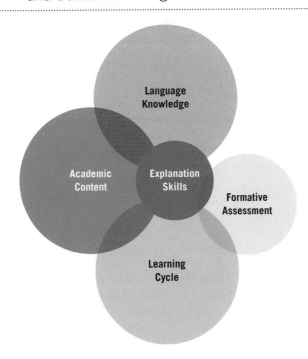

In Figure 1.1, we show the components that contribute to the development of students' explanation skills. Explanation skills are at the intersection

Key Terminology

Sociocultural Theory

Sociocultural theory is a view of learning stemming from Vygotsky's (1934/1962) integration of cognitive (i.e., mental processes), behavioral, and environmental perspectives.

Learning is socially mediated by the context in which it occurs, including by the actions of others toward the learner that may facilitate or hinder a learner's progress (i.e., internalization of new knowledge and skills).

One way that education researchers have operationalized Vygotsky's ideas about mediation has been to describe the graduated assistance (i.e., scaffolding) and routines that are set up for novice learners by more accomplished experts (i.e., teacher, peer, sibling, parent) (Wood, Bruner, Ross, 1976).

Vygotsky's theory proposes that learning takes place within the zone of proximal development (ZPD), which he describes as the distance between what a student can do independently and what he or she can do with the assistance of a more capable individual. Learning takes place when assistance is targeted to the ZPD.

Critical for later discussion of the dual roles of language and content learning are Vygotsky's ideas about the interactions between thought and language, which must be combined to perform higher mental processes (i.e., critical thinking skills).

of language knowledge (with its three interrelated levels of word, sentence, and discourse; see Chapters 4, 5, and 6 for details about these language dimensions), the academic content that is the target of the explanation (e.g., mathematics, science), and the learning cycle. Explanation skills are the result of learning that has occurred from the interaction among experience, instruction, and practice in the learning cycle.

Learning Language

Our instructional approach to language learning is grounded in sociocultural theory with its strong emphasis on the context of, and the participants in, the learning process. In an academic setting, students are constantly required to process language input from a teacher, another student, or written text. Occasionally, new knowledge is represented by nonverbal means—visuals, such as graphs, charts, representational models, and so forth—but by and large it is the interactions between student and teacher and between student and student that form the very basis of student language learning. These interactions are shaped in a variety of ways. First, teachers make modifications to their speech; for example, teachers do not make assumptions about students' familiarity with less frequently used words, and they avoid complex sentences that embed information within a longer sentence. As students' competencies increase over time, teachers (and more advanced classmates) begin to increase the complexity of their spoken language or the texts students are assigned to read, and as a result, language learning proceeds via graduated assistance or scaffolding—for example, modeling, prompting, or drawing attention to language features (Wood et al., 1976).

Second, students participate in classroom routines and join in at whatever level they are able to, be it with a single word, a set phrase, or possibly even a nonverbal gesture or representation (Bruner, 1990; Hawkins, 2004). For example, Sihan, a speaker of Mandarin and a newcomer English learner (EL) student in the second grade, is grouped with two English-proficient partners and asked to observe and then record the different parts of a plant. In this context, Sihan can be encouraged to sketch the parts of the plant so he is engaged and has the opportunity to show his content understanding. His partners can supply the names of the parts both orally and then in print by labeling the sketch. In this manner, Sihan and his partners have each collaborated in the task and fostered new language and content learning.

Araceli, a more linguistically advanced EL student, may be encouraged to discuss the observations with her partners, perhaps commenting on the color, the size, and the possible functions of the different parts of the plant. Explanations about the color, size, and function of a range of objects can be part of a classroom routine across the content areas that will provide Araceli with the necessary experience of core vocabulary and sentence structures to then extend to her engagement in the plant observation activity.

Routines are important to the development of language because they provide the learner with predictability of who and what is involved in a task. This can lessen the cognitive demands placed on students, who are then free to focus their attention on new content and the linguistic aspects of the interaction. Later, when students have acquired more language, they just have to map the language onto the already familiar classroom routines, such as pair-share, morning message, project presentations and Q&A and feedback, and collaborative inquiry projects—just as Araceli, a more advanced EL student, was able to do in the plant observation example given above.

Key Terminology
Disciplinary Discourse Practices

Disciplinary discourse practices are the "shared ways of knowing that make up [a] discipline."

—Airey and Linder (2009, p. 27)

The different content areas have each developed their own unique modes of understanding involving actions, tools, specialized vocabulary and genres, and representations of knowledge for the purpose of efficient communication among those who work within a discipline.

Successful participation in classroom routines by students who are learning English is important for fostering their positive affect toward language learning; how they feel about participating in class will be vital to how much practice they are willing to put into language learning in the future. The importance of students' positive affect has been emphasized by findings from a recent research study (James, Kobe, & Zhao, 2017). Among the important findings are that students decide whether or not to participate in classroom discussions depending on the classroom dynamic and their past experience with their peers, and the more students trust their peers, the more ready they will be to take the risks necessary to learn. The significance of trust between teacher and students is also a major factor in how well students are able to engage in learning (Van Maele, Van Houtte, & Forsyth, 2014). Consequently, teachers will need to create an inclusive, caring, and respectful classroom culture for student–teacher and student–student dialogue. Students must feel that whatever level of language they are able to produce, their contributions will be valued by their teacher and their peers and will never be subject to ridicule or sanctions.

Third, students who are engaged in authentic classroom tasks and activities are provided with a sense of communicative purpose—that is, how language functions to convey, for instance, a description, a comparison, a summarization, or an explanation. For example, students can develop an understanding of the kind of language used in a description and how details are made more vivid through the use of adjectives and adverbs, and they can learn the language used to compare and contrast phenomena—for instance, "While X shows this, Y shows that," or "X is this; on the other hand, Y is this."

These classroom learning opportunities are planned by teachers so that students can be exposed to models of, and participate in, the discourse practices of specific disciplinary content areas. These discourse-level understandings of language can even be established in advance of students' command of verbal or written forms of language as they come to understand how language is used to organize and present ideas and relationships between ideas in established ways. For example, explanations are frequently arranged into sequenced steps that provide information on causes and effects, include examples of a phenomenon, and conclude with sources of evidence for any claims made.

The box below contains student oral explanations at three phases of development en route to the most sophisticated and well-crafted explanations containing the discourse features just outlined above. We hope by the third and most sophisticated explanation in terms of discourse features, you will have grasped the mathematics task that students were asked to do! This will be a true test of the students' explanation skills used to communicate with an audience removed in time and space. The students basically needed to determine the number of colored plastic cubes given to them in a pile. It was left up to the students to figure out what strategy to use. They could choose to simply count each cube individually, skip count a set few at a time (repeated addition), or find ways to multiply the cubes (create an array of equal rows and columns, make piles of the same color and number, etc.).

Student Mathematics Explanations

Early Phase of Development

I just counted the white ones so, and the white ones if. And then there were ten, so ten plus ten equals twenty. And ten plus twenty equals thirty, forty, and fifty.

Middle Phase of Development

Use the cubes to use the cubes. Put them. Make them into a group and take two out at a time. Count them to see how many you have. Count . . . finish doing that when one—the first cluster— is in the second one. Then you'll know how many cubes there are. It's faster than using them by ones.

Advanced Phase of Development

You take the cubes and you start making a pile. And you keep going on and on until there are none left. And then however many there were when you counted. Because in division or multiplication, you can make different piles. And then for multiplication, you could get more cubes. It'll be like if you wanted groups of three and you had nine groups, so it would be three times nine.

What is perhaps most revealing about these three examples is that they are all produced by students in third grade. Due to the fact that EL students can start the development of English at any grade and given the high degree of variability in language exposure and experience, enormous differences in the sophistication of explanations can be seen across students even within one grade level.

Participation in classroom discourse can itself be a powerful mechanism for learning the other features of language (i.e., words and sentences). For example, the authenticity of the context will provide students with the motivation and the need to acquire new words and try out new sentence structures in their efforts to communicate more meaningfully and precisely. And of course, the more students are able to practice using their language skills, the more they will develop. By way of illustration: EL students in a class of newcomers to the United States were learning about subatomic particles in a science lesson. After watching a simulation, students were invited to work in pairs and come up with a question about what they had just seen. Maria and Jose were working together, and Maria started the interaction: *"For me the question is: because the s . . . the size is different. The size color is different."* Their interaction continues, and at one point Jose corrects Maria's use of the term *circles: "No why the atoms are together?"* Maria accepts Jose's correction and agrees with his question, then proceeds to add another: *"Why the electron is there round on the neutron and proton?"* (Heritage, Walqui, & Linquanti, 2015, p. 165). The students were given the opportunity to behave like scientists, developing questions from their observations, and were beginning to use some of the vocabulary they had heard that expressed concepts in their questions. While their attempts at formulating questions were not always conventional from a grammatical point of view, they had made some progress toward understanding how questions in English work, and with sensitive responses from their teacher, they were able to move forward to a more developed idea of questions in English while simultaneously developing their knowledge of subatomic particles.

We should not forget that students also learn language from their experiences outside the formal arena of the classroom. Home contexts are places where children naturally engage in explanations, often in response to parents' queries about what they learned in school that day! Informal school opportunities, such as during recess and lunchtime, also provide experiences for language learning and practice as students listen to their peers and communicate with them on a wide range of topics.

Language learning occurs in different ways across different contexts. Developing high-level skills in explanation will require recognition of the combined importance of students' own experiences, planned classroom tasks, activities and routines, and the opportunity to practice explaining for authentic communicative purposes, both written and oral.

Let us illustrate the variation in explanation skills that are demonstrated by one student in two very different contexts. Rafaella is in third grade. English is an additional language for her. She was asked to explain a personal routine—cleaning her teeth—in such a way that another child who did not know anything about teeth cleaning would be able to follow along and to explain why it was important to clean her teeth that way.

Rafaella's Teeth-Cleaning Explanation

I will ask her, "Do you know how to clean your teeth?" If she says no, I could explain her. I could tell her, "Look, first you get your brush. If you don't have one, go buy one. And after when you're done going buying one, buy a paste and a little yarn. And you get it. You put the paste first on the brush. And after you put a little bit of water, you start brushing your teeth." And why is it important? It's important because if you eat food, candy, or something that's not good for you, some food could get stuck in your teeth. And if you eat candy, they could grow cavities. And if you eat something that could stick on your teeth, and if you smile, like if you're going to take a picture, it's going to look weird.

Contrast this exquisitely detailed and well-organized explanation of teeth cleaning with Rafaella's explanation after she had solved the mathematics task involving finding out how many cubes had been presented to her.

Rafaella's Mathematics Procedure Explanation

We can use the cubes by using our fingers. And we could use them for we could get better our counting and having more numbers in your head. And they could help you counting sometimes if you don't know you could get some teachers something else for you could find out which number is it. And it could help you subtract and take away.

In this instance, she constructs an explanation that is far less developed and coherently organized than her personal routine explanation. Rafaella presumably has firsthand knowledge of and far greater personal experience with the routine she explains for cleaning her teeth. Her mathematics explanation may be impacted adversely by the challenge of completing the mathematics task, as well as the specificity of the vocabulary needed to refer to the mathematical strategy and operations she used to solve the task.

How Language Progresses

The language constructs captured by the DLLP approach include those constructs that deal with language at its earliest phase of development, such as imitation (without comprehension), single-word knowledge and usage, and the production of sentence fragments and memorized phrases, all the way through to more sophisticated productive or novel language constructs, including simple and complex sentences, making connections within and across sentences, and the organization of multiple sentences into different discourse genres or conventions (e.g., personal narratives, expository talk, opinion, or persuasion). The order in which a student's language progresses is predictable to a large degree because of the basic structures of natural languages; it is difficult to forge connections between words within and across sentences while still operating at the one- or two-word stage of language development.

Language shifts from the rudimentary to the proficient and productive in a number of different ways: Language can increase in quantity and quality; expand its repertoires for forms, structures, and functions; become increasingly accurate (conventional); exhibit changes in rate; and may follow a predictable order of acquisition (Bailey & Heritage, 2014).

Similar to the learning trajectories or progressions that have been developed for other content areas, such as mathematics (e.g., Confrey, Gianopulos, McGowan, Shah, & Belcher, 2017), the eight features or clusters of features of the DLLP approach are tied to big ideas about language concepts that emerged from our linguistic analyses of the corpus of student explanations and not to a specific set of language standards. Prior learning progressions have typically been based on students' performances on successively more difficult tasks or test items designed to measure the hypothesized order of sequence of construct difficulty—for example, in mathematics, test items to measure a hierarchy of concepts for ratio relations (Confrey et al., 2017) or the concepts undergirding proportional reasoning (Wylie, Bauer, Bailey, & Heritage, 2018). Rather than design discrete items or tasks on an assessment to measure word, sentence, and discourse features separately (e.g., testing students' abilities to spell and give definitions for a list of words or their knowledge of irregular past-tense forms in English), we chose to create tasks that simultaneously required productive language in all three dimensions to best mirror the authentic uses of language. We introduce these features in the next chapter and describe them in greater detail in Chapters 4, 5, and 6.

Integration of Language and Content

The language skills we described above do not develop in a vacuum. As we implied in previous sections, students need to talk and write about something to develop language skills, and in the academic context of school, students talk and write to learn content. The role of language to engage in deep and transferable content learning and analytical practices is emphasized in the CCRS. For example, the NGSS standards require students to ask questions, construct explanations, argue from evidence, and obtain, evaluate, and communicate information about the science they are learning (Quinn, Lee, & Valdés, 2012); the CCSS for mathematical practices ask students to explain, conjecture, and justify in making sense of problems and solving them (CCSSO, 2010; National Council of Teachers of Mathematics, 2014); and in English language arts, the CCSS include oral and written skills to inform, argue, and analyze (CCSSO, 2010). When students are learning the concepts, skills, and analytical practices of a particular discipline, they develop language skills as a means to think and also to communicate and co-regulate their learning with others (Bailey & Heritage, 2018).

While the integration of content-area learning and language is important for all students, it has particular relevance for those who are acquiring English as an additional language in school at the same time as they are learning content. Often, EL students have been required to "master" basic levels of English with the support of English-as-a-second-language (ESL) classes before they undertake any disciplinary content learning. While students entering school with little or no English will likely benefit from ESL classes for a period of time (for more information about optimal time spent in daily ESL instruction, see Lara-Alecio, Tong, Irby, Guerrero, Huerta, & Fan, 2012; Tong, Lara-Alecio, Irby, Mathes, & Kwok, 2008), the academic uses of language are the responsibility of every teacher (Bailey & Heritage, 2008; Heritage et al., 2015). Engaging EL students in worthwhile disciplinary content learning with their English-speaking peers and challenging them (with appropriate scaffolds) to develop the language specific to the kind of thinking and communication conventions of the disciplines are essential for their success in school and beyond.

Key Terminology

Emergent Bilingual

While we use *English learner (EL)* to refer to those students who have been formally identified by their school districts as likely to benefit from English language services to access the curriculum, elsewhere the education field has begun to use the term *emergent bilingual* to acknowledge that many of these students are, in fact, adding English as a new or second language to their linguistic repertoires (García, 2009).

Formative Assessment

Formative assessment is a type of assessment where the focus is on *informing* learning while it is developing, rather than measuring it or summing it up at the end of a more or less extended sequence of learning— for example, after a unit, after a course, or annually (e.g., Bell & Cowie, 2001).

Formative Assessment

In Figure 1.1 you can see that, in the context of integrated language and content learning, when students are engaged in authentic communicative activities, there are formative assessment opportunities for teachers to obtain evidence of students' skills with oral and written explanations. For example, in a third-grade classroom, the students were focusing on the structure and function of cacti in their science lessons. Toward the end of the study, the students worked in groups to create sculptures from found objects that represented their understanding of cacti structure and function. As part of their group presentations to their classmates, they wrote explanations on sticky notes. For example, Thiago, an EL student, wrote: *"I think they have spines because animals would eat them if they don't."* After receiving feedback from his peers, he put a line through *animals* and wrote *foragers.* He had learned a new word! Communicating their learning to their peers is an authentic interactive activity that helps all students learn more and provides the teacher with evidence of students' content learning and language use. With the information teachers obtain from formative opportunities, they can make plans about next instructional steps when they can intentionally provide scaffolding or models, or emphasize routines to support learning (e.g., Swaffield, 2011).

Sometimes the next instructional step might involve focusing on an aspect of explanation skills (i.e., at the word, sentence, or discourse level), while on other occasions the focus might be clearing up a misconception or assisting students to work through some difficulties they are experiencing with the academic content. In essence, formative assessment provides teachers with feedback about student learning—both language and content—which they feed forward to decisions about how to best advance learning from its current state.

Now that we have provided the basic components of the DLLP approach, let's look in more detail at our theory of action.

Theory of Action

A theory of action is a description of our intervention in terms of the relationships among inputs, outputs, and outcomes (Bennett, 2011). Figure 1.2 shows the DLLP theory of action for teacher and student outcomes.

Figure 1.2 Theory of Action for the DLLP Approach

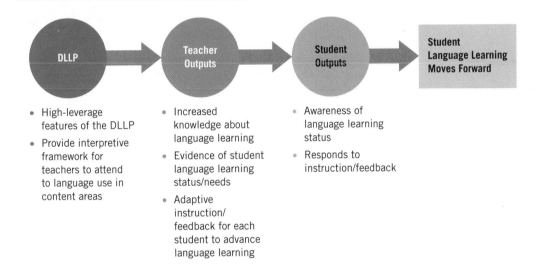

In broad terms, our theory of action hypothesizes that the input, the familiarization of the DLLP approach by teachers, will result in an increase in their knowledge of how language learning develops (output), which in turn will assist them to attend productively to student language (output) so instruction is informed by evidence obtained during formative assessment, resulting in improved language learning by students (outcome).

Our theory of action was put into practice during our DLLP implementations with different groups of teachers and those who were supporting their professional learning. From our work with these educators, we have seen how features of the DLLP approach provide an interpretive framework for teachers to attend to language use when instructing in specific content areas (e.g., mathematics, science, English language arts).

Key Terminology

Interpretive Framework

Teachers can use the DLLP approach to provide the big picture of language learning and to map the evidence of language they obtain from their students onto the DLLPs to help them *interpret* the "best fit" on the progressions to the student's language learning.

The teachers engaged their students in rich, disciplinary language instruction that incorporated word-, sentence-, and discourse-level features of the DLLP approach, described in Chapters 4, 5, and 6. Teachers felt it was worthwhile to invest in the DLLP approach for two main reasons:

1. They were able to plan and attend to language not as a separate entity, since they were already requiring students to use language in the content areas.

2. It made teachers more effective because they were intervening in learning as it was occurring.

What Teachers Say

And having this [DLLP] to look at made me more cautious to the decisions I previously made, to make sure that it's not just focusing on the content but also their oral language development.

By using the DLLP approach, teachers reported an increase in knowledge about language, language learning and instruction, and student language use. They were able to use the evidence of their students' language learning to adapt their instruction to support students' language learning. For example, in a mathematics class the students were asked *"What does division mean?"* From the students' responses the teacher was able to determine that several EL students did not have the necessary topic vocabulary to fully convey their understanding. The teacher made a note of this and decided to model specific terms, such as *repeated subtraction* and *equal groups*, in her discussions with students.

Notice that this assessment of language occurred during mathematics learning and not separate from the context in which the language was being used. This is an important point about teaching language and about formatively assessing language use.

Students in our implementation classrooms developed an awareness of language, incorporating DLLP language features in their oral and written work and transferring language knowledge and use between content areas (e.g., mathematics to science) and between language modalities (i.e., oral to written).

In summary, the DLLP approach can provide the input of high-leverage features as an interpretive framework, which results in teacher and student outputs with the goal of ultimately achieving improved language learning in the content areas.

What Teachers Say

What was fascinating to me was I was looking at science . . . [and] 90 to 95 percent of the students were using subject–verb agreement without any prompting, with describing what they were feeling. "It feels like" or "I think it feels like this," and it was just really neat to see all these complete sentences that came out of it with the subject–verb agreement from that. So my hope for next steps, probably look into how to deepen their understanding through clauses and connectors.

In the next chapter, we look at how this theory of action is operationalized by describing five key recommendations for implementing the DLLP approach.

Personal Stories

We would like to close the current chapter by sharing two personal stories about explanation. We started the chapter by answering the question: Why focus on explanation? We believe that these stories reinforce our answer by complementing the policy directions conveyed in the CCRS and associated assessments, as well as expert views of research related to explanatory talk, illustrating the educational value of explanation—a value that transfers into the world of work, with its increasing demands on complex communication and collaboration (National Research Council, 2012).

Alison's Story

The first year that the CCRS were implemented in my son's school, the principal provided a detailed overview of the mathematics and literacy curricula. She told anxious parents that mathematics was not the mathematics they had once been taught. They should not be surprised to learn that their children would be coming home with tasks involving new and varied ways to represent their mathematical understanding graphically and numerically, as well as through verbalizing their new knowledge. She explained that the students would be doing a lot more talking with each other in the classroom, too.

After the meeting, a number of parents were grouped around the foyer expressing concern. One mother was particularly disconcerted and vocalized her displeasure. Her son, instead of the teacher,

(Continued)

would be using his time in class having to teach other children how to do the mathematics. I asked what she meant. Her son, who she felt knew how to find solutions to problems already, would no longer be moving on to new and more difficult equations and word problems but would have to stop and explain his answers to other children in the classroom. "What is the point in that?" she said.

This was a rhetorical question, a bid for affirmation from our group of parents and not a literal request for an elaborate defense of the pedagogy she had just heard espoused by the principal. Unfortunately, I missed the call to parent solidarity and launched into a defense of the new practices, suggesting that her son's explanations to others would most likely help him cement or deepen his own understanding and that by teaching another child her son would make visible or audible to his teacher any of his partial understandings or misunderstandings of the mathematics.

Margaret's story is a counterpoint to Alison's and comes from her days as a K–6 school principal in Los Angeles.

Margaret's Story

In one of the sixth-grade classrooms, there was a student who was precocious in mathematics, far outpacing his classmates. His parents were naturally very concerned that he should be "challenged." To provide opportunities for this student to be truly stretched mathematically, we found a mathematics graduate student who was willing to engage with him in online conversations about mathematical problems that were considerably in advance of his peers. His parents were very pleased. However, we wanted to persuade his parents about the value of his staying with his peers in regular mathematics lessons so that he would have opportunities to explain his thinking in the lesson, something that was not his strength. His parents were not pleased at all with this suggestion and thought it was a complete waste of his time. We begged to differ, and the student stayed in the class. As the principal, I received a number of visits from his parents throughout the year, complaining about the arrangement.

Ultimately, this student went on to study mathematics at an Ivy League university, eventually gaining a doctorate in mathematics at one of the country's top schools. The year the student entered the doctoral program, we had a visit from his parents. They had come to tell us that we had been right and they had been wrong about their son staying with his classmates; they stressed that helping him become better at explaining his thinking in sixth grade had stood him in very good stead for his later mathematical education and that they were very grateful to us for this.

I was very pleased!

Together, these stories reflect themes we presented in this chapter, introducing you to the value of explanation for student language and content learning and for creating opportunities for teachers to engage in formative assessment. These ideas will be woven throughout the book as we introduce you to the ways you can support the development of students' explanation skills in content-area learning and also use explanations as part of your formative assessment practice. Teachers with whom we worked on the project told us how much they had learned about language development. They also became much more aware of the practice of formative assessment and the importance of collecting and using evidence of language and content learning.

The next chapter provides more details about the Dynamic Language Learning Progressions and how the approach grounds teaching explanation skills in the content areas.

SUMMING UP

1. Explanation is a form of expository language that is used across college- and career-ready standards to convey information about how and why things happen.

2. Explanation skills develop not in a vacuum but within academic content areas that are the target of the explanation.

3. Explanations can help clarify students' thinking and consolidate their understanding in the content areas.

4. Explanation skills require students to integrate word-, sentence-, and discourse-level knowledge and knowledge of the appropriate uses of language.

5. Students learn to develop skills in explanation through worthwhile, authentic communicative activities during content learning that require them to purposefully interact with their teachers and peers.

6. While we dedicate separate chapters to the word-, sentence-, and discourse-level skills involved in explanation, this is done for pedagogical purposes as we write the book and optimally support teacher understanding of the DLLP approach. In speech and writing, these language dimensions are integrated.

7. Routines and varied participant structures in the classroom are essential for fostering productive language experiences for all students.

8. Through formative assessment, teachers can gain from students' explanations insights into both their content understanding and their language development.

REFLECTION QUESTIONS FOR TEACHERS

1. How often do you purposely think about student explanations and intentionally make plans to include them in content-area learning?

2. How much do you think you already know about language learning? Was there anything in this chapter that was new to you? If so, what?

3. How often do you engage in formative assessment of your students' content and language learning?

4. What routines and participant structures do you already have in place in your classroom for enhancing language learning? Are there ways you might strengthen these?

5. What are you looking forward to learning more about in this book?

REFERENCES

Airey, J., & Linder, C. (2009). A disciplinary discourse perspective on university science learning: Achieving fluency in a critical constellation of modes. *Journal of Research in Science Teaching, 46*(1), 27–49.

Bailey, A. L., & Heritage, M. (2008). *Formative assessment for literacy, grades K–6: Building reading and academic language skills across the curriculum.* Thousand Oaks, CA: Corwin.

Bailey, A. L., & Heritage, M. (2014). The role of language learning progressions in improved instruction and assessment of English language learners. *TESOL Quarterly, 48*(3), 480–506.

Bailey, A. L., & Heritage, M. (2018). *Self-regulation in learning: The role of language and formative assessment.* Cambridge, MA: Harvard Education Press.

Bell, B., & Cowie, B. (2001). *Formative assessment and science education.* Dordrecht, The Netherlands: Kluwer.

Bennett, R. E. (2011). Formative assessment: A critical review. *Assessment in Education: Principles, Policy & Practice, 18*(1), 5–25.

Bruner, J. S. (1990). *Acts of meaning* (Vol. 3). Cambridge, MA: Harvard University Press.

Confrey, J., Gianopulos, G., McGowan, W., Shah, M., & Belcher, M. (2017). Scaffolding learner-centered curricular coherence using learning maps and diagnostic assessments designed around mathematics learning trajectories. *ZDM Mathematics Education, 49*(5), 717–734.

García, O. (2009). Emergent bilinguals and TESOL: What's in a name? *TESOL Quarterly, 43*(2), 322–326.

Goldman, S., & Wiley, J. (2011). Discourse analysis: Written text. In N. K. Duke & M. H. Mallette (Eds.), *Literacy research methodologies* (2nd ed., pp. 104–134). New York, NY: Guilford.

Hawkins, M. R. (2004). Researching English language and literacy development in schools. *Educational Researcher, 33*(3), 14–25.

Heritage, M., Walqui, A., & Linquanti, R. (2015). *English language learners and the new standards: Developing language, content knowledge, and analytical practices in the classroom.* Cambridge, MA: Harvard Education Press.

Hill, H. C., Blunk, M. L., Charalambous, C. Y., Lewis, J. M., Phelps, G. C., Sleep, L., & Ball, D. L. (2008). Mathematical knowledge for teaching and the mathematical quality of instruction: An exploratory study. *Cognition and Instruction, 26*(4), 430–511.

James, J. H., Kobe, J., & Zhao, X. (2017). Examining the role of trust in shaping children's approaches to peer dialogue. *Teachers College Record, 119*(10), 1–34.

Lara-Alecio, R., Tong, F., Irby, B. J., Guerrero, C., Huerta, M., & Fan, Y. (2012). The effect of an instructional intervention on middle school English learners' science and English reading achievement. *Journal of Research in Science Teaching, 49*(8), 987–1011.

Legare, C. H. (2012). Exploring explanation: Explaining inconsistent evidence informs exploratory, hypothesis-testing behavior in young children. *Child Development, 83*(1), 173–185.

Leinhardt, G. (1997). Instructional explanations in history. *International Journal of Educational Research, 27*(3), 221–232.

National Council of Teachers of Mathematics. (2014). *Principles into actions: Ensuring mathematical success for all.* Reston, VA: Author.

National Governors Association Center for Best Practices, Council of Chief State School Officers (CCSSO). (2010). *Common Core State Standards.* Washington, DC: Author.

National Research Council. (2012). *Education for life and work.* Washington, DC: National Academies Press.

NGSS Lead States. (2013). *Next Generation Science Standards: For states, by states.* Washington, DC: National Academies Press.

Osborne, J. F., & Patterson, A. (2011). Scientific argument and explanation: A necessary distinction? *Science Education, 95*(4), 627–638.

Quinn, H., Lee, O., & Valdés, G. (2012). Language demands and opportunities in relation to Next Generation Science Standards for English language learners: What teachers need to know. *Commissioned Papers on Language and Literacy Issues in the Common Core State Standards and Next Generation Science Standards,* Stanford University, Understanding Language Initiative.

Random House. (2016). *Webster's unabridged dictionary.* Retrieved from http://unabridged .merriam-webster.com/

Rittle-Johnson, B., & Loehr, A. M. (2017). Eliciting explanations: Constraints on when self-explanation aids learning. *Psychonomic Bulletin & Review, 24,* 1501–1510.

Sandoval, W. A., & Çam, A. (2011). Elementary children's judgments of the epistemic status of sources of justification. *Science Education, 95*(3), 383–408.

Snow, C. E. (1991). The theoretical basis for relationships between language and literacy in development. *Journal of Research in Childhood Education, 6*(1), 5–10.

Swaffield, S. (2011). Getting to the heart of authentic assessment for learning. *Assessment in Education: Principles, Policy & Practice, 18*(4), 433–449.

Tong, F., Lara-Alecio, R., Irby, B., Mathes, P., & Kwok, O. M. (2008). Accelerating early academic oral English development in transitional bilingual and structured English immersion programs. *American Educational Research Journal, 45*(4), 1011–1044.

Van Maele, D., Van Houtte, M., & Forsyth, P. (2014). Introduction: Trust as a matter of equity and excellence in education. In D. Van Maele, P. Forsyth, & M. Van Houtte (Eds.), *Trust and school life: The role of trust for learning, teaching, leading, and bridging* (pp. 1–36). Dordrecht, The Netherlands: Springer.

Vygotsky, L. S. (1962). *Thought and language* (E. Hanfmann & G. Vakar, Trans.). Cambridge, MA: MIT Press. (Original work published 1934)

Wood, D., Bruner, J. S., & Ross, G. (1976). The role of tutoring in problem solving. *Journal of Child Psychology and Psychiatry, 17*(2), 89–100.

Wylie, C., Bauer, M., Bailey, A. L., & Heritage, M. (2018). Formative assessment of mathematics and language: Applying companion learning progressions to reveal greater insights to teachers. In A. L. Bailey, C. Maher, & L. C. Wilkinson (Eds.), *Language, literacy and learning in the STEM disciplines: How language counts for English learners* (pp. 143–168). New York, NY: Routledge.

What I enjoyed most about this process is really bringing to light the importance of oral language. We talk about it all the time, but it's looking at these progressions in the different areas. It really makes it evident and obvious, at least to me, what are the things I can be working on in the classroom and what I should be listening in on. So that way I can incorporate it into the content that we're currently working on.

—Elementary teacher

CHAPTER 2

What Is the DLLP Approach?

The preceding quote from an elementary teacher sums up the value of the Dynamic Language Learning Progression (DLLP) approach: Working from the DLLPs, she is clear about what language she wants to focus on so she can incorporate that specific language into her content lessons. She can also listen for this language as her students discuss what they are learning. Listening to what students say is a formative assessment opportunity; the teacher can assess how students are using the target language and make instructional responses that support language development.

Let us look at an example of what this teacher means.

Notice in this excerpt from a first-grade, dual-language mathematics class how the teacher is focusing on the topic vocabulary *partition*, which her student has yet to incorporate as part of her own mathematics vocabulary. The teacher is using her exchange with the student as a formative assessment opportunity, not only to understand her mathematical thinking but also to listen for the use of specific topic vocabulary. The student uses "split them up" instead of the mathematical term *partition*. When the teacher hears the student say "split them up," rather than correcting her, the teacher uses the words *partition* and *partitioned* in her responses, modeling the terms for her student so she can hear them again in context.

Student:	I'm gonna split them up?
Teacher:	You're going to split them up. So you're going to partition them into how many groups?
Student:	Um, four.
Teacher:	Four groups?
Student:	Yes.
Teacher:	Okay. Go ahead. I'm going to come back and see how you partitioned that 92 into the four groups. I noticed the strategy you used with hundreds. Now I want to see what that strategy looks like with tens and two ones.

When the teacher returns to see the student's strategy, she will be focusing not only on the student's mathematical solution but also on the language the student uses to explain it.

In the first part of the chapter, we will describe what the DLLP approach is and how the progressions of different language features were developed. In the second part, we will provide recommendations for how teachers can implement the DLLP approach to advance language learning in the context of content-area learning in their classrooms. These recommendations come from lessons learned from two pilot implementations of the DLLPs. (See Appendix 2A for information about our pilot schools and teachers and for more details on the research study procedures.)

What Is the DLLP Approach?

The basic idea of a learning progression is well captured in this quote:

> Kids learn. They start out by knowing and being able to do little, and over time they know and can do more, lots more. Their thinking becomes more and more sophisticated. (Mosher, 2011, p. 2)

Learning progressions (or trajectories as they are often referred to in mathematics) are descriptions of how student learning in a content area develops from its most rudimentary forms through increasingly sophisticated states as students move through school (Bailey & Heritage, 2008; Corcoran, Mosher, & Rogat, 2009; Heritage, 2008; Smith, Wiser, Anderson, & Krajcik, 2006; Sztajn, Confrey, Wilson, & Edgington, 2012). Progressions lay out the significant steps that students tend to or are likely to follow as they develop knowledge and skills associated with particular content areas. As such, they describe development over an extended period of time. While they represent development in learning, progressions are not developmentally inevitable. Students' movement along the progression depends on quality teaching and learning opportunities.

Just as progressions lay out what it means to "develop" in an area of learning, the DLLPs describe how students' explanations become more sophisticated between kindergarten and Grade 6. The purpose of the DLLP approach is to provide a framework for teachers to use in support of students' language learning and formative assessment in the content areas. The DLLPs help teachers make decisions about specific language they need to focus on in particular content areas (as we saw in the opening vignette). They use the DLLPs as reference points to interpret the evidence they obtain about language from formative assessment opportunities during learning. Then with reference to the DLLPs, teachers can decide what they need to do next to promote language learning.

While the DLLP approach is relevant for all students, it has particular salience for English learner (EL) students who are acquiring language at the same time as they are engaged in content-area learning, for example, science, mathematics, social studies, and English language arts.

How Is the DLLP Approach Different From Standards?

Standards describe what students are expected to learn by the end of a year or the end of a course. Summative assessment is used to determine whether students have met the standard or not, and a range of decisions, such as placement, certification, and ranking, are made from the results of these assessments. Standards do not provide the level of detail that teachers need to plan instruction and use formative assessment integrated into instruction as a means to continuously advance student learning. Progressions can describe the intra-grade-level development of language—in other words, the incremental changes that occur in students' learning from one year's standard to the next as students become increasingly sophisticated in a particular content area. The DLLPs provide the detail necessary for teachers to pay attention to language day by day in their classrooms in any content area.

Importantly, the DLLPs are not organized by end-of-grade-level expectations as standards are. The language features that make up the DLLP approach are not specific to particular grade levels or subject areas. Instead teachers decide what language is specific and important to the content the students are learning, weave this into their teaching, and then assess its development using the DLLPs. That is, it is the content of the grade-level lessons that determines the language that gets assessed. Irrespective of grade level, teachers establish where students' language fits on the DLLPs so they can make plans about how to move language learning forward in their content areas.

In the particular case of EL students, recent English language development (ELD) standards and frameworks created by states and consortia (e.g., California Department of Education, 2012; Council of Chief State School Officers, 2012) that correspond to content standards have primarily focused on the scholastic *contexts* (i.e., mathematics, English language arts, literacy uses in science and history) in which English knowledge will be necessary. As such, the ELD standards are useful for explicitly articulating language used in service of content-area tasks and routines and are a significant improvement over previous ELD standards that often did not capture the language students frequently encounter and need in school (Bailey & Huang, 2011).

Less attention, however, has been paid to linguistic *content* (e.g., a repertoire of word types, cohesive devices in oral discourse and text, complex sentence structures) of ELD standards and how this content might progress over time as a result of learning and development. For instance, the New Language Arts Progressions of New York State (Engage NY, 2014), designed for students learning English as a new or second language, describe the instructional support students at different levels of English proficiency may need to achieve the Common Core State Standards for English Language Arts (Common Core State Standards Initiative, 2010). The productive (speaking, writing) progressions refer to "use" of information, whereas the receptive progressions refer to the "organization" of information, without further elaboration on the manner in which different features of language use and organization progress. For this reason, while ELD standards corresponding to content standards can serve as a general guide for teachers of EL students, they lack the specificity needed to describe the incremental language learning that needs to occur to support students' acquisition of English in school (Bailey & Heritage, 2014).

It may be said that what is good for EL students is good for all students. While especially relevant to EL students, by focusing on linguistic content in detail, the DLLP approach can assist K–6 teachers to support all their students' language development across the content areas.

How Does the DLLP Approach Work With Curricula?

The DLLP approach to formative assessment of language is not an ELD curriculum. The DLLP approach is not a substitute for whatever scope and sequence or basic set of plans lays out the anticipated content of ELD units and lessons. This is important to note because the progressions are focused on student explanatory language skills specifically, and EL students may need to build additional language abilities that will help them acquire other important language functions used in the classroom, such as recounting, arguing, and summarizing. While these functions will share many of the language features captured in the DLLPs for explanations, there may be aspects of language unique to these additional functions that teachers must also assist students with learning (e.g., using paraphrasing and concise superordinate category words for producing well-crafted summaries).

Also the DLLPs focus on student oral language production (and written explanations that we report on in Appendix 6F) rather than their listening comprehension and reading abilities related to explanatory discourse, although these receptive explanatory skills may be called on by teachers in their instructional responses when modeling or exposing students to more sophisticated language usage in explanations.

The DLLP approach works with existing ELD curricula to support the day-to-day monitoring of progress and individualized teaching responses given to students. Next-step decisions may be supplemental to an ELD curriculum, especially if a student needs additional support with developing certain language features. A student's "best fit" on the DLLP can be interpreted to signal a halt in the pace of the curriculum so a teacher can engage with students where they are developmentally and work more intensively on desired language features. Conversely, a teacher's interpretation of the DLLPs may suggest students are ready to advance to other more challenging aspects of an ELD curriculum.

There is a second way the DLLP approach works together with existing curricula. This specifically involves the role of the DLLPs in supporting effective formative assessment and learning in the areas of mathematics, science, English language arts, and so forth. The DLLP is intended to support *all* teachers' work, no matter the content area. In planning units and lessons, first teachers will need to examine their curricula or standards and determine what kinds of language are required for the target content learning. As teachers review the standards or curricula, it will be useful to reference the DLLPs to help them think about the language features that are needed to learn content and that can be developed within a particular unit (see Chapter 3 for an example of this planning). Teachers will need to consider the topic vocabulary students will be acquiring and the sentence structures and discourse practices that will support the particular content learning. To make sure that the language learning is manageable within the content-area learning, it will be advisable to prioritize which language learning is most *essential*. With clear priorities, teachers can then consult the DLLPs for information about the language features they have identified at the word, sentence, and discourse levels and obtain the detail that will assist them in further planning their content instruction and their formative assessment of both content and language learning.

How Was the DLLP Approach Developed?

While the term *learning progression* abounds in the education field and is used to refer to many different things, ranging from task analysis to the order in which topics should be taught, empirically based learning progressions are centered on research about how students' learning actually develops, as opposed to selecting a sequence of topics or learning experiences related to disciplinary knowledge or personal experiences in teaching (Bailey & Heritage, 2014). The DLLP is developed from empirical research about how language learning actually advances.

To create the DLLP, we generated a large corpus of data from EL students and English-only or proficient students who responded to a set of tasks we designed. These tasks asked students to explain a personal routine—teeth cleaning—and how they would solve and explain a mathematics problem. An average six oral and two written explanations in response to the tasks were collected from 324 students enrolled in grades K, 1, 3, and 5 at the time of their first explanations. You can see the tasks we used to generate the explanations in Appendix 2A.

Most students were sampled in fall and spring of the same school year. A subsample of 100 students was first sampled in the spring of the school year and then sampled at two later points (fall and the next spring) after they had transitioned into grades 1, 2, 4, and 6, respectively. This sampling provided cross-sectional data across all elementary grades and longitudinal data of up to four time points across a two-year period. We deliberately selected schools to provide diversity in student ethnicity, family income, first language (L1) background (e.g., English, Spanish, and Mandarin), L1 literacy, EL status, English proficiency, languages of instruction, and student- and school-level academic performances. In total, we collected 4,300 audio-recorded oral language explanations, which were transcribed verbatim and entered into a searchable database programmed to analyze certain language characteristics, such as sentence length, average sentence length within an explanation, parts of speech (e.g., nouns, verbs, adjectives), and use of topic vocabulary.

The data were supplemented by human linguistic coding of the initial 200 explanations collected. From our analyses of these linguistic forms, we identified eight

Key Terminology

Cross-Sectional Data

Data collected at the same point in time from individuals who differ in terms of age or grade level or some other variable of interest

Longitudinal Data

Tracks the same sample of individuals at different points in time (e.g., as they move across grade levels)

groupings of language features along the three dimensions: word, sentence, and discourse. These dimensions and their features are listed in the next section, and much more information about them will be provided in Chapters 4, 5, and 6 to help deepen teachers' understanding and prepare them for implementing the DLLPs in their classrooms.

Expert teachers were also involved in the development of the DLLP approach, providing feedback to us about the utility and feasibility as they tried out the progressions in their classrooms. Additionally, they reviewed the progressions from the perspective of their own professional knowledge, providing feedback about whether the progression made sense to them. We refined the progressions based on their feedback to ensure that the DLLP approach would be feasible and useful for other teachers.

How Often Should Teachers Use the DLLPs?

The short answer to this question is frequently. There are two main time frames for using the DLLPs, and they are not mutually exclusive. In other words, they operate in tandem. First, teachers may decide to make some anchor assessment of students' language with respect to particular language features early in the school year. This assessment can be done by intentionally eliciting certain language features during specific content-learning tasks and then determining the "best fit" for each student on the DLLPs. At two or three points in the school year, teachers can check students' current language use of these features on the same or similar tasks to keep the context comparable and, using the DLLPs, determine how much progress has been made. While this information can be used to plan continued instruction for students, the time frame in which it was obtained means that this assessment has a more summative function (i.e., summing up what students have learned over an interval of a couple of months).

The second time frame occurs on a more frequent basis and can be used in conjunction with the first. During a lesson, teachers can intentionally pay attention to how students are using certain language features, noting what they hear from each one. Then either each week or every other week, they can review their notes in light of the DLLPs to determine the "best fit" and make decisions about next steps. This time frame does not preclude teachers from making decisions *in the moment* about how to advance language learning, which is the ideal way to work with the DLLPs and will undoubtedly happen once they become familiar with the details of the DLLP language features. When teachers are able to do this, they will have high levels of expertise with the DLLPs and with formative assessment.

How Is the DLLP Approach Structured?

The DLLP approach is focused on the language that students most predictably need to succeed in school. Students use language to interact with peers and teachers in specific ways in school, as well as to engage with the content of the curriculum (Bailey & Heritage, 2008). Academic English is characterized by the use of more precise terminology, the use of complete grammatical forms, and fully explanatory discourse (e.g., Bailey, Butler, Stevens, & Lord, 2007; Schleppegrell, 2004). It is important to note that students encounter many different forms and functions of language outside the academic learning context. For example, students talk to their friends about sports and shared activities (also using highly specialized vocabulary), voice their likes and dislikes; even within classrooms, they hear language associated with nonacademic uses and functions, such as language used to manage student behavior (e.g., having to listen to and follow directions). In our prior work, we have distinguished the language demands of the school setting among ordinary conversations or social language (SL) (inside and outside of class), school navigational language (SNL) (e.g., language necessary for dealing with nonacademic aspects of the school culture, management, and logistics), and curriculum content language (CCL) (e.g., language necessary for accessing academic content). In the sidebar, we provide examples of the likely language demands in these three contexts.

While the DLLP approach was created from student language samples based on both academic and nonacademic explanations, the teacher plays a direct role in fostering growth in CCL. The DLLPs allow teachers to focus on CCL as they monitor both content and language learning. Of course development of language is not compartmentalized, so support for language growth in this academic context will spill over to other contexts of students' lives, and by the same token, language learned from experience and practice in other daily contexts (SL and SNL) will also support development of CCL.

The DLLP approach is structured around the features of the three key language dimensions:

Word: According to the Oxford English Dictionary (2018), a word is "a single, distinct, meaningful element of speech or writing." This unit of language can occur alone or in a multiword group to create a phrase or sentence.

Sentence: Words are combined into sentences that are formulated by a prescribed word order and according to grammatical rules, such as agreement in number between subjects and verbs. According to the Oxford English Dictionary (2018), a sentence is "a set of words that is complete in itself, typically containing a subject and predicate, conveying a statement, question, exclamation, or command, and consisting of a main clause and sometimes one or more subordinate clauses."

Discourse: Sentences are combined into extended talk or text. The Oxford English Dictionary (2018) defines *discourse* as "a connected series of utterances; a text or conversation." Discourse requires the organization

Key Terminology
Academic English

"Academic English is commonly regarded as a register of the language; a register is a style of the language that differs in terms of the vocabulary, grammatical structures, and organization of language to suit the context in which it is used" (Bailey, 2012, p. 5). In other words, it is "the forms and functions of the language students can expect to encounter in educational settings" (p. 4).

Examples of Possible Language Demands Encountered in SL, SNL, and CCL

SL: *I took it* [= the lunch box] *out before* [= class]. [Assumes and uses shared referents (*it, before*) when pragmatically appropriate]

SNL: *I need you all to be facing this way before we begin.* [Requires comprehension of directions]

CCL: *First, the stamen forms at the center of the flower.* [Requires comprehension and production of explanations of scientific processes, procedures, etc.]

of multiple utterances or written sentences, often into a conventional or culturally prescribed format or genre—for example, monologic discourse, such as a speech or a personal narrative, or dialogic discourse, such as a conversation or a formal debate.

A foundational premise of the DLLP approach is that students progressively learn word, sentence, and discourse dimensions of language to become skilled users of academic language, both oral and written, in their explanations. In reality, these three dimensions of language (i.e., word, sentence, discourse) operate not as independent entities but rather as mutually dependent and integral aspects of language. The DLLP approach treats them separately *only* to assist teachers in learning about them and in focusing on them for the purposes of instruction and formative assessment. There is no distinction between the three dimensions when learning and using language. The ability to acquire and coordinate the dimensions of word, sentence, and discourse features of English in sophisticated ways enables a speaker to effectively learn new content in school.

At a more detailed level are the eight progressions of high-leverage language features. We refer to these features as "high-leverage" because they are important language competencies that K–6 students need to acquire to access the academic content of the college- and career-ready standards. As the content standards become more sophisticated over a students' K–6 schooling, the high-leverage language features will also necessarily become more sophisticated. Additionally, the features are high-leverage because they organize different features of language into the readily accessible dimensions of language for teachers to focus on. Figure 2.1 shows how each of the eight high-leverage DLLP features is organized by the word-, sentence-, and discourse-level dimensions of language.

Figure 2.1 Organization of the DLLP Features Into
Three Dimensions of Language

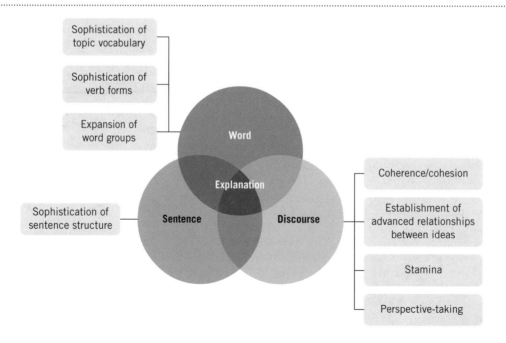

High-Leverage Features

Word

- **Sophistication of topic vocabulary**: a small core topic vocabulary progressing to a more extensive topic vocabulary and use of precise/low-frequency topic vocabulary

- **Sophistication of verb forms**: simple tensed verbs progressing to more sophisticated verb forms, such as gerunds (*cleaning*), participles (*having brushed*), and modal auxiliary verbs (*should, might*, conveying probability or obligation)

- **Expansion of word groups**: a limited repertoire progressing to an expanded array, including derived words, nominalizations (nouns formed from verbs or adjectives), adverbs, adjectives, relative clauses, prepositional phrases, and general academic vocabulary (words cutting across content areas with the same meaning, such as *report, analyze*)

Sentence

- **Sophistication of sentence structure**: simple sentences progressing to complex sentences, such as relative clauses

Discourse

- **Coherence/cohesion**: limited attempts progressing to the use of temporal connectors (*first, next, finally*) and different cohesive devices

- **Establishment of advanced relationships between ideas**: limited repertoire progressing to an expanded array, for example, through the use of causal (*because, consequently*) and contrastive (*however, while*) discourse connectors

- **Stamina**: no elaboration or lacks meaning progressing to a clear mental model of a topic with use of sufficient detail and elaboration for the listener to readily make meaning of the explanation

- **Perspective-taking**: no perspective-taking abilities progressing to the maintenance of appropriate personal pronouns (*he* referring to one student, *they* referring to several students, used unambiguously)

Key Terminology

Relative Clause

A dependent clause embedded in longer sentences, used to provide more specificity to a noun. Often begins with one of the following relative pronouns or adverbs: *who, when, whom, where, whose, why, that, which* (e.g., the groups of cubes that are piled here sum to 10).

Prepositional Phrase

A preposition followed by a noun phrase. It functions like an adjective or adverb (e.g., take a brush with toothpaste on it).

Temporal Connectors

Words and phrases that signal the sequence of events or actions in chronological order (e.g., First, create groups of five. After that, count the total number. Finally, times the number of groups by five.)

Cohesive Devices

Referential ties between words (e.g., referents introduced with full nouns, such as *the cube*, are then later referred to by unambiguous pronouns, such as *it*)

Adverbial Clause

A type of dependent clause that gives information about time, circumstance, purpose, manner, or condition (e.g., When I go to the sink, I turn on the faucet; Move the cubes from one pile to another as you count them.)

Noun Clause

Dependent clause that plays the same function in a sentence as a noun (e.g., as a subject [What I did first was sort the cubes], an object [I saw the teacher use addition], or a complement [It was easy for me to find the answer])

The forward movement along a progression is captured by the different possible ways language develops (Bailey & Heritage, 2014). These are (1) a greater amount of language, (2) language that is used where expected or called for with consistency, (3) completeness, and (4) a broad repertoire of different types for a given language form or feature. In essence, these four aspects capture the increasing breadth and depth of students' English language knowledge and use. The eight language features can be arrayed along a progression for explanation in four broad phases, taking these aspects of development into account:

- **Not Evident:** The feature is not *yet* detectable (or not used autonomously/productively; i.e., student borrows language from a prompt for an explanation), or the explanation is in a language other than English.

- **Emerging:** The feature appears but intermittently/infrequently or is largely incomplete; no repertoire of different types within a feature.

- **Developing:** The feature appears more often or is more complete; a small repertoire of types.

- **Controlled:** The feature appears where expected, is complete, and is most often used accurately; a broad repertoire of types.

Each of the high-leverage features can be monitored for these aspects of growth as Table 2.1 illustrates in the crosscutting descriptors of each of the four phases of the progression. Teachers can monitor students' language growth and needs as they go about their typical content instruction. Once opportunities for gathering evidence of student explanatory talk or writing have been identified, teachers will want to document student growth on the DLLPs in a systemic way. A simple tool for this purpose and for sharing with study teams, leadership, and parents can be found in Appendix 2B.

Table 2.1   Crosscutting Performance Descriptors of the DLLPs

DLLP Not Evident	DLLP Emerging	DLLP Developing	DLLP Controlled
• Feature not yet detectable (or not used productively) • Student explanation is in a language other than English	• Feature appears infrequently/ intermittently or is largely incomplete • Feature may be used accurately or inaccurately (errors or omissions)*	• Feature appears more often or more complete • Feature may be used accurately or inaccurately (errors or omissions)* • A small "repertoire" for the feature is evident	• Feature appears complete • Feature is most often used accurately • A broad "repertoire" for the feature is evident

*Language production may acceptably be "flawed" (Valdés, 2005) during these phases of development.

These descriptors are repeated for each of the language features but with the specificity of a given feature. In Table 2.2, we can see an example of the four performance levels for the feature *sophistication of sentence structure*. Notice how these echo the crosscutting descriptors in Table 2.1 to capture the different ways language develops but with a unique application to the sentence-level domain.

Table 2.2 DLLP for Sophistication of Sentence Structure

DLLP Not Evident	DLLP Emerging	DLLP Developing	DLLP Controlled
• One-word responses • Two or more word phrases not in English word order • Response in a language other than English • Sentence fragments placed in English word order	• Simple sentences • Compound sentences • May or may not be accurate • No use of embedding (dependent clauses)	• Must attempt sentences with complex clause structures (i.e., an independent clause) • May have repetitive use of one dependent structure, such as relative, adverbial, or noun clauses • May or may not be accurate • Simple and compound sentences mostly accurate/grammatically correct	• Use of a variety of complex clause structures, including relative, adverbial, or noun clauses • Simple and compound sentences accurate and grammatically correct • Complex clause structures mostly accurate/grammatically correct

As an illustration of the different levels of sophistication, below are some examples taken from the corpus of data used to create the DLLPs. The student's language status is included in parentheses.

No Evidence of Sophistication of Sentence Structure

"With a paste. And brushing your teeth in the bath, not in the room. And that's all." (English learner)

- Sentence fragments

"Because I have . . ." [codeswitches to Spanish]. (English learner)

- Response is mostly in a language other than English

Emerging Sophistication of Sentence Structure

"First I do the inside and the outside of my teeth. And then I do the middle of my teeth. And then I push my teeth together and I brush my teeth together. And then I rinse, swish, gargle, spit out." (English only/proficient)

- Only simple and compound sentences used

Developing Sophistication of Sentence Structure

"You need to go to the bathroom. Then brush your teeth. And you need to do it because one teeth can fall." (English learner)

- Simple sentences (accurate)

- Complex sentence with infinitive forms and adverbial clause (*because*)

Control of Sophistication of Sentence Structure

"You should clean your teeth because you could get cavities. And this is how you clean your teeth. You put some toothpaste on your toothbrush, and then put a teeny tiny bit of water on it. And then you brush for two minutes if you have that special kind of toothbrush I have. Like the one that turns around and around and around around." (English only/proficient)

- Different types of complex clause structures (relative, adverbial)

- Simple and compound sentences are controlled

- Accurate: most or all clauses are correct

As we noted earlier, the dimensions (word, sentence, and discourse) and the high-leverage language features are not separate entities during language use. They are simply treated separately in the DLLP approach to provide ease of learning and access by teachers. The DLLP approach should never be understood as a blueprint for teaching language as a series of discrete, atomistic features. Language features **should not** be taught in isolation from one another or meaningful uses of language but rather acquired in relevant, content-specific, language-rich activities and interactions. For example, instead of teaching adjectives as separate from the sentence or discourse in which they are situated, a teacher can ask: *What work does this word do here? Does it, for example, describe movement? Or does it show emotion? What other words is it connected to in order to convey a meaningful idea?* These types of questions about the work of words help uncover the various dimensions and functions of a language feature in a particular linguistic and situational context.

It's important to note that students will likely not develop high-leverage language features in lockstep; each student is going to be at a different point in his or her language learning across the array of eight DLLP features. In addition, it is unlikely that students will move categorically from one phase of the DLLPs to the next. Rather, students' language development will overlap from one phase to another. For example, the explanation below from Jimena, a young EL student, is categorized at *Developing* (Phase 3) for sophistication of sentence structure (e.g., correct use of the causal discourse connector *so* but also the incorrect use of *because* and the use of sentence fragments).

> *Because she should do it so her teeth don't get ugly and she has to do it. And how she do it is because up and down. And side.*

Given there is a mix of language elements that are present at both the *Developing* and the higher *Controlled* phases of this DLLP language feature, the "best fit" overall for this explanation on the sophistication of sentence structure progression is *Developing*. Making this judgment then allows Jimena's teacher to most effectively target instruction to those identified elements that still need instructional support for getting to an unequivocal *Controlled* level.

It is important to note also that on other features of the DLLP, this student's explanation may be placed at different phases to give the "best fit." For example, Jimena's use of the modal verb *should* suggests her repertoire of verb forms for the sophistication of verb forms progression is advancing, although we would not place this particular explanation higher than *Emerging* (Phase 2) because of the presence of inaccuracies in other verbs that may still need her teacher's attention—namely, the simple verb formation with a question marker (e.g., "How she do it"). Also in contrast with her relatively sophisticated sentence structure, Jimena's explanation would be placed as *Not Evident* (Phase 1) when it comes to having a clear mental model or stamina to provide all the necessary detailed information for a naïve listener to follow her teeth-cleaning routine.

Key Terminology
Modal Verb

Auxiliary (helping) verbs placed before a main verb. They convey notions of necessity or possibility and include *can, could, may, might, must, need, ought, shall, should, would.*

With knowledge about how language progresses from one step to another, teachers are better placed to interpret the evidence they generate in the classroom, pinpointing where individual students are with respect to vocabulary, sentence, and discourse, and to know what they need to do to advance each student's language learning from its current level.

Now that we have described what the DLLP approach is and what purpose it is intended to serve, let's look in more detail at our theory of action, a description of our intervention in terms of the relationships between inputs, outputs, and outcomes (Bennett, 2010).

From Theory to Action

Our theory of action described in Chapter 1 was put into practice during our DLLP implementations with teacher groups. From our work

Key Terminology

Interpretive Framework

Teachers can use the DLLP approach to provide the big picture of language learning and to map the evidence of language they obtain from their students onto the DLLPs to help them *interpret* the "best fit" on the progressions for the students' language learning.

with teachers, we have seen how features of the DLLPs provide an interpretive framework for teachers to attend to language use when instructing in specific content areas (e.g., mathematics, science, English language arts).

Figure 2.2 on the facing page shows how formative assessment of students' explanation skills can be made in the context of their content learning (captured by the upper arrow in the figure). Evidence of students' explanation skills, in turn, can inform teachers' instruction within the cycle of learning through instruction, student practice, and experience (signaled by the lower arrow in the figure). In addition, formative assessment includes both student self-assessment and assessment of one another's skills through peer assessment. The feedback these two aspects of formative assessment generate directly supports student practice and experience in the learning cycle. Students' own formative assessment practices rely on their autonomy and regulation of their own learning, and both presuppose and build student language abilities (Bailey & Heritage, 2018).

In the next section, we look at how integration of the DLLP approach with formative assessment of language and content learning is operationalized by describing three key recommendations for implementation. The teachers who participated in our DLLP implementations were all volunteers. We found that they had very clear ideas of what would work for them in the implementation, which have guided our recommendations below.

Recommendations for Implementing the DLLP Approach

Background Knowledge

What teachers we worked with wanted first was some background knowledge of the DLLP approach, what all the language terms contained in it meant and how each of the language features developed in sophistication. Most of them had learned about language development in their teacher education programs but not at the level of detail presented in the DLLPs. Once they had reviewed the support materials and discussed them in their meeting groups, they were ready to jump in and try something out in their classrooms. Of course, the more they worked with the DLLPs, the more knowledgeable they became and the more their confidence about their language knowledge increased.

The other area where some teachers were initially a bit uncertain was formative assessment. Like many teachers, their understanding of assessment was primarily as a frequent test administered to students to provide a score about performance. Thinking about formative assessment as an everyday classroom practice taking place as students were learning was a big mindset shift for a number of teachers. In the next chapter, we will focus specifically on describing formative assessment and how it works in the classroom.

Figure 2.2 Integration of the DLLP Approach With Formative Assessment of Language and Content Learning

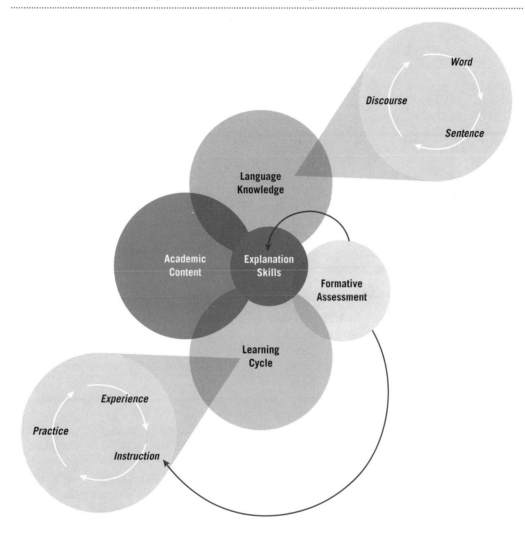

Teachers Learning in Collaboration With Their Peers

We know that teachers value the opportunity to engage in professional learning with their colleagues (Darling-Hammond, Hyler, & Gardner, 2017), and this was certainly the case in our DLLP implementations with teachers. In

SoFE

one of our implementation iterations, teachers met monthly in cross-grade-level groups over the course of two school years, in a community of practice (you can read more about communities of practice below and in Chapter 7). Typically, there were up to six participants, and they met for one hour to discuss the language features they observed in their classrooms, using the following simple protocol:

- What evidence were you looking for?

- How did you obtain the evidence?

- Using the DLLPs, what did the evidence tell you?

- What will you do/did you do to move this student's language learning forward?

- What language feature are you going to focus on next?

The teachers appreciated the protocol, which served to structure the discussion, permitting each teacher to report on his or her experience attending to the language features and select at least one new feature for the next month's round of observations. This approach also helped build a sense of commitment and accountability to the group so all teachers came to the meetings prepared to discuss what they had previously agreed would be their focus for the month.

Time is a scarce commodity in schools, and for this reason we limited our discussion time to no more than one hour per month. While this might not seem like enough time to learn about the DLLP approach and implement it for instruction and formative assessment purposes, we found that this time frame worked. The one-hour meeting gave enough time for teachers to share and reflect on their practices, and they had a month in between meetings to focus on certain language features, consult with each other as necessary, and put the DLLPs into practice.

Teachers also valued the opportunity to work across grade levels to develop an understanding of the language students were using up and down the grades. For example, in one of the group meetings, a teacher, new to the fourth-grade level, when discussing the use of causal connectors with a first-grade colleague, recognized the limited repertoire of causal connectors that her fourth-grade students were using, both orally and in their written work. She concluded that her current students demonstrated little or no advance in their use of causal connectors compared with the first-grade students' usage. As a result of what she learned during the group meeting, she decided to focus on expanding students' repertoires of connectors to more precisely express their ideas. She focused on these connectors when the students were learning about making claims and providing evidence, and she posted a chart showing the connectors in the classroom for students' reference. The teacher reported that this resource helped her students incorporate these connectors into their oral language and then ultimately into their argument writing.

As a team we were able to, you know, look at the school across all levels, one area that we were able to focus and there were some "aha" moments and we were able to develop something and meet children's needs.

Teacher Choice

We began our DLLP implementations with teachers by asking them to focus on the specific language feature *sophistication of topic vocabulary*, because we thought that would be the easiest approach for them. This turned out not to be the case! Teachers were very clear that they wanted to make their own decisions about which language features to focus on. They chose ones that would be relevant to their curricula and their current content focus. For example, one teacher chose to embed the progression for the *sophistication of sentence structure* feature during a science lesson on the students' observations of a creek's ecosystem. She reported how her lesson unfolded, illustrating how she used formative opportunities for language in the students' science learning and how she responded to students who needed more support for language use:

- I modeled sentence stems in my own language production during discussions of an ecosystem.

- I encouraged students to use sentence stems [I put a list of sentence starters on each table for use if desired] when they were writing about their observations.

- Most students adopted the sentence starters (e.g., *When looking at X, I notice Y; I observe Y . . .*) in oral sharing out following their writing.

- For those who did need more help (e.g., EL students whom I observed were only using temporal connectors in oral productions, not writing), I used small-group strategies, such as collectively looking at their writing to see where elaborated sentences could be used.

- I then decided on next steps for all students (e.g., students used different stems, depending on their language levels).

Another teacher wanted to use the existing routine of Morning Message in her kindergarten class to help her students' development within the progression of *coherence/cohesion*. Her beginning focus for this progression was temporal discourse markers. During the Morning Message session, the students routinely discuss their upcoming day or prior events with which they are already familiar. The teacher modeled the target discourse markers, which then began to show up in the students' oral productions. They asked each other questions such as *"What is your first, second, third favorite activity?"* While productions of students' own use of discourse markers may be unconventional and not necessarily related to sequencing information (the students seem to have been asking each other to rank-order their preferred activities), these first attempts can serve to acquaint the kindergartners with the necessary vocabulary for use as discourse markers, even if the execution of sequencing information still needs further development.

At a still later point in the school year, this teacher was interested in looking out for *sustainability* of her kindergarten students' acquisition of the progression features, and she tested this out across the curriculum at other points during the school day. For example, she described expressly building on her prior routine with the Morning Message by seeing whether the students' use of discourse markers would show up in their writing right after the Morning Message, and then if it would show up later in student writing of directions to make their "how-to" books. It did! It appears that these language features were not just being sustained across the day as the teacher had hoped, but they were spontaneously being generalized or extended to a different modality (from oral to written discourse) and applied to a different genre as well (from the personal narratives of the Morning Message to the procedural explanations of their own "how-to" books).

Another teacher took the progression for sentence sophistication and set goals for sentence development during her mathematics lesson planning, based on her prior observations of student needs. She incorporated a number of ways to scaffold language, including modeling specific sentence structures during her own oral production of mathematics explanations and providing sentence-starter phrasings as and when students needed them. She also supported target sentence structures across all modalities—listening, speaking, reading, and writing. Additionally, she created activities that provided a context for authentic student uptake, such as requiring students to explain their ideas about mathematics to one another while building collaborative representations of their understanding.

Initially, we provided teachers with templates to make a record of the evidence they gathered and possible action. These, too, were quickly rejected by the teachers, who preferred to experiment with their own formats. They started to develop their own ways of planning for language learning and for documenting what they heard in students' oral language during their formative assessment opportunities. For example, a primary teacher created a note-taking template, which she placed on a clipboard and used for conferences with individuals and groups and for her observations throughout the lesson. The template headings were *date, language feature, student language, language feature modeled, student response*, and *next steps* (for an additional example, see Chapter 5, Figure 5.2).

What Teachers Say

We [the teaching team] were trying to think of a way of documenting beforehand some of the sentence structures or some of the connectors that we felt would come up in the next couple of days. . . . So then it would help us to keep not only ourselves accountable for looking for evidence but also to help ensure that we were also teaching to it and embedding some of these causal connectors or going over certain sentences structures throughout our lessons. . . . So our planning guide for science begins with our core ideas, learning goals for the week, any vocabulary that would be covered. Right below we added a section for language features of focus [during the lesson].

Limit the Focus

Our third recommendation for DLLP implementation is to limit the focus on the language features. Rather than attending to all the features at once, we found that it worked much better for teachers when they focused on one feature at a time, often beginning with just one content area. Not only were teachers concentrating on teaching and formatively assessing content, but they were also having to address language learning. This simultaneous attention to content and language was definitely a challenge. Most teachers overcame the challenge by sometimes attending to content learning and sometimes attending to language learning, until they felt more confident attending to both.

What Teachers Say

I think the idea of starting small. . . . I think what helped us was focusing on one particular content area and really just trying to flesh it out. Trying to understand the balance between teaching to content and teaching to language. Not just how you are going to teach it but how you too look for the evidence.

The advantage to teachers of limiting the focus was that they were able to feel in control of the implementation and work in a way that was manageable for them, whereas initially they had felt overwhelmed by the idea of the DLLPs. Having a choice about which features to address in the context of their curriculum and focusing on one DLLP feature at a time made it possible for teachers to develop their skills in teaching and assessing content and language simultaneously.

What Teachers Say

I think for me how I've been processing it from the beginning, it seemed initially overwhelming, with all this information coming at us and trying to tackle multiple ones [features] at once. For me, what I found useful is really focusing on one and truly understanding the elements and the progression of that one and looking at how it's involved in different content areas. And then once I feel I have a good understanding of that one, then moving on to [another] one.

We also found that when teachers implemented the DLLP approach and worked with their students on one feature, it actually informed and supported development of the other features. For example, when teachers focused initially on discourse connectors, because connectors establish relationships between ideas, the teachers inadvertently began to lay the groundwork for students to use complex sentences and more consciously structure paragraphs. When students connect ideas between clauses, they bring awareness to the sentence level (e.g., with words such as *because* and *while*). When the words are used to establish specific kinds of meaning relationships between sentences (e.g., *first, next, furthermore, last*), this word work can begin to bring awareness to discourse structures.

Teachers needed practice in consciously listening for specific language features to develop an ear for them. Once they had become more skilled in listening, they were able to draw on their existing pedagogical knowledge and implement strategies based on the evidence they had obtained to further develop student language in the targeted language areas.

Another benefit of a limited focus was that by attending to a small number of target language features, teachers became aware of the contexts that would support particular kinds of language development. For example, one teacher noted that temporal connectors were easy to focus on when students were working on a narrative. During a science lesson when students were asked to classify objects into living and nonliving categories, and later asked to justify the placement of objects in those categories, the teacher noticed that the students were using words that worked to establish relationships between ideas, such as *therefore* and *so*, and words that sequenced procedures, such as *then*. Knowledge about the particular learning contexts that could generate certain features helped teachers plan for language learning and for assessing that language use.

What Teachers Say

I really think it is what your lesson consists of and what the language is that can be connected with that lesson.

Well into the project, when the teachers were reviewing the gains in their knowledge and skills, several teachers commented on how, from shaky beginnings when they needed to limit their focus to one feature at a time in one content area, they were subsequently able to adeptly handle several language features across different content areas.

What Teachers Say

Teacher A: When I see where I was last year, last year at the beginning I feel like I could only focus on one feature. I felt that I just kept on going back and it was that specific feature that I kept on focusing on over and over. I think towards the end of the year and this year I've felt much more comfortable and have been pretty flexible in terms of not only focusing so much on language being developed in one specific area, but seeing how it merges into other areas.

Teacher B: I think I would have to agree. I just think it feels as you become more confident and comfortable you can add more layers to it. Definitely.

Communities of Practice

The process we adopted for the DLLP implementations was that of a community of practice (CoP). The teachers collaborated around a common interest, exploring and sharing ideas about how to support their students' language development, all the while increasing their own professional capacities. Sharing their experiences gave them a sense of purpose and commitment to one another. Chapter 7 provides extensive background information on CoPs and how they are formed and sustained, so we will leave the details about them until then. At this point, though, we want to note the group norms that emerged from the pilot teacher meetings, which we recommend that teachers establish from the outset to help build a culture of respect and trust in their CoPs:

- Everyone makes the meetings a high priority and comes on time.

- Everyone pays attention and participates.

- Everyone acknowledges that each participant is a learner.

- Everyone acknowledges that sharing both successes and failures in a safe environment is part of individual learning, as well as helps the whole group learn.

Of course other specific norms might emerge as a result of discussion in teacher implementation groups, but we think that these are useful starter suggestions. The important point here is that group participants need to feel that they can take risks and share their failures as well as their successes in a context of mutual support without fear of negative judgments from their peers.

What Teachers Say

You have to have the opportunity to experiment with it, and take risks with it, with others, within different curricular areas.

What Benefits Can Teachers Expect From Implementing the DLLP Approach?

The DLLP approach has practical benefits for both teachers and students. Before we list the benefits we have documented, it is worth mentioning that the DLLP approach also has requirements before these benefits can be reasonably expected; time for teacher learning, experimentation and discussion, and a commitment to these from teachers and administrators are paramount for its success. The DLLP approach, when fully implemented and supported by teachers and school leaders, can

- enable teachers to choose which of the DLLP language features to focus on during content instruction;
- support effective collaboration on feedback during monthly communities of practice meetings of teachers, administrators, and other support staff;
- assist teachers in attending to both language and content development simultaneously;
- foster reflection about different language development pathways and contexts for support;
- meet the needs of each individual student.

In the next chapter, we will focus on formative assessment and how teachers can use the DLLPs for this type of assessment.

SUMMING UP

1. The DLLP approach can assist teachers to plan instruction that supports language development and to formatively assess language learning in the context of ongoing purposeful activity.

2. The DLLP language features provide a level of detail about the linguistic content of language learning that is not available in standards.

3. The language dimensions (word, sentence, and discourse) and the high-leverage features within each are not separate entities in language use and should not be taught in isolation from one another but rather should be acquired in relevant, content-specific, language-rich activities and interactions.

4. Three key recommendations for learning to implement the DLLP are (1) build background knowledge, (2) offer teacher choice in selecting features, and (3) limit the focus on features to a small number initially.

5. Implementing the DLLP approach can increase teachers' knowledge of language development.

REFLECTION QUESTIONS
FOR TEACHERS ···

1. How do you currently plan for language learning in your classroom? Based on what you have read in this chapter, how might the DLLPs be useful to you?

2. Which of the five recommendations for implementation resonates most strongly with you? Are there other factors, based on your current context, that you will want to take into account when thinking about DLLP implementation?

3. You read about challenges that teachers experienced when first implementing the DLLPs. Do you imagine that you will have the same challenges, or will they be different? Why?

4. From reading this chapter, what have you learned about language development? What do you want to read more about in subsequent chapters?

REFERENCES ···

Bailey, A. L. (2012). Academic English. In J. Banks (Ed.), *Encyclopedia of diversity in education*. Thousand Oaks, CA: Sage.

Bailey, A. L., Butler, F. A., Stevens, R., & Lord, C. (2007). Further specifying the language demands of school. In A. L. Bailey (Ed.), *The language demands of school: Putting academic English to the test* (pp. 103–156). New Haven, CT: Yale University Press.

Bailey, A. L., & Heritage, M. (2008). *Formative assessment for literacy, grades K–6*. Thousand Oaks, CA: Corwin.

Bailey, A. L., & Heritage, M. (2014). The role of language learning progressions in improved instruction and assessment of English language learners. *TESOL Quarterly, 48*(3), 480–506.

Bailey, A. L., & Heritage, M. (2018). *Self-regulation in learning: The role of language and formative assessment*. Cambridge, MA: Harvard Education Press.

Bailey, A. L., & Huang, B. H. (2011). Do current English language development/proficiency standards reflect the English needed for success in school? *Language Testing, 28*(3), 343–365.

Bennett, R. E. (2010). Cognitively based assessment of, for, and as learning (CBAL): A preliminary theory of action for summative and formative assessment. *Measurement: Interdisciplinary Research & Perspective, 8*(2–3), 70–91.

California Department of Education. (2012). *The California English language development standards*. Sacramento, CA: Author.

Common Core State Standards Initiative. (2010). *Common Core State Standards for English language arts and literacy in history/social studies, science, and technical subjects*. Retrieved from http://www.corestandards.org/assets/CCSSI_ELA%20Standards.pdf

Corcoran, T., Mosher, F. A., & Rogat, A. (2009). *Learning progressions in science: An evidence-based approach to reform* (CPRE Research Report #RR-63). New York: Consortium for Policy Research in Education (CPRE), Teachers College, Columbia University.

Council of Chief State School Officers. (2012). *Framework for English Language Proficiency Development Standards corresponding to the Common Core State Standards and the Next Generation Science Standards.* Washington, DC: Author.

Darling-Hammond, L., Hyler, M. E., & Gardner, M. (2017). *Effective teacher professional development.* Palo Alto, CA: Learning Policy Institute.

Engage NY. (2014). *New language arts Progressions of New York State.* Albany, NY: Author.

Heritage, M. (2008). *Learning progressions: Supporting instruction and formative assessment.* Los Angeles, CA: National Center for Research on Evaluation, Standards, and Student Testing. Retrieved April 8, 2018, from http://www.k12.wa.us/assessment/ClassroomAssessmentIntegration/pubdocs/FASTLearningProgressions.pdf

Mosher, F. A. (2011). *The role of learning progressions in standard-based education reform (CPRE Research Report #RB-52).* New York: Consortium for Policy Research in Education (CPRE), Teachers College, Columbia University.

Oxford English Dictionary. (2018). Retrieved from http://www.oed.com/

Schleppegrell, M. J. (2004). *The language of schooling: A functional linguistics perspective.* Mahwah, NJ: Erlbaum.

Smith, C. L., Wiser, M., Anderson, C. W., & Krajcik, J. (2006). Implications of research on children's learning for standards and assessment: A proposed learning progression for matter and the atomic-molecular theory. *Measurement: Interdisciplinary Research & Perspective, 4*(1–2), 1–98.

Sztajn, P., Confrey, J., Wilson, P. H., & Edgington, C. (2012). Learning trajectory based instruction: Toward a theory of teaching. *Educational Researcher, 41*, 147–156.

Valdés, G. (2005). Bilingualism, heritage language learners, and SLA: Opportunities lost or seized? *Modern Language Journal, 89*, 410–426.

Appendix 2A

Research Methods and Protocols

Site Selection Procedures

Five schools participated in data collection for the DLLP project. One school is a university demonstration school and was selected as a site to initially and iteratively pilot data collection protocols and teacher questionnaires, as well as conduct longitudinal data collection across school years with a subsample of students. Four additional public schools were deliberately selected from different areas of Los Angeles to attain a range of academic performances, as well as socioeconomic, racial/ethnic, and linguistic diversity within the larger sample.

Student Participants

The language progressions of explanation use in both personal routine and mathematics contexts were derived from a new longitudinal corpus of K–6 language elicited from 324 students (52% girls); 102 were identified by their schools as English learners, and 222 were English-only/proficient students.[1] The sample was ethnically diverse, with Latino students making up the largest subgroup (44.1%), followed by Caucasian (21.0%), mixed ethnicity (17.9%), Asian (9.9%), African American (4.9%), and students in none of the above ethnic groups (2.2%).

All students in the sample provided oral explanations at two time points, with some students at the demonstration school providing oral explanations at a third and fourth time point across a 2-year period.

Data Collection Protocols

Explanations play a number of different roles in exchanges (e.g., Beals, 1993). The first prompt (procedural) asks the student to tell how he or she completes the procedure of cleaning his or her teeth or solves a mathematics problem. The second prompt (justification) asks the student to tell why he or she cleans his or her teeth or why he or she chose a particular mathematics strategy. The third prompt combines these functions in an instructional explanation (along with persuasion) to ask the student to explain to a friend how to clean his or her teeth/solve the mathematics task and why he or she should clean his or her teeth/use the chosen mathematics strategy.

The language and cognitive demands associated with the third prompt are deliberately designed to be decontextualized, requiring students to explain their processes to a hypothetical student who is not present. First, students

---

[1] We collected both oral and written explanations from each student. For the current book, we focus primarily on the students' oral explanations.

had to make this realization, take account of the limited point of view of the hypothetical student, and reflect this understanding linguistically in their attempts to be explicit and fully explanatory.

In a quiet location in the students' schools, interviewers worked with individual students to elicit their oral explanations. The interviewer provided the student with as much time as the student needed to respond and then asked the simple follow-up question: "Anything else?" The interviewer allowed the student time to respond further.

Personal Routine (Cleaning Teeth)
Oral Explanation Task

Prompt 1: *Pretend I'm your teacher and tell me how you clean your teeth.*

Prompt 2: *Now tell me why you clean your teeth.*

Prompt 3: *Pretend you're talking to a friend who doesn't know how to clean his/her teeth. When you're ready, tell him/her how to do it and why he/she should do it.*[2]

The mathematics explanation data were generated using a task that was designed to elicit language for mathematical reasoning as it is reflected in the Common Core State Standards for mathematics (National Governors Association Center for Best Practices, Council of Chief State School Officers, 2010).[3] Specifically, the students were expected to interact with mathematical concepts of counting and cardinality and express their reasoning through oral explanations (Bailey & Heritage, 2014). Students were presented with a quantity of Unifix Cubes (plastic interlocking blocks) and asked to find the total number of cubes. To account for differences in cognitive demand across grades, the quantity of cubes differed by grade: 6 cubes for kindergartners; 10 cubes for first graders; 50 cubes for second, third, and fourth graders; and 100 cubes for fifth and sixth graders. The mathematics task was designed to be as equivalent as possible at each grade level so students' explanations would be suitable for comparative linguistic analyses. Students were told to find the total using whatever strategy they wished.

To solve the mathematics task, students could follow one or more of several possible procedural strategies: (1) group the cubes; (2) select a number to group them by; (3) connect the cubes; (4) push aside the cubes; (5) calculate the total by counting, repeated addition, or multiplication; and (5) give a final answer. Interviewers took detailed notes of what the student was doing with the cubes during the activity (e.g., sequence of procedural steps, whether they grouped cubes by color, arrayed them in rows and columns, etc.).

---

[2]Pronouns referring to the classmate were matched to participant's gender.

[3]The Counting and Cardinality Kindergarten CCSS Mathematics Standards 4 & 5, which read in part: "Understand the relationship between numbers and quantities; connect counting to cardinality" and "Count to answer 'how many?' questions about as many as 20 things arranged in a line, a rectangular array, or a circle, or as many as 10 things in a scattered configuration; given a number from 1 to 20, count out that many objects" (National Governors Association Center for Best Practices, Council of Chief State School Officers, 2010).

After providing the total number of cubes, the interviewer began the mathematics oral explanation task by telling the child, "Now I'm going to ask you a few questions. Please give your best explanation for each one."

Mathematics Oral Explanation Task

Prompt 1: *What did you do to find out how many cubes there are?*

Prompt 2: *Why did using the cubes this way help you find out how many there are?*

Prompt 3: *Pretend you are talking to a classmate who has never done this activity. When you're ready, tell him/her how to use the cubes to find out how many there are and why using the cubes this way helps him/her.[4]*

istock.com/ieva

Data Processing and Management

Verbatim transcriptions of the oral digital recordings were made by trained graduate assistants, and then the parsing of the speech stream into utterances was verified by a second trained transcriber. A web-based corpus management and analysis system, the Dynamic Relational Graphical Ontological Networks (DRGON), was created for the project (see, for details, Bailey, Blackstock-Bernstein, Ryan, & Pitsoulakis, 2016). DRGON is an adaptation of the Ontological Relations Builder (ORB) system, an automated ontology generation software suite that was developed at the National Center for Research on Evaluation, Standards, and Student Testing (Mousavi, Kerr, & Iseli, 2011).

Data Analyses

The DRGON system was programmed to use the Stanford Natural Language Processing (NLP) (Klein & Manning, 2003) to parse and identify parts of speech. Lexical-level measures included frequency and type of general academic vocabulary and frequency and type of topic-related vocabulary (personal routine or mathematics). Other manually analyzed characteristics of the explanations were informed by our prior work (the Academic English Language Project, e.g., Bailey, Butler, Stevens, & Lord, 2007; the Evaluating Validity of English Language Assessment Project, e.g., Heritage & Bailey, 2011) and that of others cited in various sections below.

We also coded salient features of the explanations that emerged from initial analyses. These features go beyond the frequency and rate measures extracted by NLP to also code language as it is used within an explanation as a whole. Two hundred explanations had previously been rank-ordered by the research team blind to the background characteristics of the students. The team first worked independently and then reached consensus to form a preliminary progression of increasingly sophisticated explanations.

---

[4]Pronouns referring to the classmate were matched to participant's gender.

Characteristics that explanations shared at similar points on the continuum were then identified at the word, sentence, and discourse levels and represented in eight recurring linguistic and discourse features or, in some cases, clusters of related features that we argue capture students' abilities to use language in increasingly sophisticated ways for explanatory purposes (Bailey & Heritage, 2014).

While we have located several features in the word dimension of the DLLP approach, they may also involve some sentence-level processing (e.g., nominalization that changes the part of speech by transforming a verbal component into a nominal component) and are more accurately denoted as morphosyntactic features of the explanations. Topic-related vocabulary was defined as vocabulary specific to the personal routine or mathematics task (e.g., *toothbrush, rinse* for personal routine, and *count, equal* for mathematics task) and *essential* to making meaning of the explanation or related to it (i.e., not as critical to meaning making). Some words that are used as different parts of speech (e.g., *brush* [noun] and *brush* [verb]) were counted separately depending on their use. In addition, we treated all forms of a semantic or word family (e.g., *organize, organizing, organized*) as separate lexical items rather than represent them just by a root word (*organize*), because our work includes early developmental phases of word learning when students may be adding new entries into their mental lexicons as individual, unique terms.

Subcategories of words also included cross-disciplinary words (i.e., general academic vocabulary) and discipline-specific words (e.g., specialized or technical vocabulary; Bailey et al., 2007). General academic vocabulary was defined as vocabulary that can cut across two or more content areas (Bailey et al., 2007) and retain the same meaning (e.g., *organize, effective*). Much of this vocabulary was confirmed by a school district grade-level word list for general academic vocabulary. "Vivid" vocabulary (i.e., evocative imagery and rhetorical flourishes) was also identified as a significant characteristic contributing to the sophistication of student explanations.

Explanations with a variety of verb tenses, signaling linguistic complexity, employed the use of modals and complex verb tenses. The focus on verb tenses begins with the simple present and past tenses and shifts to increasingly more complex tenses (e.g., the future perfect progressive *will have been going*). Modal verbs signal the speaker's or author's stance toward a topic (Halliday & Martin, 1993; Schleppegrell, 2004).

At the sentence level, we identified simple, compound, complex, and compound-complex sentences. These represent a progression from simple to complex structures, ranging from simple declarative and negative sentences to multiple embedded clauses within a sentence (Bailey & Heritage, 2008; Owens, 1996; Scott, 1988).

At the discourse level, we documented how coherent explanations were organized and demonstrated control of information and connections between propositions (i.e., presentation of information and/or ideas in a logical or accurate sequential, chronological, or causal order). The frequency and different types of discourse connectors (e.g., causal connectors, such as *because, so*, and temporal connectors, such as *then, after*) were identified for the role they played in the logical organization of discourse and creation of relationships between ideas (e.g., Christie, 2012; French, 1988; Halliday & Hasan, 1976; Jisa, 1987).

Cohesion was achieved through control of cohesive devices, such as accurate pronominal referential ties (e.g., *it, them*, used to refer to *brush* and *teeth*), within and across sentences. We noticed how students needed a mental model of what they were explaining and the tenacity to fully explain that representation of their ideas so a naïve listener (or in the case of written explanations, a reader) could make meaning. We called this aspect of explanations stamina, analogous to the stamina concept in reading (e.g., Braman, 2008). Perspective-taking (i.e., first person: *I* and *we*; second person: *you*; and third person: *the boy/girl* and *he/she*) was a significant element of student explanations and contributed to their linguistic complexity. For example, inconsistent perspective-taking was noted when a child shifted back and forth (inappropriately) between first, second, and third person during an explanation.

These characteristics were organized into eight high-leverage features or in some instances clusters of several features. These features were then coded for each explanation by the researchers and trained graduate student assistants as being at one of four points on the DLLP progression: *Not Evident* (i.e., not yet detectable, may use only language from the prompt, or give a non-English response), *Emerging* (i.e., occurs infrequently/intermittently, incomplete, with no repertoire of types; may be inaccurate), *Developing* (i.e., occurs more often, more complete, with a small repertoire of types; may be inaccurate), or *Controlled* (i.e., occurs where expected or in obligatory contexts, complete, with broad repertoire of types, most often used accurately).[5]

Reliability

The trained coders double-coded random selections of the oral and written explanations at several different points during the DLLP development stages. An example of one such session of double-coding calculated reliability on 45 (14%) personal routine explanations from the data corpus at time point 1 and an additional 19 (6%) mathematics explanations from time point 1 (see Bailey, Blackstock-Bernstein, & Heritage, 2015). Interrater reliability expressed as the number of agreements divided by the number of agreements and disagreements for each DLLP feature for personal routine explanations ranged from .70 for coherence/cohesion to .93 for sophistication of topic-related vocabulary, with a mean of .84, and for mathematics explanations ranged from .74 for stamina to .95 for control of perspective-taking, with a mean of .86. Additionally, Cohen's kappa, which takes account of chance agreement, ranged for personal routine explanations from .57 for coherence/cohesion to .87 for sophistication of topic-related vocabulary, and for mathematics explanations ranged from .63 for stamina to .88 for control of perspective-taking. The mean kappa for the eight features was .73 and .76 for personal routine and mathematics explanations, respectively. The resulting kappas are considered moderate-high for the personal routine and substantial for the mathematics task (Landis & Koch, 1977).

---

[5]Conventional or accurate usage is not taken into account while language is still emerging or developing, in line with notions of "flawed" (Valdés, 2005) or imperfect language being appropriately anticipated at these phases of development.

REFERENCES ··

Bailey, A. L., Blackstock-Bernstein, A., & Heritage, M. H. (2015). At the intersection of mathematics and language: Examining mathematical explanations of English proficient and English language learner students. *Journal of Mathematical Behavior, 40*, 6–28. http://dx.doi.org/10.1016/j.jmathb.2015.03.007

Bailey, A. L., Blackstock-Bernstein, A., Ryan, E., & Pitsoulakis, D. (2016). Data mining with natural language processing and corpus linguistics: Unlocking access to school-children's language in diverse contexts to improve instructional and assessment practices. In S. El Atia, O. Zaiane, & D. Ipperciel (Eds.), *Data mining and learning analytics in educational research* (pp. 255–275). Malden, MA: Wiley-Blackwell.

Bailey, A. L., Butler, F. A., Stevens, R., & Lord, C. (2007). Further specifying the language demands of school. In A. L. Bailey (Ed.), *The language demands of school: Putting academic English to the test* (pp. 103–156). New Haven, CT: Yale University Press.

Bailey, A. L., & Heritage, M. (2008). *Formative assessment for literacy, grades K–6: Building reading and academic language skills across the curriculum.* Thousand Oaks, CA: Corwin.

Bailey, A. L., & Heritage, M. (2014). The role of language learning progressions in improved instruction and assessment of English language learners. *TESOL Quarterly, 48*(3), 480–506.

Beals, D. (1993). Explanatory talk in low-income families' mealtime conversations. *Applied Psycholinguistics, 14*, 489–514.

Braman, K. (2008). Reading stamina: Energy needed to fuel reading. *RocketReader Newsletter.*

Christie, F. (2012). *Language education throughout the school years: A functional perspective.* Malden, MA: Wiley-Blackwell.

French, L. A. (1988). The development of children's understanding of "because" and "so." *Journal of Experimental Child Psychology, 45*, 262–279.

Halliday, M. A., & Hasan, R. (1976). *Cohesion in English.* London, UK: Longman.

Halliday, M., & Martin, J. (Eds.). (1993). *Writing science: Literacy and discursive power.* Pittsburgh, PA: University of Pittsburgh Press.

Heritage, M., & Bailey, A. L. (2011). *English language proficiency assessment foundations: External judgments of adequacy. Evaluating the Validity of English Language Proficiency Assessments.* Enhanced Assessment Grant, U.S. DOE, Evaluating the Validity of English Assessments (EVEA) Project Deliverable. Retrieved from http://www.eveaproject.com/doc/Generic%20ELPA%20Foundations%20Document%20FINAL%208%202%2010.pdf.

Jisa, H. (1987). Sentence connectors in French children's monologue performance. *Journal of Pragmatics, 11*(5), 607–621.

Klein, D., & Manning, C. D. (2003). Accurate unlexicalized parsing. *Proceedings of the 41st Meeting of the Association for Computational Linguistics* (pp. 423–430).

Landis, J. R., & Koch, G. G. (1977). The measurement of observer agreement for categorical data. *Biometrics, 33*, 159–174.

Mousavi, H., Kerr, D., & Iseli, M. (2011). *A new framework for textual information mining over parse trees* (CRESST Report 805). Los Angeles, CA: University of California, National Center for Research on Evaluation, Standards, and Student Testing (CRESST).

National Governors Association Center for Best Practices, Council of Chief State School Officers (CCSSO). (2010). *Common Core State Standards.* Washington, DC: Author.

Owens, R. E. (1996). *Language development: An introduction*. Needham Heights, MA: Allyn & Bacon.

Schleppegrell, M. J. (2004). *The language of schooling: A functional linguistic perspective*. Mahwah, NJ: Lawrence Erlbaum Associates.

Scott, C. M. (1988). Spoken and written syntax. In M. A. Nippold (Ed.), *Later language development: Ages 9 through 19* (pp. 49–95). Boston, MA: College Hill.

Valdés, G. (2005). Bilingualism, heritage language learners, and SLA research: Opportunities lost or seized? *Modern Language Journal*, *89*(3), 410–426.

Appendix 2B

Directions for Teachers' Tool for Documenting Language Features in the Classroom for Formative Purposes

Gathering evidence of student language use and progress during instruction is a critical aspect of the DLLP approach. This tool is designed to help you gather and document evidence of your students' learning on one to two DLLP language features that you focus on for a given month.

Use this tool to help you record your observations of students giving an explanation. Explanations are multifunctional and can address the what, how, and why of psychological states, phenomena, actions, events, and processes. See below for purposes of explanations (based in part on Beals, 1993).

Explanation Purpose	Definition
Main Purposes	
Procedural/process	How you/I do something
Justification	Why you/I do something
Embedded/Additional Purposes	
Cause and effect	Why something happened
Description/definition	What something is like/means
Evidence	How I know something
Intention	Why I am saying/doing/asking
Internal state	Why I want/feel . . .

Source: Beals (1993).

Explanations are integral to and required in all academic disciplines. For example, students should be able to use explanations to demonstrate the following in these subjects:

- *English language arts*—conceptual knowledge and their English language proficiency skills

- *Mathematics*—mathematical concepts, procedures, and reasoning

- *Science*—scientific inquiry, procedures, and casual forces of a phenomenon

- *Social studies*—causes of an event or movement and analysis and interpretation of sources

You may adjust this tool to better fit your style of observational note-taking. If you do adapt this tool, please keep the following elements in your version of the tool for recording language features in the classroom.

Language feature: Record the high-leverage language feature you are working on with your students this month. We recommend that you work on no more than one to two language features a month with your target students.

Oral or written: Please indicate if the students were using the language feature(s) orally (e.g., in discussion or oral discourse) or in written form (e.g., quick write, essay writing).

Description of use: Describe the activity or tasks students were engaged in when you were observing language feature use. Also include student participant structures during the activity or task. For example, were students working in small groups, pairs, or individually?

Context of use: This refers to the subject area (e.g., English language arts, mathematics, science, social studies) in which you made the observation. Please include as much detail as you can, such as "mathematics—learning about common denominators for multiplying fractions; science—ecosystems; social studies—Civil War."

Student example(s) of use: Record target students' oral or written language use of the feature you are working on this month.

Teacher comments/notes: This is a space for you to jot down any other relevant comments and notes about the student, the activity, next steps, analysis of evidence of student progress in using the language feature, and so forth.

REFERENCE

Beals, D. (1993). Explanatory talk in low-income families' mealtime conversations. *Applied Psycholinguistics, 14,* 489–514.

NOTE

Based in part on Beals (1993). This and related resources are available at https://www.dllp.org/index.php/resources/pilot-teacher-resources.

dllp
dynamic
language
learning
progressions

Tool for Documenting Language Features in the Classroom for Formative Purposes

Teacher: _____ Grade: _____

School: _____ Month: _____

				Instances When Language Feature Is Used by Focus Student(s) in the Classroom			
Focus Student Name	Date	Language Feature	Oral or Written	Content Area	DLLP Phase for Feature	Description of Evidence (e.g., What were students doing? What was the activity? How were they grouped?)	Student Example(s) of Use (record student quotations, location of audio file [e.g., audio file #3], etc.)	Teacher Comments/ Notes (e.g., next steps in instruction)

*Good teaching is forever being on the cutting
edge of a child's competence.*

—Jerome Bruner

CHAPTER 3

Formative Assessment

Formative assessment, often referred to as assessment *for* learning, is assessment that is intended to inform learning as it is developing. It is different from assessment for summative purposes, which is intended to measure what students have achieved at the end of a period of learning—for example, at the end of a unit, a course, a quarter, or the year. The quote on the facing page from Jerome Bruner (n.d.) goes to the heart of formative assessment. If teachers are to be effective, then they must be consistently on the "edge" of students' learning so they can continuously keep learning moving forward. Knowing the "edge" of students' learning as they are learning so teaching can be matched to the students' needs is the core aim of formative assessment.

Formative assessment was promoted in the 1980s (Crooks, 1988; Natriello, 1987; Sadler, 1989) as a way to connect the two assessment activities of making judgments about student learning and providing students feedback intended to move learning forward. A major landmark in establishing formative assessment as an explicit domain of practice was Paul Black and Dylan Wiliam's (1998) extensive research review, which presented clear evidence for formative assessment as an essential component of classroom work that can raise standards of achievement. Since then, research, research reviews, theory, and practice-based evidence have reinforced Black and Wiliam's claim that formative assessment, when well implemented, is a powerful engine for promoting student achievement. As a result, formative assessment has firmly taken hold in many places across the world.

To clarify what formative assessment is, as distinct from other forms of assessment, below are quotes from three leading scholars in the field from three different countries.

What Is Formative Assessment?

Formative assessment's prime concern is with the here and now of learning. It occurs in the flow of activity and transactions in the classroom.

—Sue Swaffield (2011, p. 441),
University of Cambridge, England

(Continued)

As we can see, these scholars situate formative assessment as part of ongoing, everyday classroom practice. Teachers obtain evidence of learning through dialogue, demonstration, and observation to keep learning moving forward. Formative assessment is a practice used by teachers *and* students. We will unpack these ideas more later in the chapter. However, we want to underscore here that formative assessment is not more frequent testing that tells teachers whether their students "got it or didn't get it" (Otero, 2006) so they can "reteach" if the students didn't get it. Instead, formative assessment is about gaining insights into students' initial, emerging, or partial understanding and skills during a lesson so teachers can make decisions about the appropriate pedagogical actions intended to advance learning from its current "edge." As we learned in Chapter 2, the purpose of the Dynamic Language Learning Progression (DLLP) approach is to assist teachers in interpreting students' oral and written language in content lessons so they can decide on appropriate action to progress in language development.

Given the predominance of grading practices in American schools, one other point about formative assessment to note here is that it is not part of a grading process; let us be clear that formative assessment is not used to give grades. This is because grades provide a summative evaluation of learning, whereas formative assessment is the means teachers use to gain insights into student learning during learning. So teachers need to save any thoughts about grading until the end of the learning sequence. It is unfair to grade students *while* they are in the process of learning.

The teachers we worked with on the DLLP approach were initially a bit uncertain about formative assessment. Like many teachers, their understanding of assessment was that it is a test administered to students to provide a score on performance. Thinking about formative assessment as an everyday classroom practice was a big mindset shift for a number of teachers.

We found that Figure 3.1 helped teachers frame ideas about formative assessment and how to implement the process in their classrooms. The figure shows that formative assessment is grounded in three key questions teachers must ask themselves regardless of the content being assessed (Atkin, Black, & Coffey, 2001; Hattie & Timperley, 2007; Sadler, 1989):

- **Where am I going?** (In this context, what is my language learning goal for students in this content-area lesson?)

- **Where am I now?** (In this context, what does this evidence reveal about this student's language relative to the DLLPs?)

- **Where to next?** (In this context, based on my interpretation of the evidence, what do I need to do in my instruction to advance this student's language learning?)

As Figure 3.1 shows, there are several elements that make up the process of formative assessment: (1) learning goals and success criteria, (2) obtaining evidence, (3) interpreting evidence, (4) giving feedback, and (5) contingent teaching and learning. Let us now consider each one.

Figure 3.1 The Formative Assessment Process

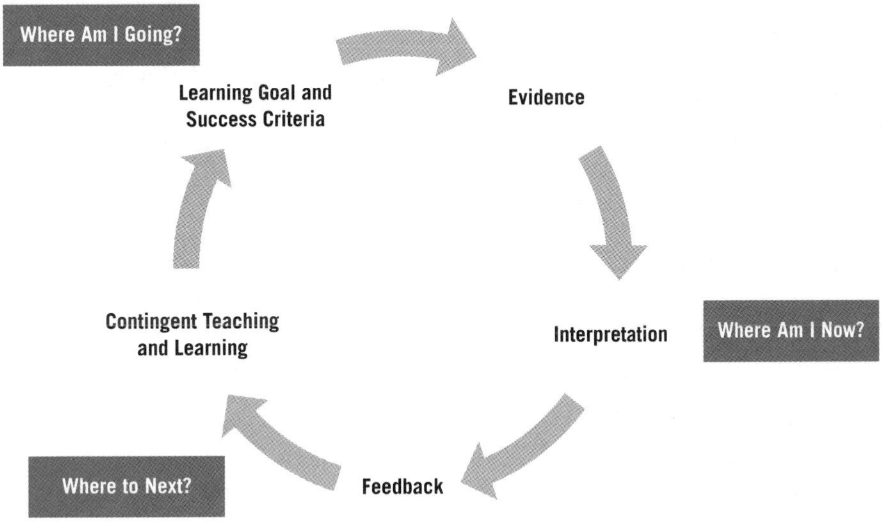

Source: Adapted from Heritage (2010).

Learning Goals and Success Criteria

Formative assessment begins (as do learning and instruction) with clear learning goals and success criteria. Teachers clarify the intended language learning (the goal), not what the students are going to do (the activities). The learning goal needs to be lesson-sized and connected to a bigger picture of learning. For example, establishing advanced relationships is a much larger goal within a particular content area than the lesson-sized goal in mathematics of "*using conditional connectors 'if . . . then' and 'whenever . . . then.'*" This is a manageable goal that is valuable to learn within the context of establishing advanced relationships in mathematics. There will be other opportunities for students to incrementally acquire a wider range of connectors in support of developing sophistication with this particular language feature.

Once the goal is clarified, then teachers have to decide how they will know if the students are acquiring the targeted language. To establish success criteria, teachers need to ask *"What are the indicators that I will be looking and listening for to tell me if the students are making progress toward the goal?"* For example, success criteria related to the goal of *using conditional connectors "if . . . then" and "whenever . . . then"* might be that students can use the connectors in a mathematical explanation and say how and why the connectors work in the sentence. The learning experiences the students will need to reach the goal are planned once the goal is clearly established.

Key Terminology

Construct

What the assessment is intended to measure (e.g., reading comprehension, mathematical reasoning)

Content Relevance

The degree to which the assessment provides a relevant and representative sample of the construct

Construct Underrepresentation

The degree to which the important aspects of the construct are not represented well or left out of the assessment

Construct-Irrelevant Variance

The degree to which performance on the assessment is influenced by irrelevant factors, such as skills that are ancillary or tangential to the intent of the assessment (e.g., reading speed on a reading comprehension test) (adapted from Linn & Miller, 2005, pp. 78–79)

Eliciting Evidence

Teachers intentionally plan formative assessment opportunities to elicit students' oral language in the context of learning activities in the classroom. This requires them to create situations that enable students to produce oral language (e.g., peer discussions), to offer prompts that elicit language (e.g., questions), and to engage students in tasks that necessitate use of the target language in authentic contexts for a real purpose (e.g., provide explanations for their solutions).

Ideas from traditional education measurement, such as content relevance, construct underrepresentation, and construct-irrelevant variance (see sidebar), can be applied to eliciting evidence in a formative assessment context in the sense that the evidence-gathering opportunity should be aligned with the learning goal (the construct being addressed), it should be an appropriate representation of the construct, and it should include the important dimensions of the construct. In other words, the strategy should not be so broad that it contains dimensions that are irrelevant to the construct (e.g., language features that are not the focus of learning) or too narrow that it fails to include the important dimensions of the construct (e.g., using a strategy or opportunity that does not give students the chance to use the language that is the focus of the learning goal). Selecting the appropriate evidence-gathering opportunity to meet these conditions requires teachers to be very clear about what is to be learned and what evidence is needed to determine their students' current learning status.

In the way issues of fairness and bias are applicable in traditional measurement approaches, they are also relevant to formative assessment. Because students' learning does not develop in lockstep, formative assessment is inevitably personalized, and teachers will need to employ strategies that tap into the individual student's learning. Whatever formative assessment opportunities a teacher selects, they should account for the range of students present in the class so all students have the opportunity to show where they are in their language learning and have the prospect of moving forward from their current status. Similarly, formative assessment opportunities should not include any elements that would prevent some students from showing where they are relative to content goals, such as the use of language they cannot understand or are unfamiliar with, which is particularly important in the case of English learners. In these cases, teachers would be introducing construct-irrelevant variance into their assessments and interpretations of student content learning.

Another important concern in relation to instructional decisions in formative assessment is "sufficiency of information" (Smith, 2003, p. 30). In this regard, teachers have to be confident that they have enough information about the student's language learning to make a reasonable judgment about the current status of that learning. In practical terms, this might mean that before making a judgment about learning, a teacher has evidence from a student representation in a content area, from observations of the student constructing the representation or discussing it with peers (gaining insights into both language and content), and from probing questions about the nature of the representation—why the student constructed it in a particular way and what it means (acquiring information about the student's explanations). Multiple sources of evidence in relation to the goal and criteria are likely to provide a more accurate picture of learning than just one instance of assessment.

Interpreting and Using Evidence

Once teachers have evidence of the target language use, they interpret the evidence with reference to the DLLPs to determine the "best fit" for each student. Teachers ask the question *"Based on the evidence I have, where does this student's language development seem to fit best on the progression?"* Locating the "best fit" is not an exact science. If the decision about the "best fit" from one instance of assessment does not seem right based on further evidence, the teacher can make changes to his or her decision without impacting the student's learning, as would be the case if this happened in high-stakes tests, such as the annual summative assessments of standards. Deciding on the "best fit" relies on teachers' clinical judgment, not an external source that creates scores, as in most other forms of assessment. Their judgment provides them with feedback about their students' language that they can then feed forward into making decisions about how to respond contingently to their students.

Responding contingently means that teachers make a decision about the instructional action that is matched to the "edge" of students' learning, as revealed by the interpretation of evidence, with the aim of advancing learning. Contingent responses include planning new learning experiences, taking immediate pedagogical action (e.g., modeling, prompting, explaining), and providing feedback to students that helps them understand where they are relative to the goal (Bailey & Heritage, 2008; Heritage, 2013). Let us illustrate this practice with another example of a student's oral explanation to a friend of how to brush his teeth and why he should do it:

> *He should he does it like this, he has to get the pasta [= paste in Spanish], put it in the toothbrush and brush and then spit it out. And he should do that for, for his breath could smell good and his teeth to be white.*

A target of a teacher's assistance based on this evidence could be to help the student gain control of modals *should* and *would* by modeling correct use of them (e.g., *would* for *could*) and engaging students in opportunities to use modals during learning activities.

Giving Feedback to Students

Feedback is not intended to indicate to students that their language use is either correct or incorrect. Rather, the purpose of feedback is to help students understand what they are doing well in relation to the learning goal (e.g., *"I noticed in our discussion today that you were using one of the verb forms we have been thinking about."*) Then the students need to understand what *they* can do to improve (e.g., *"In our next discussion, can you try to use more of those verb forms when you are explaining your ideas?"*)

Feedback should focus on the learning and not be ego involving (e.g., *"I think you are a great student"* or *"You really messed up today."*)

Contingent Teaching and Learning

In terms of language development, it is unlikely that teachers will make just one instructional response and students will move forward. We just don't learn language that way. Rather, multiple responses on multiple occasions can support students in acquiring the particular target language features.

Making contingent responses was something that our pilot teachers found they could do from the very beginning of their DLLP implementation, and they believed this was one of the most critical contributions of the DLLP approach to their teaching. Even while they were still learning to grasp the ins and outs of the eight different DLLP features, they used the DLLP approach to calibrate their instructional responses and prevent inappropriately teaching beyond their students' zones of proximal development (ZPD) (see Chapter 1 for more about the ZPD).

What Teachers Say

From the get-go the DLLP can prevent missteps in trying to take a student from, say, an early level straight to advanced. You do that and you lose the student. The DLLP can help make sure you appropriately build up to the Controlled phase. You don't need to know or work with any more than a single feature to immediately use the DLLP to do that.

Student Role in Formative Assessment

The three questions that ground the process of formative assessment (*Where am I going? Where am I now? Where to next?*) are equally applicable to students as to teachers. Because formative assessment involves students as active participants, teachers need to help students understand the goals and the success criteria they are pursuing. For example, to understand the goal of expanded word groups, students will need to hear what expanded word groups sound like, discuss the use of prepositions and adjectives in explanations, and learn how an expanded word group can help convey meaning in an explanation. When they understand the goals and criteria, with intentional teaching and structures, they can assess where they think they are in their language acquisition and, in consultation with their teacher, set goals for further development.

Understanding goals and criteria helps students provide feedback to their peers to assist peers' learning. Similarly, when students understand the goals and criteria, they are better placed to use the feedback that has been provided to them by either their teacher or their peers. Engaging students in the assessment and learning process is a hallmark of teacher expertise in formative assessment. Teachers who are expert practitioners in formative assessment share with their students responsibility for moving learning forward; learning is recognized as a social process and becomes a joint responsibility. Chapters 4, 5, and 6 provide examples of how teachers can provide opportunities for self-assessment and peer feedback in the context of language learning.

One of the reasons formative assessment works is that the principles of learning that underlie and are implemented in formative assessment practices are firmly supported by cognitive research. Simply put, these principles are

Key Terminology
Metacognition

Thinking about one's thinking; processes used to plan, monitor, and assess one's skills and understanding

1. start from a learner's existing understanding (i.e., the "edge" of learning);

2. involve the learner actively in the learning process (students know what they are learning and why they are learning it, and they are active participants in learning, as opposed to passive recipients);

3. develop the learner's overview (i.e., metacognition)—this requires that students have a view of the purpose of their learning, understand criteria of quality of achievement (success criteria), and engage in self-assessment; and

4. emphasize the social aspects of learning (i.e., learning through interactions with others, particularly important for learning language) (Black, Wilson, & Yao, 2011).

To illustrate how these principles are implemented and what formative assessment looks like in action, in the next section we provide an extended example of classroom practice.

Example of Formative Assessment in Action

Ms. Silva planned a 4-week English language arts unit to provide rich language learning opportunities for her fifth-grade students, 50% of whom were designated English learners.

The college- and career-ready standards her unit addressed were as follows:

- Write arguments to support claims in an analysis of substantive topics or texts using valid reasoning and relevant and sufficient evidence.

- Produce clear and coherent writing in which the development and organization are appropriate to task, purpose, and audience.

- With guidance and support from peers and adults, develop and strengthen writing as needed by planning, revising, editing, rewriting, or trying a new approach.

- Conduct short research projects that use several sources to build knowledge through investigation of different aspects of a topic.

- Recall relevant information from experiences or gather relevant information from print and digital sources; summarize or paraphrase information in notes and finished work, and provide a list of sources.

- Draw evidence from literary or informational texts to support analysis, reflection, and research.

These standards were addressed in the context of the students' particular interest in environmental concerns. There were several language features that Ms. Silva thought could be developed over the course of the unit, lesson by lesson. These were

- Use of word groups (i.e., doing interesting things with words)

- Sophistication of verb forms (varied and precise use of verbs in context)

- Sophistication in sentence structure (varied and precise use of sentence structure)

- Coherence/cohesion (the explicit ordering of sentences and the varied and precise ways the text is tied together by cohesive devices)

- Establishment of advanced relationships between ideas (varied and precise use of discourse connectors, e.g., *because, however, in contrast*)

These language features would be the focus of her formative assessment opportunities so she could incrementally advance students' capabilities from whatever point on the DLLPs they had reached.

Her first lesson of the unit was what she calls an "entry event," which was to ask students to read and respond to quotations focused on environmental issues. For example, one was a quotation from a Native American proverb:

Treat the earth well; it was not given to you by your parent; it was loaned to you by your children. We do not inherit the earth from our ancestors; we borrow it from our children.

Ms. Silva provided guiding questions for the students to reflect on particular quotations and think about their responses:

- What does this quotation mean to you?

- What connections can you make to what is happening today?

- Is this quotation relevant today?

After reading the quotation from the proverb, one student wrote:

This quotation means to me that we should stop Global Warming because the earth was not given to us to do what we want with it. The earth was loaned to us to live in and take care of for our children.

Ms. Silva then held a class discussion about the students' responses.

In this entry event, Ms. Silva had two formative assessment opportunities for language: the students' discussion and their written responses. Throughout the unit there were many such opportunities. For example, Ms. Silva provided the students with articles to read about environmental issues and current solutions so they could apply prior knowledge on what is evidence and reading for evidence. As they were reading she also encouraged them to think about how they could be change agents in the world in support of the environment. There were peer discussions and class discussions on their reading and their ideas, providing opportunities for Ms. Silva to assess their reading for evidence skills and the students' language use.

Next in the unit, she took them through a research process, modeling through a think-aloud how to formulate a research question from their reading and discussions. After the students had developed and refined their own questions in response to feedback from Ms. Silva and their peers, they conducted their research using a variety of sources—including books, articles, digital resources, and interviews with adults—took notes along the way, and then synthesized their findings. During the research process, Ms. Silva built in various opportunities for the students to engage in self-assessment. For example, on several occasions she asked them to make an assessment of the notes they had gathered and determine whether they had enough information to answer their research question and how they knew. This self-assessment was also a formative opportunity for Ms. Silva; from the students' responses she was able to see how the students were understanding the research process.

The last phase of the unit was a focus on students' own writing based on their research. Ms. Silva taught mini lessons on developing arguments, building counterarguments, and using evidence to support claims. Now it was the students' turn to use their findings and construct an argument, counterarguments, and support for their claims with evidence from their research.

One-on-One Conferences
as Formative Assessment

One of the formative assessment opportunities Ms. Silva regularly uses is one-on-one conferences with students during their independent writing time. While she cannot conference one-on-one with all her students during one session of independent writing, she manages to meet with each student over a span of three to four class periods to assess where they are in their writing, to provide individual feedback (which she discusses with the student and then writes on a sticky note for them to refer to later), or even to work with the whole class on teaching points that have emerged through her assessment conferences. When Ms. Silva provides feedback to individuals, other students who are sitting nearby listen in, often using the feedback they hear to improve their own writing. She also has a policy that before students meet with her, they have to obtain feedback from a peer. Students use the peer's and Ms. Silva's feedback to refine their writing in an iterative process.

During one of the independent writing sessions, Ms. Silva had a conference with Joshua, an English learner. She had decided to focus on Joshua's sentence structures at the same time she was assessing the development of his writing. Her general impression was that Joshua had made some advances in his sentence sophistication, but she wanted to make a more precise assessment of this language feature. Prior to this segment of their interaction, Ms. Silva had asked Joshua to share what he was working on, and he had replied that he was "looking for his reasons," observing that when he found more reasons, he "got more counterarguments." As their conversation continued, Ms. Silva was satisfied that he understood the concepts of *reasons, argument*, and *counterargument* and was able to use precise topic vocabulary in his explanations.

Ms. Silva then built on Joshua's discussion of arguments and counterarguments, and asked why some people might not want to join the fight against global warming.

Ms. S: Okay, and what are some of the reasons why they might not want to be a part of this [fight against global warming]?

Joshua: Because sometimes people don't care, or they're just, like, really mad.

Ms. S: And why would you say that?

Joshua: 'Cuz you know how people are really busy sometimes, and sometimes they're, like, concentrating on their work more than other stuff that are happening so they, like, like, put them to the side and work on what they are going to work on, like their work.

Ms. S: That's right. (Nods) So, do you think there are some people that don't believe in global warming?

Joshua: Yeah, they're, like, some people that really need to recycle and waste lots of stuff.

Ms. S: They waste things, so do you think there are people who don't believe there is anything wrong with not recycling?

Joshua: Yeah.

Ms. S: And do you think that could be another counterargument?

Joshua: (Nods)

Ms. S: That they just don't believe that there is anything wrong or that they don't believe that there is anything happening to the earth.

Joshua: Mm-hm. (Slightly nods) Or, like, they just, like, look up in the sky and it seems normal, so they just say the world is normal and they don't care about the global warming.

Ms. S: And everything's fine, right? (Nods while speaking)

As she listened to Joshua, Ms. Silva noticed that while he was expressing a sophisticated idea—the world looks normal when people look at the sky, so they do not perceive an issue with global warming—his language reflected a small repertoire of discourse connectors (*'cuz, so*), which he used correctly, and that he mainly used simple sentences, with occasional issues of clarity or vagueness with actions and objects—for example, *"work on what they are going to work on, like their work"* and *"waste lots of stuff."* She also noticed that he had included some sophisticated verbs in his explanations (*concentrating, recycle, busy, waste*). Based on this evidence, Ms. Silva determined that the "best fit" on the DLLPs for Joshua was the Developing phase of sophistication of verb forms and sentence structure, as well as establishing advanced relationships between ideas. To advance his language capabilities, she decided to work on two key aspects: (1) increasing his repertoire of discourse connectors to get him to a higher level of expressing advanced relationships and (2) increasing the clarity and precision in how he expressed the object of his sentence structures (noun phrases) to move beyond such uses as *"lots of stuff."* She noted that he also needed support in sentence structure sophistication, and she determined that feature as a focus for him—although not immediately, because she did not want him to have too many priorities at once. Ms. Silva complimented Joshua on his writing and gave him feedback on what she had observed about his language, letting him know which language aspects she wanted him to work on next.

After Ms. Silva thanked Joshua for the conversation, she made very quick notes in her ring-binder file about what she had observed and what she planned to do next for him. As it turned out, there were several students who would benefit from the same next steps, so she decided she would do some intentional language modeling and provide feedback to the students on these aspects when she next conferenced with them. In future conferences, she would ask Joshua how he thought he was progressing with respect to these two language features, examine the degree of Joshua's and others' uptake of discourse connectors and precise noun phrases in oral and written language, and provide feedback intended to make the students aware of these aspects of language, how well they were using them, and how they could advance in their use.

The process Ms. Silva used with Joshua was repeated with all of her students. However, because of the range of language levels in her class, her focus was not always the same. She was intentionally monitoring students' language production and making decisions about specific areas of focus for formative assessment and next steps.

At the end of each independent writing session, Ms. Silva asks the students to do a quick-write about their progress relative to success criteria and what they need help with. She reviews these at the end of the day and makes decisions about any mini lessons that are necessary or whom she needs to conference with during the next writing session.

Once the students had completed their writing assignments, this unit concluded with the students thinking about their own agency in contributing to climate change and what they could do personally to combat it and to help the environment.

Now that we have seen formative assessment in action, below we summarize in Table 3.1 what formative assessment is and what it is not.

Table 3.1 What Formative Assessment Is and What It Is Not

Formative Assessment Is . . .	Formative Assessment Is Not . . .
Generating evidence *intentionally* in the course of continuous teaching and learning, through observation, listening, discussion, questioning, and review and analysis of tasks/work	Giving a test at the end of an instructional cycle or on a predetermined basis (e.g., quarterly, annually)
Gauging how student learning is progressing while students are in the process of learning	Evaluating student achievement at the end of a sequence of learning
Using evidence contingently to inform immediate and near-immediate teaching and learning	Using test data to make decisions about medium- and long-term instructional and/or curricular plans
Providing ongoing descriptive feedback to students	Assigning grades
Involving students in the assessment process through self-assessment and peer feedback	Telling students the results of a test

Classroom Culture

In Chapter 1, we discussed the importance of an inclusive classroom culture for student language learning. This idea is worth reiterating in the context of formative assessment implementation. In practicing formative assessment, teachers and students need to create a classroom culture characterized by the norms of

- mutual trust between teacher and students and among students;
- feelings of safety to reveal students' language status, display their understanding of content, and express and challenge ideas;
- respect for the assets students bring to the classroom from their own cultures and communities; and
- supportive, collaborative relationships.

Teachers establish these norms by modeling respect toward students in their interactions; by showing that they value the students' ideas through careful, interpretive listening to students' responses; and through the routines and structures that are established in the classroom. In this regard, teachers make the behavioral expectations for learning in the classroom clear, including how students work with and learn from peers. Teachers incorporate the students' lived experiences into the classroom, drawing on their cultural backgrounds and their community resources. They set high expectations for students by providing challenging, rigorous learning opportunities that are matched to each individual's level of learning to support learning of, and formative opportunities for, language and content.

Teacher Expertise

If formative assessment as described in this chapter is new to teachers, then it will take time to develop expertise. Even teachers who are seasoned implementers of formative assessment tell us that they are still learning and refining their practices. Of course, this is to be expected of accomplished teachers who have a mindset of continuous professional learning and growth. The DLLP approach is intended to provide the structure for formative assessment, but the skills to do it effectively will require teachers to reflect and practice, as we saw the teachers doing in Chapter 2.

Bronwen Cowie (2016) refers to the expertise teachers need to engage in high levels of formative assessment as *connoisseurship*—a level of skill that enables them to access information on student learning, orchestrate an extraordinary number of complex judgments in the course of a lesson, and implement appropriate and immediate actions in response to evidence. Undergirding this high level of orchestration are several competencies:

- Strong, flexible disciplinary knowledge

- The ability to prioritize content to focus on key learning targets

- An understanding of which formative assessment strategies are most effective for the content learning at hand

- Knowledge of how student learning of that content develops

What Experts Say

Teachers require the professional knowledge and skills to: plan for assessment; observe learning; analyze and interpret evidence of learning; give feedback to learners and support learners in self-assessment. Teachers should be supported in developing these skills through initial and continuing professional development.

—Assessment Reform Group (2001, p. 3)

The DLLP approach supports teachers in developing knowledge about the discipline of language development and how students' language learning increases in sophistication along eight high-leverage features. With this understanding teachers can prioritize the learning goals to advance language in content-area learning. In short, the DLLP approach is a major resource for developing skills in formative assessment. The addition of teachers' commitment to enhancing their skills through sustained collaboration with colleagues, practice, and reflection will result in genuine expertise and *connoisseurship*.

In the next chapter, we move to Part II of the book, where we examine the three dimensions of language, word, sentence, and discourse that are incorporated into the DLLP approach. We will begin by looking in detail at the word features of the DLLP approach.

SUMMING UP

1. Formative assessment is a process, not a test, intended to inform ongoing teaching and learning, not to provide a summative judgment about what has been learned at the end of a longer sequence of learning.

2. Grading is not part of a formative assessment process.

3. A teacher's planning should provide for formative opportunities for both teacher and students to obtain and use information about progress toward learning goals during a lesson.

4. Planning should also include strategies to ensure that students understand the goals they are pursuing and the criteria that will be applied in assessing their learning. How students will receive feedback and how they will take part in assessing their learning should also be planned.

5. Evidence of learning is interpreted by teachers to make contingent pedagogical responses, including providing feedback to students that helps them take actions to move forward.

6. An inclusive classroom culture is essential for effective formative assessment.

7. The DLLP approach provides the structure for teachers to engage in formative assessment, but to develop expertise, teachers will need to engage in sustained practice and reflection.

REFLECTION QUESTIONS FOR TEACHERS

1. How does what you have read about formative assessment in this chapter square with your own thinking? What is the same? What is different?

2. How often do you engage in formative assessment? After reading this chapter, what are areas of formative assessment you think you could strengthen in your classroom practice?

3. What aspects of formative assessment, using the DLLP approach, do you think will be or are already the most challenging for you? Why?

4. How do you think you might overcome these challenges?

5. What routines and participant structures do you already have in place in your classroom to support formative assessment?

REFERENCES

Assessment Reform Group. (2001). *Assessment for learning: 10 principles.* Cambridge, UK: Author.

Atkin, J. M., Black, P., & Coffey, J. (2001). *Classroom assessment and the National Science Education Standards.* Washington, DC: National Academy Press.

Bailey, A. L., & Heritage, M. (2008). *Formative assessment for literacy grades K–6: Building reading and academic language skills across the curriculum.* Thousand Oaks, CA: Corwin.

Bell, B., & Cowie, B. (2001). *Formative assessment and science education.* Dordrecht, Netherlands: Kluwer.

Black, P., & Wiliam, D. (1998). Assessment and classroom learning. *Assessment in Education: Principles Policy and Practice, 5,* 7–73.

Black, P., Wilson M., & Yao, S.-Y. (2011). Road maps for learning: A guide to the navigation of learning progressions. *Measurement: Interdisciplinary Research and Perspectives, 9*(2–3), 71–123.

Cowie, B. (2016, April). Connoisseurship in assessment for learning. Presentation at Special FAST SCASS Conference, Portland, Oregon.

Crooks, T. J. (1988). The impact of classroom evaluation practices on students. *Review of Educational Research, 58,* 438–481.

Hattie, J., & Timperley, H. (2007). The power of feedback. *Review of Educational Research, 77*(1), 81–112.

Heritage, M. (2010). *Formative assessment: Making it happen in the classroom.* Thousand Oaks, CA: Corwin.

Heritage, M. (2013). *Formative assessment: A process of inquiry and action.* Cambridge, MA: Harvard Education Press.

Klenowski, V. (2009). Assessment for learning revisited: An Asia-Pacific perspective. *Assessment in Education: Principles, Policy, & Practice, 16*(3), 263–268.

Linn, R. L., & Miller, M. D. (2005). *Measurement and assessment in teaching.* Upper Saddle River, NJ: Pearson Education.

Natriello, G. (1987). The impact of evaluation processes on students. *Educational Psychologist, 22,* 155–175.

Otero, V. (2006). Moving beyond the "get it or don't" conception of formative assessment. *Journal of Teacher Education. 57*(3), 247–255.

Sadler, D. (1989). Formative assessment and the design of instructional systems. *Instructional Science, 18,* 119–144.

Smith, J. (2003). Reconsidering reliability in classroom assessment and grading. *Educational Measurement: Issues and Practice, 22*(4), 26–33.

Swaffield, S. (2011). Getting to the heart of authentic assessment for learning. *Assessment in Education: Principles, Policy & Practice, 18*(4), 433–449.

Features of the DLLP Approach

Part II is a thorough treatment of the three dimensions of language (i.e., word, sentence, discourse) that are incorporated in the Dynamic Language Learning Progression (DLLP) approach. Recall from Part I that the DLLP approach traces the steps students are likely to move along as they develop sophistication in the high-leverage language features for the purpose of explanation. As teachers begin the process of attending to these features that students are using in explanations, they can use the DLLP approach for the purpose of formative assessment and contingent teaching in response to assessment evidence. While we have devoted separate chapters to the three dimensions, they should not be viewed as independent entities but rather as mutually dependent and integral aspects of language. The word, sentence, and discourse dimensions are pulled apart and treated in three different chapters for professional learning reasons, but for students there is inherently no rigid demarcation among the three dimensions when learning, using, and developing language. For the chapter on discourse features, we are joined by our colleague Gabriela Cardenas.

This chapter begins the series of chapters devoted to the three dimensions of language and focuses on the word-level DLLP features that include sophistication of topic-related vocabulary, sophistication of verb forms, and expansion of word groups. It is important to remember that although these features are described within the word dimension, they also may involve some sentence- and discourse-dimension processing because students will rarely hear or use words in isolation from sentence- and discourse-level aspects of language. In fact words are embedded in a larger language context that may involve different modes of communication (oral or written) and different text or discourse types and that will be influenced by the different content areas (mathematics, science, history/social science, or English language arts; e.g., Valdés, Bunch, Snow, & Lee, 2005). Also, language features with small units of meaning (e.g., words types) can be the building blocks for language features that contain larger units of meaning, such as phrases, clauses, sentences, groups of sentences, and whole texts or discourse practices (e.g., personal narratives, conversations, and expository or informational language).

Handle them carefully, for words have more power than atom bombs.

—Pearl Strachan Hurd

CHAPTER 4

Word Features of the DLLP Approach

A word is a unit of language that carries meaning. Much of what you know when you say that you know a language is the words of that language. Knowing words, or collectively the vocabulary of a language, is a critical foundation for both effective oral language and literacy (Beck & McKeown, 1991; Blachowicz & Fisher, 2004; Nagy & Townsend, 2012). A word can be used alone or combined with other words to create a larger unit of meaning (i.e., a phrase or idiom). In the case of imperatives (i.e., commands), a single word—as a verb—also constitutes an entire sentence. Below, we see single words used to affirm, name, describe, request, or command, and combinations of words into two-word or longer phrases used to label, used to describe objects, events, or actions, and in the case of the last phrase, used figuratively (i.e., a nonliteral meaning).

- Correct
- Penguins
- Protractor
- Green
- Contagious
- Listen!
- Good job!
- Repeated addition
- Tornado formation
- Yesterday's English lesson
- Sitting on the edge of the canyon
- The heart of the matter

Word choice differentiated the sophistication of the explanations in our oral language corpus. Semantic refinement, whereby words are used in more precise ways, progresses over time (Verhoeven & Perfetti, 2011). The use of nouns and verbs that were specific to a topic, and the use of varied and precisely referenced objects, processes, and so forth (versus vague, repetitive, and imprecise words) marked the linguistic complexity of student oral explanations. Increase in the range of verb forms was also a characteristic of the development of student explanations. More sophisticated explanations included a variety and complexity of verb tenses. Finally, at the word level, expanded use of a range of different word groups, such as adverbs, adjectives, prepositions, and academic vocabulary cutting across content areas, to name just a few, was also documented. As the box below shows, knowledge of words and how to use them plays a role in a range of English language development or proficiency (ELD/P) standards, such as those published by the New York State Department of Education (2014) and the California Department of Education (2012), as well as in college- and career-ready standards, such as the Common Core State Standards (National Governors Association Center for Best Practices, Council of Chief State School Officers, 2010).

Examples of ELD/P Standards Related to Vocabulary

New York: New Language Arts Progressions (ESL/New Language) Grade 6: Speaking and Listening 1: Emerging ELD Level

Speaking-Centered Activity: Use **preidentified words and phrases** and the previously completed graphic organizers to complete sentence starters that pose and respond to questions and require elaboration and detail, within rules established for collegial discussion, when speaking in partnership and/or small groups.

California: ELD Standards, Grade 1: Section 2: Elaboration on Critical Principles for Developing Language and Cognition in Academic Contexts Part I: Interacting in Meaningful Ways. Emerging ELD Level

B. Interpretive 7. Evaluating language choices. Describe the language writers or speakers use to present an idea (e.g., **the words and phrases used to describe** a character), with prompting and substantial support.

Examples of College- and Career-Ready Standards Related to Vocabulary

Common Core ELA: Reading Informational Texts, Kindergarten

Craft and Structure K.4: With prompting and support, ask and answer **questions about unknown words** in a text.

Common Core Mathematics: Grade 2

Geometry A3: Partition circles and rectangles into two, three, or four equal shares, describe the shares **using the words *halves, thirds, half of, a third of*, etc.**, and describe the whole as two halves, three thirds, four fourths. Recognize that equal shares of identical wholes need not have the same shape.

Sources: New York State Department of Education (2014); California Department of Education (2012); National Governors Association Center for Best Practices, Council of Chief State School Officers (2010).

This chapter contains a number of examples of the word-level features that are tied to teachers working in different content areas and grade levels, with students who are at different language development levels. The three features of the word dimension—sophistication of topic-related vocabulary, sophistication of verb forms, and expansion of word groups—are treated in three separate sections of the chapter. Combined, these features allow teachers to focus on building the necessary depth and breadth of knowledge and use of words tied to academic content learning.

While a number of the ELD/P standards explicitly focus on word-level language at the earliest stages of the English proficiency continuum, words, of course, continue to be essential at any level of language proficiency, across all grades and content areas, and continue to be acquired throughout our lifetimes. It is therefore critical that teachers are assisted with making instructional decisions about word-level knowledge and skills: which to focus on and when, what supports to use with which students, and how to monitor students' development of vocabulary as it progresses in their classrooms day by day. The DLLP approach is designed to make teachers intentional about their teaching of all language dimensions, including vocabulary, as it is encountered in planning for and providing content instruction.

After reading this chapter, you will

- understand the purpose of focusing on student progression in the three word-level DLLP features;

- develop skills in identifying word types;

- gain an understanding of how word types progress along the DLLP word-level features: sophistication of topic-related vocabulary, sophistication of verb forms, and expansion of word groups; and

- develop skills in placing student oral language samples on each of the three DLLP word-level features.

In the next section, we describe how focusing on topic-related vocabulary allows teachers to trace the increasing sophistication of students' use of vocabulary in the different content areas from the *Not Evident* phase through to the *Controlled* phase in support of formative assessment and contingent teaching. The DLLP approach puts the focus on students' learning topic-related vocabulary in the context of authentic language use (e.g., words used to solve with a peer the calculation of angles of a triangle or to describe the motivations of the character Zero in *Holes*) and not simply words learned as discrete entities on a weekly vocabulary or spelling test list.

Section 1: Sophistication of Topic-Related Vocabulary

Definition: Varied and precise vocabulary use, including the use of technical and vivid vocabulary words

Progression: Small core topic-related vocabulary progressing to a more extensive topic-related lexicon and use of precise and low-frequency topic-related vocabulary

How to Choose Topic-Related Vocabulary for Formative Assessment

Key Terminology

Semantics

The meanings carried by words or phrases

Lexical Items

Another term used to mean "words"

Lexicon

An individual's store of known words; can be receptive (comprehension) or productive (expressive)

Noun Declension

Changes (inflections) made to nouns or pronouns to mark derived forms, for example, plurality in English; can be regular (*cube-cubes*) or irregular (*tooth-teeth*)

Verb Conjugation

Changes (inflections) made to verbs to mark grammatical forms, for example, person and number agreement (*I add, she adds, they add*) and tense in English. Tenses can be regular (*add-added*) or irregular (*take-took*)

In the DLLP research project, we defined topic-related vocabulary as vocabulary specific to the personal routine or mathematics tasks that were used to create our data corpus for the development of the DLLPs (see Appendix 2A for more information about the tasks). A specific task or activity will most likely have a predictable set of essential or core vocabulary. For example, as you might imagine, *toothbrush* and *water* were ubiquitous in the teeth-cleaning personal routine we asked students to explain for the DLLP project, and *count, add,* or *multiply* (depending on which mathematics strategy students chose) and *number* were essential topic-related vocabulary for the mathematics task they explained to us. There will also be a larger set of words that may be less central to a topic and may not have been relevant to a students' experience (e.g., *floss* and *rinse* may or may not be used, depending on whether a student does either in his or her personal routine, and *row* and *column* may not be used if a student is grouping cubes to multiply, not using an array). Deciding which vocabulary should be considered essential or merely related is where teachers need to use their knowledge of the content area they are teaching and assessing for both language and content learning. Content teachers are best positioned to make the choice between the words students need to convey their content learning and the words that may be optional in a given activity and that students can either omit or substitute with a word from their everyday lexicon without loss of content meaning making. Support for acquiring the wide range of topic-related vocabulary that, while not essential but still highly relevant for a well-crafted explanation of a task, will of course be necessary as students move along the DLLP for sophistication of topic-related vocabulary. Many textbooks conveniently bold key topic words. We do not recommend this be the sole source for word choices, but if teachers need assistance with identifying topic-related vocabulary for their grade levels and lessons, this is a place to start.

To implement the DLLP for sophistication of topic-related vocabulary, we counted words that are used as different parts of speech (e.g., *brush* [noun] and *brush* [verb]) separately depending on how the students used them in their explanations while completing the tasks. In addition, given that students in grades K–6 are still acquiring the English language as either their first or second language, we treated all forms of a semantic family (e.g., *organize, organizing, organization, organized*) as separate lexical items rather than representing them just by the root word (*organize*).

It is probable that some children, and in particular English learner students, are still acquiring such words as separate lexical entries in their personal lexicons, rather than as root forms with word derivation and grammatical inflection rules used to form other words from them (e.g., noun declension and verb conjugation). In other words, we acknowledged when students used all the different forms a word can take, regardless of whether they overtly knew the rules or patterns by which the related words are made.

When students produce a sophisticated explanation, it contains more varied and precise vocabulary use. Along the progression, children's word choices move from including only the most essential vocabulary and some topic-related vocabulary to increasingly technical (including specialized/content-specific) vocabulary and "vivid" vocabulary words, which enliven an explanation or strongly evoke an image.

In the DLLP progression, topic-related vocabulary comprises four subfeature components. Examples of the subfeatures from the students' personal routine (i.e., teeth cleaning) and mathematics task explanations are listed below:

Essential topic-related vocabulary: The relatively small, core set of topic-related vocabulary words most speakers or writers are likely to rely on for the listener or reader to understand the topic being explained (e.g., *brush, toothpaste, water* for a personal routine and *count, blocks, numbers* for the mathematics task)

Topic-related vocabulary: Words that could typically be used to explain details about the topic (e.g., *gums, germs, floss* [noun or verb], *solve, group* [noun or verb], *array* [noun or verb])

Technical topic-related vocabulary: Words not likely to be encountered outside a discipline or subdiscipline context (e.g., *crowns, dentures, enamel, prime number, remainders, subtract*)

Vivid vocabulary: Words that evoke imagery (i.e., rhetorical "flourishes," e.g., *swirl, gurgle, fuzzy, pea-sized, scrambled, scattered*)

Development of the Sophistication of Topic-Related Vocabulary

Table 4.1 on the next page shows how the sophistication of topic-related vocabulary develops from DLLP *Not Evident* to DLLP *Controlled* phases.

Examples of Student Explanations With "Best Fit" Placement on the Sophistication of Topic-Related Vocabulary DLLP

Following Table 4.1 are some examples of topic-related vocabulary taken from the DLLP data corpus of student explanations in response to the personal routine (teeth cleaning) and academic (mathematics) tasks. The student's language status is included in parentheses. The bullets following examples provide details of the use of the language feature and why we considered the explanation a "best fit" at that phase of the progression.

Table 4.1 DLLP for Sophistication of Topic-Related Vocabulary

DLLP Not Evident	DLLP Emerging	DLLP Developing	DLLP Controlled
• No use of topic (essential or otherwise) vocabulary in English or only repeating vocabulary from prompt	• Use of some essential topic-related vocabulary not from prompt*	• Mostly accurate use of a variety of topic-related vocabulary (including essential topic vocab not from prompt and some precise, topic-related words beyond the essential) • Use of sufficient topic-related vocabulary (including words from prompt) to make the context clear • Possible use of imprecise general terms in place of technical (specialized content-specific) vocabulary or ambiguous deictic referents (e.g., *it, that, these*) in place of topic words	• Appropriate and accurate use of a variety of precise topic/technical vocabulary (comprising essential topic vocab not from prompt as well as many words beyond the basic, including at least one technical word) • Possible use of low-frequency words that enliven the explanation or evoke an image (aka vivid vocab)

*Prompt is broadly defined as any question or comment that students respond to.

No Evidence of Sophistication of Topic-Related Vocabulary

[Researcher: Pretend you're talking to a friend who doesn't know how to clean her teeth. When you're ready, explain to her how to do it and why she should do it.]

"Because she should do it so her teeth don't get ugly. And she has to do it. And how she do it is because up and down. And side." (English learner)

- Only use of topic-related vocabulary is repeated from prompt (*teeth*)

[Researcher: Pretend you are talking to a classmate who has never done this activity. When you're ready, tell him how to use the cubes to find out how many there are and why using the cubes this way helps him.]

"With, with you want to work like you have something to do with. . . . With you want to work like you have something to do with." (English learner)

- Topic-related vocabulary not mentioned at all

Emerging Sophistication of Topic-Related Vocabulary

"He should do it because you want to have clean teeth. And if he doesn't know how to brush his teeth, then teach him because you want know how to brush

your teeth. And that's all. You have to brush your teeth with a toothbrush and you could brush your teeth because you could lose your tooth." (English-only/proficient student)

- Use of four essential topic-related vocabulary words (*clean* [adjective], *brush, toothbrush, tooth*)

- Note: Use of *clean* is as an adjective and thus is not repeated from the prompt (verb)

"You need to put the cubes in the top and count them. It helps you for you can count." (English learner)

- Use of one essential topic-related vocabulary word (*count*)

- Note: Use of *cubes* is repeated from the prompt and is not counted toward the number of "productive" topic-related vocabulary words

Developing Sophistication of Topic-Related Vocabulary

"He should clean his teeth because he could have cavities. And he has to clean his teeth because he would . . . He has to brush his teeth. Then get a drink of water. Then brush his teeth again. Then get a drink of water. Then brush your teeth again. And then get a drink of water, and that's it." (English-only/proficient student)

- Use of three topic-related vocabulary words, including one (*cavities*) that is technical and more advanced than the essential topic-related vocabulary (*brush, water*)

"Okay. You should do them by ten because it's a lot more faster positive and and even quicker because because it helps you get . . . 'cause the more you do stuff by tens, the more easy counting stuff will be for you."

[Researcher: And can you tell him how to do it?]

"You, you grab ten cubes then get another ten cubes. And then when there're no more cubes, and they're all grouped by ten, you count them out. And then you see that there is a hundred." (English learner)

- Use of three topic-related vocabulary words, including one (*even*) that is technical and more advanced than the essential topic-related vocabulary (*count[ing]*); additional topic-related vocabulary (*grouped*) also used

- Note: Use of *cubes* is repeated from the prompt and is not counted toward the number of "productive" topic-related vocabulary words

Controlled Sophistication
of Topic-Related Vocabulary

"So first of all, why you should brush your teeth. For one thing, you get cavities and those hurt. I'm not experiencing it, but those hurt. Second, why cavities are caused, bacteria that go [makes sound] about your teeth and those are bad bacteria. Well, that's enough."

[Researcher: Right, and then last, how . . .]

"How do you brush your teeth. I would basically demonstrate it, so pretend this pencil is my toothbrush. So I do it on the tongue and then the back of my teeth, the middle, and the front."

[Researcher: Anything else?]

"That's basically how I do it. But even though I usually do it a much shorter amount of time, you have to brush for at least a minute, though I usually do it for definitely less than a minute. However, it seems, I still haven't gotten any cavities yet even though I don't brush my teeth that well." (English-only/proficient student)

- Use of five topic-related vocabulary words, including three (*cavities, bacteria,* and *tongue*) that are more advanced than essential topic-related vocabulary (*brush, toothbrush*). Two of these are technical (*cavities* and *bacteria*)

"I'll just sort them by color, and then count how many each one has without adding them up because you might get confused. And then if each one has the same amount I will sort them by color and if each color has the same amount, then you could add them up all together. For instance, this one has ten. Each color has ten in total. And then since you know what ten plus ten . . . Since you know each one has ten, you could count the each groups by ten and for this one you will get a hundred." (Former English learner)

- Use of nine topic-related vocabulary words, including two (*add[ing], total*) that are technical and go beyond the essential topic-related vocabulary (*count, ten, hundred*). Additional topic-related vocabulary was also used (*groups, sort* [as a verb], *plus, amount*)

In Appendix 4A, we have included several student explanations and invite you to read these, make note of the types of vocabulary the students were using, and then attempt to place the explanations on the DLLP for sophistication of topic-related vocabulary. At the end of the appendix is an annotated version of each explanation giving what we think is the "best fit" on the DLLP and our rationale.

Mapping the Distribution of "Best Fit" Placement on the Sophistication of Topic-Related Vocabulary DLLP

Figure 4.1 shows the distribution of explanations produced by elementary-age students in the DLLP research project across the different DLLP phases. This figure includes the explanations of students across the range of English proficiency levels in the project corpus. Students were responding to the academic prompt in which the topic-related vocabulary required of them to solve a mathematics task included the words for 0 to 100, *block(s)*, *count(ing)(ed)*, and *number(s)*. We created this graphic for research purposes so we would learn about the distribution of students' topic-related vocabulary sophistication. The "best fit" for the majority of explanations is placed at the *Developing* phase. Less than 15% of explanations produced by students are at the *Controlled* phase, and this group includes native English speakers and students who were already in the sixth grade. Very few students had yet to use any of the topic-related vocabulary we deemed essential, although a large number (33%) of the explanations still contained little expected topic-related vocabulary and were placed at the *Emerging* phase of the DLLP. Our recommendations in the next paragraph for how to interpret the DLLP emerged from these research findings.

Figure 4.1 Distribution of "Best Fit" Placement
of Oral Explanations on the DLLP for
Sophistication of Topic-Related Vocabulary

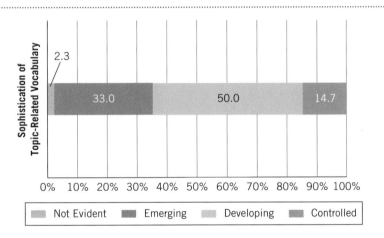

Teachers can use this graphic to help guide their expectations for where students' explanations might be placed on the sophistication of topic-related vocabulary DLLP feature. By clearly identifying ahead of time what topic-related vocabulary is expected in the tasks and activities teachers assign students, they can be mindful of what vocabulary students use as they conference with them or listen to them working in pairs or groups. Choose a core set of words that would be essential to the task and listen for additional topic-related vocabulary that students also use. The sophistication in student usage for this DLLP feature comes from students' increasing repertoire of words beyond the core words teachers would minimally anticipate, as well as their eventual greater accuracy in word usage.

Using the Sophistication of Topic-Related Vocabulary DLLP Feature to Generate Actionable Information to Assist Student Progress

Here we provide two examples of how teachers responded to evidence of students' topic-related vocabulary.

> Through her conversations with and observations of her students, Ms. Blake noticed they were frequently struggling to use the mathematics-related vocabulary from her lesson. She found that the "best fit" for their language production on the DLLP for this feature was still *Emerging*. Based on this evidence, she decided to focus on mathematics-related vocabulary because, as she explained, her students "were currently explaining around the word instead of using the word." In this context, rather than meeting the teacher's goal of using precise mathematics vocabulary, students were instead paraphrasing concepts. What is evident here is the teacher's attention to students' acquisition of vocabulary for mathematics learning and her intention to focus on target topic words in subsequent lessons.

> Returning to the extended vignette in Chapter 3, at the point in the unit when the students had read articles about environmental issues and current solutions, Ms. Silva asked them to discuss in small groups what they had learned from their reading. As she listened to their discussions, she noticed that many of the students were using very limited topic-related vocabulary, mainly from everyday language, to describe concepts they had understood from their reading. For example, she heard them talking about "dirt" (instead of pollution), "keeping" (instead of preservation), and "care" (instead of conservation). While she was pleased that the students seemed to understand the concepts, she realized that they had not yet appropriated the topic-related vocabulary from either their reading or prior discussions they had engaged in during their study of environmental issues. She determined that many of her students were at the *Emerging* level in topic-related vocabulary for this area of study. Her next step in developing the students' topic-related vocabulary was to draw attention to specific words as she used them; for example, when she used the word *pollution*, she reminded the students that this word referred to how air, water, or land had been made "dirty" or been damaged by humans. She also noted when students used these words accurately during their discussions or during her one-one-one conferences and gave them constructive feedback.

Student Self- and Peer Assessment of Sophistication of Topic-Related Vocabulary

Formative assessment of content learning has placed students' assessment of their own learning at the forefront of this assessment approach (Andrade, 2010). Assessing one's progress in language development is no exception. Students can listen to their peers' explanations in large-group and small-group discussions and make check marks against a list of topic-related vocabulary (five to six words only for an effective focus) when they hear specific words, and then let their peers know which they have used and which they still need to incorporate in their explanations. A variant would be to do this as partners, taking turns listening to each other during alternate lessons.

Students can also be supported in reviewing their own written explanations to check for more precise and less precise vocabulary use. In fact, feedback on self-evaluations more generally has been proven effective as a strategy for improving elementary students' accuracy of judgments about their own learning (van Loon & Roebers, 2017). In the cases where they think the vocabulary could be more precise, they can make revisions, ask a peer or a teacher for an appropriate substitution, or reread the text. They can also do the same thing for peer feedback. Peers can read each other's work and provide feedback about the effective use of precise topic-related vocabulary and where improvements could be made. This will likely have a reciprocal effect in helping peers with their own topic-related vocabulary development.

Students can also be encouraged to complete a self-assessment prompt after the end of a lesson or at the close of the day, such as the ones that follow:

- When I was talking today in class, I used this topic-related vocabulary: [list words].

- I don't think I know the precise word for _____ because I used this word: _____.

- My vocabulary goal for tomorrow is to _____.

- I would like help with vocabulary from _____ [fill in peer's name].

With the right kind of guidance and given ways to build up familiarity and experience, elementary-age students as young as second grade can self-assess using the DLLP approach (Pitsoulakis Goral & Bailey, 2016, in press). In our research project, while we found significant associations only between sixth graders' self-assessment and our own evaluations of the students' oral explanations (suggesting these students could self-assess quite effectively), students in the younger grades were still able to complete the self-assessment activity, if not always with the same degree of agreement with our placement of their explanation performance. Nonetheless, they had begun the process of becoming aware of their own language use, which we believe will lead to more accurate self-assessment the more students practice.

Students who participated in the DLLP research project were taught how to identify the "best fit" for their oral explanations on the sophistication of topic-related vocabulary feature in a series of four steps.

> **Step 1:** Working individually, the students were given a visual representation (different stages of a developing flower) and age-appropriate descriptions of the four-phase progression. Appendix 4B provides this graphic for teachers' use.

> **Step 2:** We then modeled the process of using a learning progression to place oral explanations at the different phases, giving our rationale and using counters as placeholders to mark the "best fit" on the graphic as you would on a game board.

> **Step 3:** Students were then supported in assessing other students' explanations through guided noticing, an activity that can make implicit knowledge explicit and has been used successfully in other language-related fields, such as second-language acquisition (Collins, 2007). The students heard the audio recordings of explanations from other students at a range of placements on the DLLP for the sophistication of vocabulary feature, and as we placed these explanations on the DLLP game board, students were prompted to give their own rationale for the placements. This activity helped make them familiar with explanations at different phases of development and gave them an important point of comparison for their own vocabulary production.

> **Step 4:** In a final step, students listened to and then independently found the "best fit" for their own oral explanations on the DLLP.

What Experts Say

Extending the use of language learning progressions to self-assessment allows students to conceptualize where they are on the path of language development and where they need to go.

—Pitsoulakis and Bailey (2016, p. 5)

Through this teaching process, the DLLP was taken from an abstract concept to a series of concrete examples, making the course of the progression accessible for mid- to late-elementary-age students to use during their own self-assessments (Bailey, Blackstock-Bernstein, Ryan, & Pitsoulakis, 2016). Completion of the self-assessment task still led to a valuable learning experience for nearly all the students we worked with, even if they did not always make placements on the sophistication of topic-related vocabulary progression identical to the ones we had identified for their explanations. For example, one second grader said of her explanation of a mathematics task, *"I didn't use too much math words. I used too much 'count.' . . . I use 'count' a lot. . . . I need more math words."* She recognized that the sophistication of topic-related vocabulary feature includes the use of varied words and could identify an area of growth (*"I need more math words"*). Like this young student, nearly all students were able to identify both strengths and areas for improvement within their explanations, and they were able to express their evaluation of their performance using the very success criteria we had laid out in the DLLP for this language feature. In addition, some were able to articulate the broader purpose of aligning self-assessment with a learning progression. We highly recommend teachers adopt the scaffolded self-assessment process described above on a regular basis so this becomes part of the classroom routine for students. A variant of this self-assessment process that is likely more realistic is for students to listen to or read each other's explanations in real time rather than use newly recorded explanations for each topic or lesson.

What Students Say

It is telling me that I can still grow. I can still make my way up to the perfect explanation, but it's at my rate, not at anyone else's. It's my rate and it's my record so I can keep it and make sure I keep getting better and better.

—Third-grade student

In the next section, we turn our attention to how students develop sophisticated verb forms to enrich the word-level language of their explanations and how teachers can assist in this process.

Section 2: Sophistication of Verb Forms

Definition: Varied and precise verb use, including the use of complex verb forms

Progression: Simple-tensed verbs progressing to the inclusion of gerunds, participles, and modals

Sophisticated explanations include a variety of verb forms. Children move from the use of verbs in sentence fragments (i.e., omitting expected subjects and objects of verbs) through the repetitive use of simple verb forms (e.g., present, past, negation, and infinitives) to a range of more complex verb forms (e.g., modals, present participles, perfect tense verbs, and gerunds).

A list of all verb types, both simple and complex, that are part of the DLLPs (the subfeature components) follows (Butler, Bailey, Stevens, Huang, & Lord, 2004). Table 4.2 lists simple verb forms that are most frequently used in English. Examples are given for each.

Table 4.2 Simple Verb Forms in the DLLP Approach With Examples

Simple Verb Forms	Examples
Present	I brush my teeth.
Past	I brushed my teeth.
Future	I will brush my teeth.
Negation	I don't eat candy.
Infinitives	I like to brush my teeth.
Progressive	I am brushing my teeth. (Present) I was brushing my teeth. (Past) I will be brushing my teeth. (Future)

Examples of Modal Verbs

Modal verbs include the following:

Can

Could

Dare to

Had better

May

Might

Must

Need to

Ought to

Shall

Should

Will (only if used in rare instance to convey author stance/habit [e.g., *Boys will be boys*], rather than as the auxiliary verb for the future tense, which is not a modal usage)

Would (including contraction, e.g., *I'd*)

Complex Verb Forms

We provide more details with examples of the complex verb forms that are necessary to identify the *Developing* and *Controlled* phases of the DLLP.

Modals: These verbs are auxiliary (helping) verbs that do not always require an infinitive before the main verb that follows. See the sidebar for a full list of modal verbs.

Participles: These verbs play the role of an adjective or adverb and modify a noun or noun phrase. For example:

> And then I do <u>circling</u> motions all around my teeth.

> The number of cubes <u>remaining</u> is easy to count.

> <u>Having brushed</u> my back teeth, I do the front ones one more time.

Perfect tense: These include present, past, and future tenses of verbs. For example:

> *Present perfect*: They <u>have brushed</u> their teeth every day.

> *Past perfect*: I <u>had brushed</u> three times a day until I hurt my gums.

Future perfect: She <u>will have brushed</u> her teeth by the time I see her.

Gerunds: A gerund is a verb form that can be used in place of a noun phrase. For example:

> <u>Brushing</u> is easy.
>
> I don't like <u>flossing</u>.
>
> <u>Counting</u> cubes is fastest.

Development of Sophistication of Verb Forms

Table 4.3 shows how the sophistication of verb forms develops from the DLLP phase *Not Evident* to the DLLP phase *Controlled*. Development occurs along the same crosscutting parameters already mentioned in Chapter 2, with students using a greater variety of verbs with greater accuracy by the final phase of the progression.

Table 4.3 DLLP for Sophistication of Verb Forms

DLLP Not Evident	DLLP Emerging	DLLP Developing	DLLP Controlled
• No verb use in English OR • Simple verbs used in sentence fragments (may be used inaccurately)	• Use of simple verb types (including simple present, past, and future tense as evidence of different types), negation, and infinitive verbs in mostly accurate usage • Complex verb forms (i.e., modals) may be borrowed from prompt and repeat the phrasing exactly	• Repetitive use of small set of verb types (i.e., relies on some complex verb types [not necessarily the same verb word itself], such as modals, past/present participles, perfect verbs, or gerunds) • May be used accurately or inaccurately	• Mostly correct use of many, varied verb types • A combination that includes evidence of correct usage of simple and complex verb types

Examples of Student Explanations With "Best Fit" Placement on the Sophistication of Verb Forms DLLP

Below are some examples taken from the DLLP corpus of oral explanations for both a personal routine and mathematics task. The student's language status is included in parentheses.

No Evidence of Sophistication of Verb Forms

"I clean too fast me. And you need get the water. Put at your mouth. Do this. Then skip it out." (English learner)

- Use of simple verbs
- Errors in verb usage (*need, get,* and *skip*)

- Note: Use of *clean* is repeated from the prompt and is not counted toward the number of "productive" verb forms

"Six." (English learner)

- No use of verb forms

Emerging Sophistication of Verb Forms

"You need to get your toothbrush. Clean it with water. Brush it however you want, but you need to still brush it. And you should do it because you don't want your teeth to get dirty and to fall off and to get cavities." (English learner)

- Use of simple verbs and infinitives
- Use of modal verbs (*need*); one borrowed from prompt (*should*)

"Maestro . . . my teacher told me that I just have to help you do these things. Not that help you. You have to. . . . I'mma break them apart and you have to count them by colors, by colors and match them together. So if if you you have to use this, you have to connect them together because it's easier how to do it. And my teacher told me to tell you that." (English learner)

- Use of simple verbs and infinitives
- Repetitive use of *have to* before a range of infinitive verbs (*help, count, match, use, connect*)
- Notice use of *I'mma* as a contraction of "I am going to"— possibly an unanalyzed whole or chunk

Developing Sophistication of Verb Forms

"I clean my teeth by taking my toothbrush and taking toothpaste. And then putting the toothpaste on, then washing my toothbrush. Then putting it in my mouth and then rubbing everywhere. And then I finish, and I spit it out. Basically I drink water first. And then I just gargle it in my mouth. And then I spit it. And then I am done, and I go out of the bathroom." (English-only/proficient student)

- Use of simple verbs
- Use of gerunds (*taking, putting, washing, rubbing*)

"Um, so you like put, put the cubes in in a group of by their color. And then when they're all in the groups, you can count how many they're in in all. Like, for example, they're all ten or just count them all up together."

[Researcher: Can you tell her why this way helps?]

"It helps this way because it's more organized or so you can you can concentrate this way better. And like you would know what group this thing goes in if you lose one and then you put it back in its place." (English-only/proficient student)

- Use of simple verbs
- Use of different modal verbs (*can, would*)

Controlled Sophistication of Verb Forms

"Because you should brush your teeth. And then if you're done, you put water in your toothbrush. And then you start brushing your teeth all over again."

[Researcher: And can you tell him why he should do it?]

"Because it's so important." (English learner)

- Use of present participle (*are done*)
- Use of gerund (*brushing*)
- Use of modal borrowed from prompt (*should*)

"Count it like you can count it uh by tens because then you could um make it like way easier. And if um you get stuck, you can retry it again by another by another number. First of all, I tried it by ones. But it didn't work. So I was just slow. Then I counted it by threes. Then I wanted a little easier. But then I um uh then I went by tens and then it was way easier. And now um I know that."

[Researcher: Can you tell him why this way helps?]

"Why? Um it helps because if you have in in if in your life you have to count how much marbles or like stuff you need, you could count it by other numbers. So it, it would be faster."

[Researcher: Anything else?]

"Um you could make it make it into. Let's say you could have put it in estimates. So then like when you estimate something, then you could find uh if if you could see if if your answer's right. If it's not, you could try again." (Former English learner)

- Use of a range of modal verbs (*can, could, would*) with a range of verbs (in this instance, *count, make, retry, try*)
- Use of present perfect (*have put*)

In Appendix 4C, we have included several student explanations and invite you to read these, make note of the types of verb forms the students used, and then attempt to place the explanations on the DLLP for sophistication of verb forms. At the end of the appendix is an annotated version of each explanation giving what we think is their "best fit" on the DLLP and our rationale.

Mapping the Distribution of "Best Fit" Placement on the Sophistication of Verb Forms DLLP

Figure 4.2 shows the distribution of mathematics explanations produced by students placed on the sophistication of verb forms progression. The "best fit" for the majority of explanations placed them at the *Developing* phase. However, almost 39% of students' explanations were at the *Controlled* phase. Less than 1% of explanations were placed at the *Not Evident* phase, and very few explanations were considered to be still *Emerging*. This means that in this cohort of K–6 students, most were at least attempting one or two complex verb forms, even though they might still have contained some inaccuracies. Clearly, teachers can still do much to support the continued acquisition of more sophisticated verb forms so students can express their knowledge and ideas more articulately.

Figure 4.2 Distribution of "Best Fit" Placement of Oral Explanations on the DLLP for Sophistication of Verb Forms

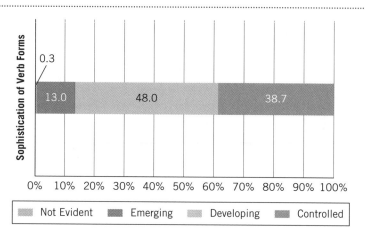

Next, we provide recommendations for this further development of verb forms.

Using the Sophistication of Verb Forms DLLP Feature to Generate Actionable Information to Assist Student Progress

During a social studies unit, Ms. Deane's second-grade students were studying architecture of the local community. In this lesson, they were working in groups composed of English learners and native English speakers to construct some of the structures they had studied. One of the goals of the construction was that students would collaborate and negotiate the design and execution of their structures. As the students worked together, Ms. Deane circulated, listening in on the students' conversations. She was pleasantly surprised to hear the students using modal verbs during their work time together. She heard students say *"You might put that there," "What would happen if you put the block here?" "I could put that there."* Although she had been modeling the use of modal verbs as a focus of her instruction to assist students' negotiation skills, she had not anticipated that her English learner students, in particular, would pick them up so quickly, even though some of their syntax was not entirely accurate. What she realized was that the context she had established in creating structures encouraged the students' use of modal verbs. She thought the "best fit" on the DLLP for these students was closer to the *Controlled* level than the *Developing* level and decided to use their example as a spur to other students' usage, as well as to their continued and expanding usage.

At the end of the work time, she gathered the students together and provided feedback on what she had heard: *"As I was listening to your conversations today, I noticed that many of you were using words like* might, could, *and* should," and then she gave them specific examples of the sentences in which these words were used. She asked the students to think about the "work" of the verbs in the sentence and to turn to a partner and share ideas. When the class came back together, Ms. Deane asked students to contribute the ideas they had discussed. One student said, *"They make other students listen to you,"* and others agreed. Ms. Deane pursued this idea, asking for more information about what they meant. Another student offered, *"Well, they're not telling you what to do—it's more like asking if they agree."* Yet another student said, *"Yeah, like suggesting, not telling."* Ms. Deane repeated some of the sentences that she had heard students use, asking them to listen again to see if they thought that ideas the students had presented were what these words were doing. There was general agreement among the students. Ms. Deane concluded by asking students to listen for these words when they talked with each other in later lessons. She also made a note for herself to remember to point out these verbs and the work they were accomplishing when she heard them in students' speech or saw them in written work in the future.

What Teachers Say

Not just the questions I pose for them but the different modeling to show different examples of subjects and verb agreements . . . Just being more explicit and direct with the examples I think has really made a difference. And being mindful of that within the lessons I'm already planning. So it's not like these are separate entities, these are all part of whatever mini lesson or whatever activity we're doing. I'm just looking at ways to draw that in as well.

Student Self- and Peer Assessment of Sophistication of Verb Forms

Self- and peer assessment can be undertaken for this language feature in the same ways we described above for topic-related vocabulary. Students can listen to their peers' explanations in large-group and small-group discussions and make check marks against a target list of sophisticated verb forms when they hear specific words, then let their peers know which they have used and which they still need to incorporate in their explanations.

Students can also be supported in reviewing their own written explanations to check for more or less sophistication in verb forms and do the same in providing peer feedback with suggestions for improvement.

Students can also be encouraged to complete the same self-assessment prompt shown earlier but modified for sophistication of verb forms:

- When I was talking today in class, I used these sophisticated verb forms: [list words].

- My vocabulary goal for tomorrow is to _____.

- I would like help with sophisticated verb forms from _____ [fill in peer's name].

In the final section of this chapter, we examine how students use a wider variety of word types given time and with increased English proficiency.

Section 3: Expansion of Word Groups

Definition: Use of greater variety of word groups (i.e., "doing interesting things with words")

Progression: A limited repertoire progressing to an expanded array including derived words, nominalizations, adverbs, adjectives, relative clauses, prepositional phrases, and general academic vocabulary

Increasingly complex explanations contain a greater variety of word groups, expanding the breadth and depth of students' repertoires of vocabulary. Children's explanations may first include only simple forms of nouns (i.e., not derived from other parts of speech) and everyday, basic verbs (e.g., *go, put, do*). As their explanations develop, they begin to incorporate a variety of different lexical characteristics. The expansion of word groups feature includes students' use of

- words derived from a root word (e.g., *electric-electricity, electrical, electrician*);

- nominalizations (i.e., special case of nouns formed from verbs or adjectives, such as *multiplication* from the verb *multiply, goodness* from the adjective *good*);

- a range of adverbs, adjectives, and prepositional phrases used to modify and elaborate on verbs and nouns; and

- general academic vocabulary (i.e., words that cut across content areas yet are commonly encountered and acquired in academic contexts, for instance, *analyze, observation, examine*).

In this final section of the word dimension of the DLLPs, we explain how the expansion of word groups feature captures the ways students' lexical repertoires are added to over time and across the content areas that are important for their academic learning.

Subfeature components with examples are listed below:

Nominalizations: Nouns that are converted from verbs or adjectives (e.g., *floss-flossing [is good for you], clean-cleaning [takes time], well-wellness, add-addition*)

Derived words: A morphologically derived word contains a derivational affix (either a prefix before or a suffix after the root word) that changes the meaning of the root word. Often the grammatical category (part of speech) is also changed by the addition of an affix. Examples of derived words that change grammatical category are *easy/easily, modern/modernize, glory/glorify.* Examples of derived words that do not change grammatical category are *dentist/dentistry, mathematics/mathematician*—all are nouns.

Prepositional phrases: A preposition followed by a noun phrase. The object of the preposition can be a noun, a pronoun, a gerund phrase, a wh-clause (e.g., *with whom, for which*), or a compound noun phrase (e.g., *group by the reds and blues*). Prepositional phrases function like an adjective or adverb (e.g., *take a brush with toothpaste on it; brush your teeth by flossing them; caused by bacteria; count them with my fingers*).

Key Terminology
Morphology

Morphemes are the smallest unit of meaning in a language—often simply a whole word but they can be word endings (e.g., *-ness*) and affixes that carry meaning (e.g., *un-*), or inflections on words needed for grammatical marking (e.g., tense, plurality, gender).

Relative (adjectival) clauses: Relative clauses are dependent and cannot stand alone. They function as adjectives. Relative clauses contain a subject and a verb and often begin with one of the following relative pronouns or adverbs: *who, when, whom, where, whose, why, that, which.* For example:

The number that I counted was 50.

I would tell my friend who has braces to clean her teeth really well.

Adjectives: Words that describe or modify a noun (e.g., *healthy teeth, whole life, front teeth*)

Adverbs/adverbial phrases: Words that modify a verb or an adjective, often giving information about when, where, why, or under what conditions something happens or happened (e.g., *move the toothbrush slowly across your mouth; I brush back and forth; now you can count them again*)

General academic vocabulary: Words or phrases used in academic contexts that occur across various content areas (e.g., *combine, demonstrate, for instance, likely*) and retain the same meaning

Key Terminology
Reduced Relative Clause

A relative clause in which the relative pronoun (*that, who,* or *which*) is omitted. For example, *"Putting them in an array makes one line (that) I can count easily."*

Development of Expansion of Word Groups

Table 4.4 shows how expansion of word groups develops from DLLP *Not Evident* to DLLP *Controlled* phases.

Table 4.4 DLLP for Expansion of Word Groups

DLLP Not Evident	DLLP Emerging	DLLP Developing	DLLP Controlled

• Explanation has only morphologically simple nouns (i.e., with no derivational complexity or modifiers) and everyday, basic verbs (with no modifiers)
 	
• At the most, only repetitive use of the same one preposition
 	
• No use of general academic vocabulary
	• Some use of expanded word groups, including evidence of any one of the following word groups:
	  ○ Nominalizations
	  ○ Derived words
	  ○ Prepositional phrases (use of more than one preposition type)
	  ○ Relative (adjectival) clauses
	  ○ Adjectives in noun phrases and adverbs to modify verbs
	
	• Either may or may not use general academic vocabulary
	
	OR
	
	• Use of general academic vocabulary without other expanded word groups
	
	• May or may not be used accurately (semantically or grammatically)
		• Widening repertoire of different word groups
		
		AND
		
		• Some general academic vocabulary terms mixed in with everyday, casual terms
		
		• May or may not be used accurately (semantically or grammatically)
			• Wide repertoire of different word groups, showing that student can do interesting things with words
			
			AND
			
			• General academic vocabulary used mostly instead of everyday, casual terms
			
			• Mostly used accurately (semantically or grammatically)

Examples of Student Explanations With "Best Fit" Placement on the Expansion of Word Groups DLLP

Below are some examples taken from the DLLP data corpus. The student's language status is included in parentheses. The bullets following examples provide details of the use of the language feature and why we considered the explanation a "best fit" at that phase of the progression.

No Evidence of Expansion of Word Groups

"I first get my toothbrush and put it in water. Put toothpaste on. Then brush in the front, in the sides, then my tongue and the top. And I wash my toothbrush. And then put it away and the toothpaste away. And I take a towel, and I wipe my mouth." (English-only/proficient student)

- No evidence of expanded word groups
- Repetitive use of preposition *in* only

"Just count them like one, two, three, four, five. Or if you know how to count by twos, you can count by twos, like two, four, six, eight."

[Researcher: And can you tell him why this way helps?]

"'Cause you'll. Well y-you should try to um do the twos cause that might help you, you know what I mean, to count by twos." (English-only/proficient student)

- No evidence of expanded word groups

Emerging Expansion of Word Groups

"He could do it by just putting paste on his brush, putting water on it. And then brush his teeth for like 20 minutes. And then get water in a cup. And then spit it out twice. He should do it so his bones and his teeth and parts of his body can stay healthy." (English-only/proficient student)

- More than one type of expanded word group: variety of adverbs, prepositional phrases, one nominalization (*parts of his body*); no general academic vocabulary (required for the *Developing* phase)

"So you can learn and, and count. Uh uh umm um to learn and count when you grow, you could count and learn."

[Researcher: Anything else?]

"And so you could get to the number two thousand. And to learn about all the numbers. And to show your mom and your dad and your brother or your uncles. And your grannies and your tias [aunts]. Whoever you show them."

[Researcher: Can you tell your friend how to do it?]

"Um" [no further response]. (English learner)

- More than one type of expanded word group: adjectives, prepositional phrases; no general academic vocabulary (required for the *Developing* phase)

Developing Expansion of Word Groups

"I will ask her, do you know how to clean your teeth? If she says no, I could explain her. I could tell her, 'Look, first you get your brush. If you don't have one, um um go buy one. And after when you're done going buying one, buy a paste and a like a little yarn and you get it, you put the paste first on the brush. And after you put a little bit of water, you start brushing your teeth.' And why is it important? It's important because if you eat like food, candy, or something that's not good for you, you or like some some food could get stuck in your teeth. And if you eat candy, they could grow cavities. And if you eat something that could stick on your on your teeth and if you smile, like if you're gonna take a picture, it's gonna look weird." (English learner)

- Use of several different expanded word groups: variety of adjectives, prepositional phrases, and one relative clause

- One general academic vocabulary term (*explain*) (more are required for the *Controlled* phase, relative to the number of everyday, casual terms)

"Okay, um if a easy way is to connect all the red ones. Wait, 1, 2, 3, 4, 5, 6, 7, 8, 9, 10. Okay um the a easy way is to connect connect them, the row, each color and it whatever um the first color has, um whatever the number that the first color has, I think it, the others colors could have the other one. The same amount. So this one had 10, but I accidentally put a white one. But if I were to, there's a red one left. So if I would have put the red one where the white one goes, and take the white one out, um there would've been 10 still. So you need to find out how much colors there are in total. Then um you multiply by tens, so 10, 20, 30, 40, 50."

[Researcher: And why does using the cubes this way help him?]

"Um, it helps us so it doesn't fall off, and so it doesn't get mixed. And so you could stick it up or sideways, so it doesn't get mixed up with the other colors. So you don't say um so you don't count them wrong by accident." (English learner)

- Use of several different expanded word groups: variety of adjectives, adverbs, prepositional phrases, and one relative clause
- Two general academic vocabulary terms used (*connect, amount*) (more are required for the *Controlled* phase, relative to the number of everyday, casual terms)

Control of Expansion of Word Groups

"So first of all, why you should brush your teeth. For one thing, you get cavities and those hurt. I'm not experiencing it, but those hurt. Second, why cavities are caused. Bacteria that go [makes sound] about your teeth and those are bad bacteria. Well, that's enough. How do you brush your teeth? I would basically demonstrate it, so pretend this pencil is my toothbrush. So I do it on the tongue and then the back of my teeth, the middle, and the front. That's basically how I do it. But even though I usually do it a much shorter amount of time, you have to brush for at least a minute, though I usually do it for definitely less than a minute. However, it seems, I still haven't gotten any cavities yet even though I don't brush my teeth that well." (English-only/proficient student)

- Use of several different expanded word groups: a variety of adverbs, adjectives, derived words, prepositional phrases, relative clauses, and one nominalization (*a much shorter amount of time*)
- Use of six different general academic vocabulary terms (e.g., *experiencing, demonstrate*)

"Okay. Well the way to use the cubes is to sort them out by colors into, into individual groups. So ten, ten, ten, ten, ten, and so on. Wait, I've done a final count now and there's ninety. Okay."

[Researcher: All right. So telling him how to do it.]

"Okay. So the way you do it is you take um each color and then, well take each cube from each color, and then uh you take, you sort out all the colors and then count how many one group of colors has. And then, uh you find, find out how many groups of each color there is. Well, you find how many groups of ten. Well there's a certain amount of colors and if you sort them on to certain amount of groups, then you multiply how many cubes there are in each group by the amount of groups that there is."

[Researcher: And why does using the cubes . . . Can you tell him why using the cubes this way is the best way?]

"Oh um because using, using the cubes this way is the best way because you can easi- um you can easily use your multiplication skills to find it instead of having to add them all together, which would probably take a long time. And uh basi- people recognize colors more than random little cubes all sorted out in different, in different um, in different ways." (Former English learner)

- Use of several different expanded word groups: a variety of adverbs, adjectives, derived words, prepositional phrases, one relative clause, and six nominalizations (e.g., *the way to use the cubes; a certain amount of colors; using the cubes this way*)
- Use of seven different general academic vocabulary terms (e.g., *individual, probably*)

In Appendix 4D, we have included several student explanations and invite you to read these, make note of the types of word groups the students were using, and then attempt to place the explanations on the DLLP for expansion of word groups. At the end of the appendix is an annotated version of each explanation once again giving what we think is the "best fit" on the DLLP and our rationale.

Mapping the Distribution of "Best Fit" Placement on the Expansion of Word Groups DLLP

Figure 4.3 shows that the overwhelming majority of explanations for the mathematics task were placed at *Emerging* for "best fit" on the progression of expansion of word groups. This means the elementary students in the DLLP project often had more than one word group type (e.g., derived words, adverbs, nominalizations) but tended not to use general academic vocabulary in their explanations. A small number of explanations was placed at *Developing*, and just over 10% of the explanations had yet to show any evidence of expanding the variety of words. Less than 1% of mathematics explanations produced by the cohort of K–6 students were placed at the *Controlled* phase that requires the use of many different word types and also the more extensive use of general academic language where opportunity arises. Students at each of the first three phases of the DLLP have room to grow, and teachers must be aware of instructional and formative assessment strategies to promote rich language experiences and practice among their students.

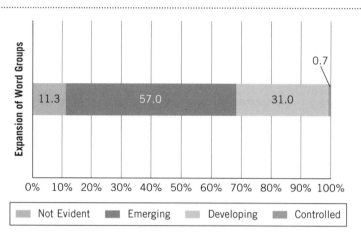

Figure 4.3 Distribution of "Best Fit" Placement of Oral Explanations on the DLLP for Expansion of Word Groups

	Not Evident	Emerging	Developing	Controlled

What Teachers Say

What we've found is that they are using the words, they get excited when they use the words, but it's interesting because it seems to take a few months, right? So right now, they're starting to use "process" and "erosion" in language. But we saw those words at the beginning of the year, so it took like 2 months, for it to really sink in and percolate, and now suddenly its part of their language.

Using the Expansion of Word Groups DLLP Feature to Generate Actionable Information to Assist Student Progress

In a fourth-grade class, Mr. Dobson was working on the language feature expansion of word groups with his students. The students had been reading and discussing a range of narratives that included what Mr. Dobson termed "luscious language"—language that is very vivid and conveys strong images to the reader. In this lesson, Mr. Dobson had been reading aloud a narrative about a thief who had been stealing all kinds of things from the local community. Everyone in the community believed that Mr. Johns was the culprit. Bryce and Lisa, the two main characters in the narrative, were determined to find him. At this point in the narrative, the teacher stopped the reading and asked the students to do a quick write about what they thought would happen next. He asked them to pay attention to "luscious language" in their writing.

This is what one of his students wrote:

> It was a very cold night. The moonlight was on the walls of the houses. There was ice covering the ground. Bryce and Lisa got out of their beds

to catch Mr. Johns. Then they heard something scream. Bryce turned round to see a big cat, bigger than even a person. It came slowly towards them. Before they could do anything, the cat had got Lisa and ran off with her. Bryce watched. He was still and quiet.

The feedback the teacher provided to the student was

You have been very imaginative about what happens next in the story—this is great!

I see there are places where you could expand your word groups. Can you think about how to use expanded word groups to make more of a contrast between the size of the cat and Bryce and Lisa. I'll check in with you later to see what you have come up with.

Student Self- and Peer Assessment of Expansion of Word Groups

All the self- and peer assessment strategies described above for topic-related vocabulary and verb forms can be applied in this context as well. Students can also use the tool in Figure 4.4 for peer and self-assessment in the expansion of word groups the students have been working on. For peer use, the wording would be changed to "my peer/classmate" instead of "I." Students could also discuss their responses on the tool in a one-on-one conference with teachers or even as a whole class. In addition, the teacher could prompt a reflection at the end of a discussion, for example, by asking what language students heard that belonged to one of the focal word groups.

In the next chapter we will see how the DLLP approach is applied to students' development of sentence structures and how to formatively assess this language feature.

Figure 4.4 Self-Assessment Chart for Expansion of Word Groups

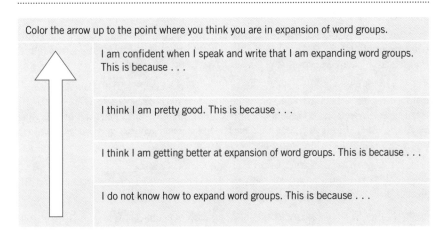

Color the arrow up to the point where you think you are in expansion of word groups.

I am confident when I speak and write that I am expanding word groups. This is because . . .

I think I am pretty good. This is because . . .

I think I am getting better at expansion of word groups. This is because . . .

I do not know how to expand word groups. This is because . . .

SUMMING UP

1. Words are a single, distinct, meaningful element of speech or writing.

2. There are three features of the word dimension in the DLLP approach: sophistication of topic-related vocabulary, sophistication of verb forms, and expansion of word groups.

3. Words are embedded in a larger language context that will be influenced by the language needed in different content areas (mathematics, science, history/social science, or English language arts).

4. The DLLP approach is designed to help teachers make intentional decisions about vocabulary learning in content areas.

5. Students can be supported to assess their own use of words and decide on their next steps in language development.

REFLECTION QUESTIONS FOR TEACHERS

1. How does what you have read about word usage and knowledge in this chapter square with your own thinking? What is the same? What is different?

2. How often do you plan for and intentionally teach vocabulary in context during content instruction? Topic-related vocabulary? Verb forms? Different word groups?

3. How do you assess students' vocabulary formatively?

4. After reading this chapter, in what ways will you plan for vocabulary instruction and assessment?

REFERENCES

Andrade, H. L. (2010). Students as the definitive source of formative assessment: Academic self-assessment and the self-regulation of learning. In H. L. Andrade & G. J. Cizek (Eds.), *Handbook of formative assessment* (pp. 90–105). New York, NY: Routledge.

Bailey, A. L., Blackstock-Bernstein, A., Ryan, E., & Pitsoulakis, D. (2016). Data mining with natural language processing and corpus linguistics: Unlocking access to school-children's language in diverse contexts to improve instructional and assessment practices. In S. El Atia, O. Zaiane, & D. Ipperciel (Eds.), *Data mining and learning analytics in educational research* (pp. 255–275). Malden, MA: Wiley-Blackwell.

Beck, I. L., & McKeown, M. G. (1991). Conditions of vocabulary acquisition. In R. Barr, M. Kamil, P. Mosenthal, & P. D. Pearson (Eds.), *Handbook of reading research* (Vol. II, pp. 789–814). White Plains, NY: Longman.

Blachowicz, C., & Fisher, P. (2004). Vocabulary lessons. *Educational Leadership, 61*(6), 66–69.

Butler, F. A., Bailey A. L., Stevens, R., Huang, B., & Lord, C. (2004). *Academic English in fifth-grade mathematics, science, and social studies textbooks* (CSE Tech. Rep. No. 642). Los Angeles: University of California, National Center for Research on Evaluation, Standards, and Student Testing (CRESST). Available at www.cse.ucla.edu

California Department of Education. (2012). *The California English Language Development Standards: Kindergarten through Grade 12.* Sacramento, CA: Author.

Collins, L. (2007). L1 differences and L2 similarities: Teaching verb tenses in English. *ELT Journal, 61*(4), 295–303.

Pitsoulakis, D., & Bailey, A. L. (2016, April). Extending learning progressions to self-assessment: Students finding 'best fit' for learning and instruction. Paper presented at the annual meeting of the American Educational Research Association, Washington, DC.

Pitsoulakis Goral, D., & Bailey, A. L. (in press). Student self-assessment of oral explanations: Use of language learning progressions. *Language Testing.*

Nagy, W., & Townsend, D. (2012). Words as tools: Learning academic vocabulary as language acquisition. *Reading Research Quarterly, 47*(1), 91–108.

National Governors Association Center for Best Practices, Council of Chief State School Officers. (2010). *Common Core State Standards.* Washington DC: Author.

New York State Department of Education. (2014). *New Language Arts Progressions.* Albany, NY: Author.

Valdés, G., Bunch, G. C., Snow, C. E., & Lee, C. (2005). Enhancing the development of students' language(s). In L. Darling-Hammond, J. Bransford, P. LePage, K. Hammerness, & H. Duffy (Eds.), *Preparing teachers for a changing world: What teachers should learn and be able to do* (pp. 126–168). San Francisco, CA: Jossey-Bass.

Van Loon, M. H., & Roebers, C. M. (2017). Effects of feedback on self-evaluations and self-regulation in elementary school. *Applied Cognitive Psychology, 31*(5), 508–519.

Verhoeven, L., & Perfetti, C. A. (2011). Introduction to this special issue: Vocabulary growth and reading skill. *Scientific Studies of Reading, 15*(1), 1–7.

Appendix 4A

Practice Finding the "Best Fit" on Sophistication of Topic-Related Vocabulary

Read the following example explanations from K–6 English learners and attempt to place them on the DLLP (*Not Evident, Emerging, Developing,* or *Controlled*) for sophistication of topic-related vocabulary. Use the descriptors for the progression in Table 4.1 (page 82). Be sure to think of a rationale for each of your placements. For comparison, our placements and rationale are revealed on the following page.

Example 1:

Because his teeth need to be clean. And the bottom too, and his tongue. And he needs to clean in the sides. And then he needs to brush them every day. Then he has to clean the other side.

Example 2:

She should do it so her teeth don't get ugly. And she has to do it. And how she do it is because up and down. And side.

Example 3:

You could use it so you don't get— so they're separated right? So then you have to put them in groups so that you wouldn't be confused. So that's why you use this.

Example 4:

Put them how you think you can multiply them, like by twos or fives or tens or six or however you think. And if they're equal, if each group has the same amount of cubes then you just count them. You don't count them but you multiply them or just add them however you want. And then when you're done counting them, after that that's your answer about how many cubes you got. So it is important to have it this way, so then it's easier instead of you going one by one and counting them one by one.

Suggested "Best Fit"

Example 1: Developing Topic-Related Vocabulary Sophistication

- Use of some topic-related vocabulary (*bottom, tongue, sides*) beyond just core or essential vocabulary (*brush*)

- Note: *Clean* and *teeth* are repeated from the prompt and not counted as "productive"

Example 2: No Evidence of Topic-Related Vocabulary Sophistication

- Topic-related vocabulary repeated from the prompt (*teeth*) and not counted as "productive"

- While *side* is additional topic-related vocabulary and *ugly* is vivid vocabulary, these are not effective in the absence of essential vocabulary to comprehend the explanation

Example 3: Controlled Topic-Related Vocabulary Sophistication

- Use of topic-related vocabulary beyond the essential (*count, twos, fives,* etc.), including technical vocabulary (*multiply, equal, add*), and additional topic-related vocabulary (*amount, answer*)

Example 4: Emerging Topic-Related Vocabulary Sophistication

- Does not use essential topic-related vocabulary to make the context clear

- Use of some additional topic-related vocabulary (*separated, groups*)

Appendix 4B

Student Self-Assessment DLLP Graphic

Source: DLLP project.

Appendix 4C

Practice Finding the "Best Fit" on Sophistication of Verb Forms

Read the following example explanations from K–6 English learners and attempt to place them on the DLLP (*Not Evident, Emerging, Developing,* or *Controlled*) for sophistication of verb forms. Use the descriptors for the progression in Table 4.3 (page 91). Be sure to think of a rationale for each of your placements. For comparison, our placements and rationale are revealed on the following page.

Example 1:

You do it because so it can help you find out how many there are in all and so you can learn more of the numbers.

[And can you tell her how to find out how many there are?]

How many there are in all? There's six. There are in all. There are six.

[Can you tell her how you found that out?]

I found that out because I was counting them. By counting them.

Example 2:

And he do it right. It go get dirty.

[And can you tell him how to do it, because he doesn't know how?]

Slow.

Example 3:

It helps you count.

[Can you tell him how to do it to find out how many there are?]

Put them together.

Example 4:

You know why you need to brush your teeth, friend? You need to brush your teeth, otherwise your teeth will all fall out. First you need to get all the germs out, and then drink some water and then spit it in the sink. And then you have a weird toothbrush. So you think.

[And can you tell him why he should do it?]

Because your tooth will fell all out.

Suggested "Best Fit"

Example 1: Controlled Verb Form Sophistication

- Use of modal verb (*can*)
- Use of gerund (*counting*) in addition to simple verbs

Example 2: No Evidence of Verb Form Sophistication

- Use of simple verbs in sentence fragments
- Inaccuracies in verb use (e.g., *do, go*)

Example 3: Emerging Verb Form Sophistication

- Use of simple verbs

Example 4: Developing Verb Form Sophistication

- Repetitive use of modal verb (*need*) in addition to simple verbs and infinitives
- Some inaccurate verb use (e.g., *because your tooth will fell . . .*)

Appendix 4D

Practice Finding the "Best Fit" on Expansion of Word Groups

Read the following example explanations from K–6 English learners and attempt to place them on the DLLP (*Not Evident, Emerging, Developing,* or *Controlled*) for expanding word groups. Use the descriptors for the progression in Table 4.4 (page 98). Be sure to think of a rationale for each of your placements. For comparison, our placements and rationale are revealed on the following page.

Example 1:

I think you should just count them randomly because if you put them in stacks or you put them in groups of color, it's just going to take much longer. And when you count them solo, it's going to take shorter.

[Can you tell her how to do it?]

You just have to count the cubes. It doesn't matter how you count them. You just put them in whichever one you can. You just put them in a pile, and the pile starts growing until you get your final answer.

Example 2:

You have to clean your teeth for they could be clean. And you have to get the brush and do it like this.

Example 3:

You need to count them by one. Like that. You can do it to help you. Now so you can know how many is the answer.

[Can you tell how?]

Just counting. Just you get the thing and count it. Also it's in the paper just do it with the fingers. If you need more fingers, you can do drawing to draw.

Suggested "Best Fit"

Example 1: Developing Expansion of Word Groups

- Use of four types of expanded word groups (adverbs, derived words, prepositional phrases, adjectives)
- Use of two general academic vocabulary terms (*randomly, answer*)

Example 2: No Evidence of Expansion of Word Groups

- No evidence of expanded word groups

Example 3: Emerging Expansion of Word Groups

- Use of two types of expanding word groups (prepositional phrases, adjective)
- Use of one general academic vocabulary term (*answer*)

Note: There were no oral explanations by English learners placed as "best fit" at the *Controlled* phase on the DLLP for expanded word groups.

The grammar of English offers alternative options for making different kinds of meanings in different contexts.

—Mary Schleppegrell

CHAPTER 5

Sentence Features of the DLLP Approach

In this chapter, we provide the background and detailed descriptions of the Dynamic Language Learning Progression (DLLP) for sophistication of sentence structure so teachers can formatively assess this feature in the content areas they teach. This feature of the DLLP approach focuses on how students formulate increasingly complex sentences and how their teachers can support their grammatical and syntactic development to do this.

Sentences comprise words that are combined by a prescribed word order and according to grammatical rules that convey information about such things as tense, number, and plurality (e.g., agreement between a noun and a verb for the number of people or things involved).

Sentences can be as short as one word—*Brush! Add!*—or they can be longer and complicated. Complex sentences often string together words of different phrase types and always embed one clause or sentence within another. In the sentence below, the main verb *have* makes an appearance only at the very end of the sentence, and all that comes before it are embedded clauses, which are dependent on the last independent clause.

> *If I count the first row first that has 5 in it and times that by all the rows, then I have 30.*

To elaborate a little more, sentences comprise one or more clauses; a clause contains a subject that is a noun or a pronoun and a predicate that is the tensed (finite) verb (i.e., the verb must convey past, present, or future action or state). An independent clause conveys a complete thought and can stand alone as a complete sentence (e.g., *I add*). A dependent, or subordinate, clause does not convey a complete thought and is not considered a complete sentence (e.g., *Because I added*). A dependent clause usually functions within the sentence as a noun or adjective or adverb to modify the main noun or verb, and it is often signaled by a word that indicates its dependent status (e.g., *when, that, because, though, if*).

The arrangement and relationship of the combined clauses create different types of sentences: simple, compound, complex, and compound–complex sentences. A phrase contains no tensed verb (e.g., *the best solution*) and is not considered a standalone sentence. A sentence fragment may contain only part of the required syntactic ordering or grammatical elements needed to

Key Terminology

Syntax

The conventions used by speakers to combine individual words to create sentences and phrases

Grammar

The overall structure of sentences, including the syntax and the morphological inflections placed on words to convey tense (e.g., past tense regular form +*ed*), plurality (e.g., typically +*s*), number agreement between nouns and verbs (e.g., S*andra goes; the students go*), possessives (e.g., *Maria's book*), and so forth

Quick Review of Sentence Types

[Conjunction is in italics; main verb is in bold; embedded clauses are underlined.]

- **Simple**: Contains one independent clause (one main verb); for example, "I **put** toothpaste on the toothbrush."

- **Compound**: Contains two or more independent clauses, typically joined by a conjunction (FANBOYS → *for, and, nor, but, or, yet, so*) or with punctuation, such as a colon, semicolon, or dash; for example, "Then I **get** a cup *and* I **spit** out the water."

- **Complex**: Contains an independent clause and one or more dependent clauses; for example, "They **should do** it <u>because it cleans their mouth</u>."

- **Compound–complex**: Contains two or more conjoined independent clauses and one or more dependent clauses; for example, "<u>Once you're done</u>, you **can use** floss, *but* I just **go** ahead *and* **do** mouthwash."

formulate a conventional sentence (e.g., *my teeth clean; sum group*). Collectively, shifts from use of phrases and simple sentences through to compound–complex sentences represent a progression from rudimentary to more challenging structures (Bailey & Heritage, 2008; Owens, 2015; Scott & Stokes, 1995).

In our research project, we documented how more sophisticated explanations displayed an increase in the use and variety of sentence structures (Bailey, 2017). In our data, we found utterances that comprised just phrases and fragments, as well as simple, compound, complex, and compound–complex sentences across the different students' explanations. In terms of sentence types specifically, utterances formed simple statements or declarative sentences (e.g., *I have 30 cubes*), simple questions or interrogative sentences (e.g., *Are your teeth clean?*), command or imperative forms (e.g., *Stack the cubes up!*), and simple sentences with negation (e.g., *I don't floss*) through to sentences using complex syntax. These included sentences with multiple embedded clauses (e.g., *And then <u>when you're done putting them in groups</u>, you **can add up** the cubes in each group <u>because this will be easier for you</u>*) [main verb formulation of the sentence is in bold; embedded clauses are underlined].

As the box on the facing page shows, formulating a variety of sentence structures for different purposes features in a range of English language development or proficiency (ELD/P) standards and across the academic content standards. For example, from kindergarten onward students are expected to formulate questions during their science learning (NGSS Lead States, 2013). Students must be aware of the conventions of English grammar (National Governors Association Center for Best Practices, Council of Chief State School Officers [CCSSO], 2010) and use complete sentences in their recounting of their own or vicarious experiences (California Department of Education, 2012). They must also know how to structure simple, compound, and complex sentences (CCSSO, 2012).

The chapter also includes examples of student explanations from different content areas and at different grade and language development levels.

The next section describes the different sentence structures in greater detail, providing numerous examples to help build understanding and familiarity with the variety of clause types that make up the sentence structures. We also describe how teachers can trace the increasing sophistication of students' syntax and grammar from the *Not Evident* phase through to the *Controlled* phase of the DLLPs. This is best done during the teaching of authentic content lessons, which studies have shown can differ in terms of the types of sentence structures they tend to favor depending on the content (Bailey, Butler, Stevens, & Lord, 2007; Christie, 2012; Fang & Schleppegrell,

2010; Schleppegrell, 2004). For example, Bailey and colleagues (2007) reported that in terms of what sentence types and complexity students were exposed to in fifth-grade texts, mathematics texts had significantly shorter sentences and far simpler sentence structures than either science or social studies texts and had fewer complex sentence structures. Paying close attention to the sophistication of sentence structure across the entire curriculum will help ensure students are given the opportunity to develop the full range of sentence-level language skills encountered in school.

Examples of ELD/P Standards Related to Sentence Structure

California: ELD Standards, Grade 2: Section 2: Elaboration on Critical Principles for Developing Language and Cognition in Academic Contexts: Part I: Interacting in Meaningful Ways: Bridging ELD Level

12. Selecting language resources a. *Retell texts and recount experiences* **using increasingly detailed complete sentences** *and key words.*

CCSSO: ELP Standards, Grade 4: Standard 10, Level 5

Produce and expand simple, compound, and complex sentences.

Examples of College- and Career-Ready Standards Related to Sentence Structure

Common Core ELA-Literacy (All Grades): College and Career Readiness Anchor Standard for Language 1

Conventions of Standard English: *Demonstrate command of the conventions of standard English grammar and usage when writing or speaking.*

NGSS: Kindergarten: Earth and Space Sciences

K-ESS3-2 Earth and Human Activity: *Ask questions to obtain information about the purpose of weather forecasting to prepare for, and respond to, severe weather.*

Sources: California Department of Education (2012); Council of Chief State School Officers (2012); National Governors Association Center for Best Practices, Council of Chief State School Officers (2010); NGSS Lead States (2013).

After reading this chapter, you will

- understand the purpose of focusing on student progression in the sentence-level DLLP feature,

- develop skills in identifying sentence types,

- gain an understanding of how sentence structures progress along the DLLP sentence-level feature, and

- develop skills in placing student language samples on the DLLP sentence-level feature.

Sophistication of Sentence Structure

As discussed above, the sentence structures we use in English range from simple constructions to very complex formulations. We can think of these structures as the different architectural configurations of sentences on which we hang our words.

Definition: Use of sentences with varied structures, including both simple and complex

Progression: Shift from reliance on one-word responses and sentence fragments to simple sentence constructions to a mix of simple and complex (embedded clauses) constructions

Simple Sentences. These sentences comprise a noun as the subject (S) and a single main verb (V) with the option to be followed by another noun as the object (O). Simple sentences can optionally be added to by any number of prepositional phrases (*with, on, in*, etc.), and any number of adjectives or adverbs can be inserted next to the nouns and the verb, respectively. However, these additions do not make the sentence structure itself any more complex; rather, they just add to the amount of information conveyed and the overall sentence length. For example, "Anna (S) drinks (V) tea (O)" and "Danny (S) deliberately takes (V) a long nap (O) with his shoes on" are both simple sentences in terms of their basic structures, but the second sentence has hung more words on the frame. The inclusion of the adverb *deliberately* tells us something extra about how he is taking the nap, and the adjective *long* tells us even more about the nature of his sleep. Finally, an entire prepositional phrase, "with his shoes on," reveals yet more about Danny's napping style. Clearly, because a sentence is simple does not mean it is simplistic. It is important to understand that the simplicity is found in the form or structure of the sentence itself and not in the meaning being conveyed. Some of the simplest sentences—*Believe in me; I do; I love you*—are among the most profound we will ever speak or hear!

Compound Sentences. These sentences require the coordination or joining of two simple sentences, for example, "Anna drinks tea, and Danny takes a nap." In this instance, *and* is a coordinating conjunction that connects the two simple sentences to make one longer compound sentence.

Complex Sentences. In contrast to the two sentence constructions above, complex sentences require embedding one sentence (or clause) within another so the embedded component is dependent on (or subordinate to) the main or independent clause. The embedded clause could not stand alone if the independent clause were to be removed. For example, "Anna drinks tea that Danny made." In this instance, "that Danny made" is embedded within the independent clause "Anna drinks tea" with its main verb and would not make sense if it were to stand alone.

Compound–Complex Sentences. The most sophisticated syntactic structures combine compound and complex forms within one sentence, for example,

"Anna drinks her tea and she waits because Danny is sleeping." "Because Danny is sleeping" is a dependent clause embedded within the main clause "she waits," which itself is joined to "Anna drinks" by the conjunction *and*. Each of these different sentence types and what their internal structures involve are further explained below.

Clauses Defined

A clause contains a subject and a verb (denoting an event, action, activity, or state). An independent clause can stand alone as a complete sentence; typically, a dependent (or subordinate) clause cannot stand alone. Independent clauses can occur in coordinate structures joined by a conjunction (e.g., *and, or, but*) or a semicolon, colon, or dash (Butler, Bailey, Stevens, Huang, & Lord, 2004). Types of dependent clauses include relative (adjectival) clauses, adverbial clauses (e.g., time, condition, purpose), and noun clauses (functioning as subjects or objects of other clauses or phrases). We further illustrate each of these below.

Relative (adjectival) clauses describe a noun as adjectives do.

Examples:

The number <u>that I counted</u> was 50.

I would tell my friend <u>who has braces</u> to clean her teeth really well.

Adverbial clauses give information about time, circumstance, manner, and condition.

Examples:

<u>When I go to the sink</u>, I turn on the faucet.

Move the cubes from one pile to another <u>as you count them</u>.

<u>If she doesn't do it</u>, she's going to have a lot of bacteria in her mouth.

You don't want to get cavities <u>because they really hurt.</u>

I clean my teeth <u>so (that) I don't get cavities.</u>

Noun clauses have the same functions in sentences as nouns standing alone (e.g., used as a subject, object, or complement).

Examples:

<u>What I did first</u> was sort the cubes. (Subject)

I saw <u>the teacher use addition</u>. (Object)

It was easy <u>for me to find the answer.</u> (Complement)

Development of the Sophistication of Sentence Structure

Table 5.1 shows how the sophistication of sentence structure develops from DLLP *Not Evident* to DLLP *Controlled* phases. Where we place explanations on the DLLP for sophistication of sentence structure, we make an important demarcation between using complex sentences versus not using these sentences. To progress to the *Developing* phase of the progression, students need to have attempted at least one complex sentence, even if they have yet to accurately control these more challenging structures.

Table 5.1 DLLP for Sophistication of Sentence Structure

DLLP Not Evident	DLLP Emerging	DLLP Developing	DLLP Controlled
• One-word responses • Two-or-more-word phrases not in English word order • Response in a language other than English • Sentence fragments placed in English word order	• Simple sentences • Compound sentences • May or may not be accurate* • No use of embedding (dependent clauses)	• Must attempt sentences with complex clause structures (i.e., an independent clause and at least one dependent clause) • May have repetitive use of one dependent structure, such as relative, adverbial, or noun clauses • May or may not be accurate* • Simple and compound sentences mostly accurate/ grammatically correct	• Use of variety of complex clause structures, including relative, adverbial, or noun clauses • Simple and compound sentences accurate/ grammatically correct • Complex clause structures mostly accurate/ grammatically correct

*Language production may acceptably be "flawed" (Valdés, 2005) during these phases of development.

Examples of Student Explanations With "Best Fit" Placement on the Sophistication of Sentence Structure DLLP

Below are some examples taken from the DLLP data corpus. The student's language status is included in parentheses. The bullets following examples provide details of the use of the language feature and why we considered the explanation a "best fit" at that phase of the progression.

No Evidence of Sophistication of Sentence Structure

[Researcher: Pretend you're talking to a friend who doesn't know how to clean her teeth. When you're ready, explain to her how to do it and why she should do it.]

"With a paste. And brushing your teeth in the bath, not in the room. And that's all." (English learner)

- Sentence fragments

[Researcher: Pretend you are talking to a classmate who has never done this activity. When you're ready, tell him how to use the cubes to find out how many there are and why using the cubes this way helps him.]

"By putting them together." (English-only/proficient student)

- Sentence fragment

Emerging Sophistication of Sentence Structure

"First I do the inside and the outside of my teeth. And then I do the middle of my teeth. And then I push my teeth together and I brush my teeth together. And then I rinse, swish, gargle, spit out." (English-only/proficient student)

- Only simple and compound sentences used

"You need count them and, and then count them like this. And go no go keep it check. You need count them in line."

[Researcher: Can you tell him why?]

"Why you know? Why? You know you go have to figure it out." (English learner)

- Simple and compound sentences
- One reduced relative clause (implied *that* before "you go have to")

Developing Sophistication of Sentence Structure

"You need to go to the bathroom. Then brush your teeth. And you need to do it because one teeth can fall." (English learner)

- Simple sentence (accurate)
- Complex sentences with infinitive forms and subordinate adverbial clause (*because*)

"Okay. Well, you can you can use well if you know how to count by tens, you can use you can make 10 you can put 10 blocks. Uh well you can make put 10 of those blocks and make a one strip. And then you keep on making them until you are until you run out. And then you go 10, 20, 30, 40, 50."

[Researcher: And can you tell her why that way helps?]

"Okay. So, it's easy because you can just go 10, 20, 30, 40, 50 and not have to add some, some other numbers. And so that's my easy strategy." (English-only/proficient student)

- Simple and compound sentences (accurate)

- Complex sentences with *if* (implied *then*) clause and subordinate adverbial clause (*because*)

Control of Sophistication of Sentence Structure

"You should clean your teeth because you could get cavities. And this is how you clean your teeth. You put some toothpaste on your toothbrush, and then put a teeny tiny bit of water on it. And then you brush for two minutes if you have that special kind of toothbrush I have. Like the one that turns around and around and around, around." (English-only/proficient student)

- Variety of different types of complex clause structures: relative ("that turns around . . ."), subordinate adverbial (*because*)

- Simple and compound sentences are controlled

- Accurate: Most or all clauses are grammatically correct

"You can count it by tens because then you could make it way easier. And if you get stuck, you can retry it again by another number. First of all, I tried it by ones. But they don't work. So that was slow. Then I count it out by threes. Then I wanted a little easier. But then I went by tens and then it was way easier. And now I know that done. It helps because if in your life you have to count how much marbles or stuff you need, you could count it by other numbers. So it would be faster. You could make it into. Let's say you could put it in estimates. So then when you estimate something, then you could see if your answer's right. If it's not, you could try again." (English learner)

- Different types of complex clause structures, including adverbial (*because*) and *if* . . . [*then*] clauses

- Simple and complex sentences are controlled

- Accurate: Most or all clauses are correct.

In Appendix 5A, we have included several student explanations and invite you to read these, make note of the different sentence structures the students were using, and then attempt to place the explanations on the DLLP for sophistication of sentence structure. At the end of the appendix is an annotated version of each explanation giving what we think is the "best fit" on the DLLP and our rationale.

Mapping the Distribution of "Best Fit" Placement on the Sophistication of Sentence Structure DLLP

Again we are able to provide a big-picture view of the distribution of students' explanations on the DLLPs, this time for their development of sophistication in sentence structure (see Figure 5.1). This includes students at all levels of English proficiency responding to the mathematics explanation task we gave them. The vast majority of explanations were at either the *Developing* or *Controlled* phases. Very few student explanations were placed at the *Not Evident* phase, and just over 11% were placed at the *Emerging* phase.

Figure 5.1 Distribution of "Best Fit" Placement of Oral Explanations on the DLLP for Sophistication of Sentence Structure

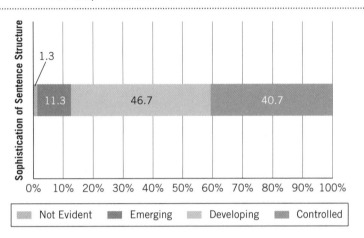

This distribution is consistent with the language research conducted on the syntactic development of school-age children (e.g., Nippold, Hesketh, Duthie, & Mansfield, 2005). While many children acquiring English as their only or dominant language have much of the syntax and grammar of the language in place by the time they start formal schooling, some sentence structures are less frequently encountered, so knowing which word is the subject and which the object is less straightforward. For example, the frequency of production of relative clauses (e.g., *The owls that live in the desert are small*) continues to increase into adulthood (Nippold et al., 2005). Passive sentences with their word order reversal and object cleft constructions with their unusual object-first word order are particularly challenging. The reason we would use such less-common structures is to place emphasis on the object of the sentence. Maybe we are already talking about flowers or columns in an array and want to maintain those topics as our key focus. These structures are more challenging than the common SVO word order of English sentences that children come to rely on and are not acquired until well into later childhood and the early teen years (Dick, Wulfeck, Krupa-Kwiatkowski, & Bates, 2004).

In the next section, we describe how teachers have applied the sophistication of sentence structure DLLP to their day-to-day instruction and formative assessment practices.

Key Terminology

Passive Sentences

Reverse the typical word order of the sentence (SubVerbObj → OVS; e.g., *The flower is pollinated by the bee*)

Object Cleft Constructions

Follow the unusual word order of OSV (e.g., *It's the column that the red cube is forming*)

Using the Sophistication of Sentence Structure DLLP to Generate Actionable Information to Assist Student Progress

During a community of practice meeting, Ms. Garcia, a first- and second-grade Spanish–English dual-immersion teacher, spoke of setting "expectations for doing more" with language and reported seeing this awareness develop in her students over time as well. Ms. Garcia regularly uses one-on-one conferences with her students to obtain actionable information about their language use in mathematics. For some time, Ms. Garcia has been focusing on increasing the sophistication of some of her students' sentence structures.

Figure 5.2 Example of Teacher Planning of Language Opportunities in Context (Conferencing Notes)

Conferencing Log

Language Use Observations

Date	Language Feature	Evaluating Sentence Structure	Sentence Structure Modeled: (T) Teacher (P) Peer	Student Response After Modeling
10/25	Worked on explaining his own work	"Alex 63 and 54 is Audrey so I bring them together and I get 11 tens"	Q: What do we know about Alex and Audrey? (P) Since ___ has ___ and ___ has ___, I decided to _decompose_ both the ___ and ___.	They go trick or treating and got candy. Alex got 63 candies and Audrey got 54 candies. I break the #'s and I got my answer
11/06		"Diego & Tyler collect (collected) rocks from the garden. Diego collected 33 rocks & Tyler collected 66 rocks. Since I have to join the 33 and 66, I first decomposed both the numbers."	Q: What will you do next? [Then] I joined the ___ and the ___	Then I joined the tens & the ones together and I got my answer
11/14	Worked on Responding to the work of others			

Next Steps:

Still using simple sentences to explain how he solved a problem

NEXT → Simple sentences often need to be expanded w/ modifiers to create a clear picture in the listener's mind

[NEXT] Provide more opportunities for the use of complex sentences. Model for support (Partner with Sean)

help with articulation

work on paraphrasing w/ prompts

Source: Used with permission.

Figure 5.2 shows the template she uses to make notes about sentence structure during the conferences. The notes are organized under the headings "Language Feature," "Evaluating Sentence Structure," "Sentence Structure Modeled," and "Student Response After Modeling." There is also a space for her to write the next steps she wants the student to take in language learning. Once she has made notes, she uses the DLLP approach to determine the "best fit" so she can decide on these next steps. For this particular student, her next step was to "*provide more opportunities for the use of complex sentences. Model for support (Partner with Sean. Work on paraphrasing with prompts).*"

Another way Ms. Garcia generates actionable information about her students' sentence structures is to have them first generate oral language and then put it in writing. For example, during a science lesson, in their discussion about marine life, the students formulated questions they wanted to investigate further (see Figure 5.3). They then wrote their individual questions and arrayed them across the floor. Ms. Garcia could quickly see the sophistication of the sentence structures they were using and determine the next steps she wanted to take in terms of language support.

Figure 5.3 Examples of Student Question Formulations About Marine Life Captured by a Teacher for Further Discussion

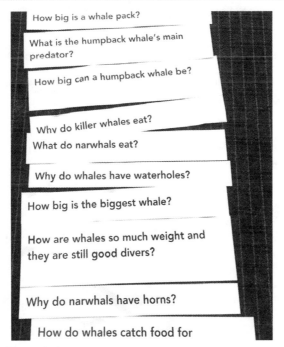

Source: Used with permission.

Another example is taken from Ms. Brown's second-grade reading lesson. The students were working on developing reading fluency. Over several weeks they had assembled criteria for fluency, and in this particular lesson, the students read to each other in pairs and provided feedback to their peers about their fluency. This was a formative assessment opportunity for Ms. Brown to listen to the feedback and, in particular, the students' use of sentence structure.

As she listened, she quickly documented what she heard her students say. Some of the sentences she wrote, with the students' initials as identifiers, were as follows:

J: *I kinda heard you read with meaning, like understanding the words. "I'm puzzled," I kinda heard you get stuck on that.*

D: *Yeah, it was good. You read it like a telling sentence when you read a punctuation mark.*

S: *You read a little choppy. So, the other feedback from what I've heard, you did pretty good. You need to read words accurately and at the just right speed.*

At the end of the lesson, she reviewed her documentation with two purposes in mind. First, she wanted to get a picture of the types of sentence structures her students were using. Second, she wanted to know the kind of feedback they were giving to each other. Feedback to peers had been a recent focus in the class, and students had been practicing providing feedback by giving it to her based on her read-alouds to the entire class. With a clear picture of each aspect from her documentation, she was able to make plans to build on her students' sentence structure usage and to hone their skills in giving peer feedback.

What Teachers Say

I have seen them [students] go [from] very simple sentences to more compound–complex sentences without having it being a focus. Yes, its compound sentences but it's also teaching the words that make them compound sentences and having them understand them and use and apply them in so many different contexts and then talk about them as a use within a sentence.

Student Self- and Peer Assessment of Sophistication of Sentence Structure

Templates and protocols can provide a useful structure when students provide feedback to peers. For example, Figure 5.4 on the facing page shows a template Ms. Garcia uses for peer feedback; one student is providing feedback to another about her mathematics. The structure, which Ms. Garcia's students are very familiar with, includes a put-up (P), a question (Q), and a suggestion (S). (In Figure 5.4, the student writes: P: *I like how you trieyed your very best to get the anser right but it was a little topsy turvy. Q: How do you know thats the right anser? S: Next time could you try and read the problem carefully.*) A similar structure could also be used for older students. On another occasion this same template could be used for peer feedback about language use.

Protocols and templates can also assist students with self-assessment. For example, structured protocols for self-assessment of language could include questions such as these:

- Did you meet your language learning goal today?
- How do you know?

Or

- What did you find challenging about language learning goals in today's [mathematics, science, English language arts] lesson?

- What are you not sure about?

- What help do you think you need in the next lesson?

- Who or what do you think can help you?

It is important to remember that, in addition to templates and protocols, teachers need to provide time in the lesson for students to do self-assessment about language learning and provide peer feedback. Students also need to be given time to use the feedback, otherwise it will be of little value.

Knowledge of sentence structure should be considered core knowledge for teaching and is probably one of the most challenging or intimidating areas of language knowledge that teachers encounter. However, if teachers are to support the progress of their students' language, they will need to know about sentence structure and how it develops. Knowing about the differences between simple, compound, and complex sentences and their respective clause structures will advantage teachers in helping their students develop increasingly sophisticated language, so it is worth the time and effort to develop expertise in this area.

Figure 5.4   Example of Peer Feedback

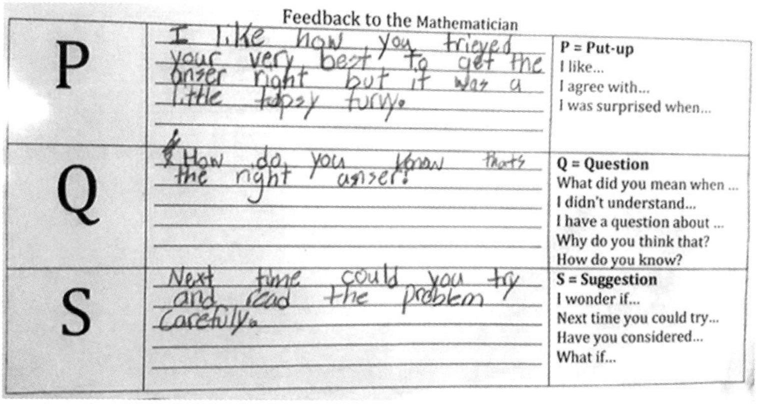

....

Source: Used with permission.

In the next chapter, we build on sentence structure expertise to focus on discourse features that rely on students' abilities to combine sentences into longer stretches of talk or text—in other words, how sentences are arranged into larger organizational structures to convey elaborated ideas and deeper meaning of the content material students encounter.

SUMMING UP

1. Sentences are made up of a series of words in connected speech or writing that form a grammatically complete expression or thought.

2. Sentences comprise one or more clauses, and the arrangement and relationship of combined clauses create different types of sentences: simple, compound, complex, and compound-complex sentences.

3. Formulating a variety of sentence structures for different purposes is featured in a range of ELD/P standards and across the academic content standards.

4. Supporting students to develop increasing sophistication of sentence structure is best done in authentic content lessons.

5. Teachers can use the DLLP approach to generate actionable information about students' sentence structures and decide on next steps to secure progress in their development.

REFLECTION QUESTIONS FOR TEACHERS

1. How does what you have read about sentence structure in this chapter square with your own thinking? What is the same? What is different?

2. How often do you plan for and intentionally teach a variety of sentence structures in context during content instruction?

3. How do you assess students' sophistication of sentence structure formatively?

4. After reading this chapter, in what ways will you plan for sentence structure instruction and assessment?

REFERENCES

Bailey, A. L. (2017). Progressions of a new language: Characterizing explanation development for assessment with young language learners. *Annual Review of Applied Linguistics*, 37, 241–263.

Bailey, A. L., Butler, F. A., Stevens, R., & Lord, C. (2007). Further specifying the language demands of school. In A. L. Bailey (Ed.), *The language demands of school: Putting academic English to the test* (pp. 103–156). New Haven, CT: Yale University Press.

Bailey, A. L., & Heritage, M. (2008). *Formative assessment for literacy, grades K–6: Building reading and academic language skills across the curriculum*. Thousand Oaks, CA: Corwin.

Butler, F. A., Bailey A. L., Stevens, R., Huang, B., & Lord, C. (2004). *Academic English in fifth-grade mathematics, science, and social studies textbooks* (CSE Tech. Rep. No. 642). Los Angeles:

University of California, National Center for Research on Evaluation, Standards, and Student Testing (CRESST). Retrieved from http://cresst.org/publications/cresst-publication-3013/?_sf_s=butler

California Department of Education. (2012). *The California English language development standards*. Sacramento, CA: Author.

Christie, F. (2012). *Language education throughout the school years: A functional perspective*. Oxford, UK: Wiley-Blackwell.

Council of Chief State School Officers. (2012). *English language proficiency (ELP) standards with correspondences to K–12 practices and Common Core State Standards*. Washington, DC: Author.

Dick, F., Wulfeck, B., Krupa-Kwiatkowski, M., & Bates, E. (2004). The development of complex sentence interpretation in typically developing children compared with children with specific language impairments or early unilateral focal lesions. *Developmental Science, 7*(3), 360–377.

Fang, Z., & Schleppegrell, M. J. (2010). Disciplinary literacies across content areas: Supporting secondary reading through functional language analysis. *Journal of Adolescent and Adult Literacy, 53*(7), 587–597.

National Governors Association Center for Best Practices, Council of Chief State School Officers. (2010). *Common Core State Standards*. Washington, DC: Author.

NGSS Lead States. (2013). *Next Generation Science Standards: For states, by states*. Washington, DC: National Academies Press.

Nippold, M. A., Hesketh, L. J., Duthie, J. K., & Mansfield, T. C. (2005). Conversational versus expository discourse: A study of syntactic development in children, adolescents, and adults. *Journal of Speech, Language, and Hearing Research, 48*(5), 1048–1064.

Owens, R. E., Jr. (2015). *Language development: An introduction* (9th ed.). Boston, MA: Allyn & Bacon.

Schleppegrell, M. J. (2004). *The language of schooling: A functional linguistics perspective*. New York, NY: Routledge.

Scott, C. M., & Stokes, S. L. (1995). Measures of syntax in school-age children and adolescents. *Language, Speech, and Hearing Services in Schools, 26*(4), 309–319.

Valdés, G. (2005). Bilingualism, heritage language learners, and SLA: Opportunities lost or seized? *Modern Language Journal, 89*, 410–426.

Appendix 5A

Practice Finding the "Best Fit" on Sophistication of Sentence Structure

Read the following example explanations for K–6 English learners and attempt to place them on the DLLP (*Not Evident, Emerging, Developing*, or *Controlled*) for sophistication of sentence structure. Use the descriptors for the progression in Table 5.1 (page 120). Be sure to think of a rationale for each of your placements. For comparison, our placements and rationale are revealed on the following page.

Example 1:

Why he should brush his teeth? So he doesn't get cavities neither, and he doesn't get sick, or he doesn't get cancer in his teeth.

[Okay. Can you explain to him how to do it?]

You brush your teeth back and forth like that. You do it from the back to everywhere, even your teeth in the back. And you do it on your teeth then from the back and from the top. Then you're done. You get water. You put it in your mouth to spit it out and you're done.

Example 2:

By counting them like I did or just by estimating. Or counting by twos or fives or tens.

[And why does using the cubes that way help him?]

Counting more faster and easier.

Example 3:

You need to get your toothbrush, put some paste and put a little bit of water. And you go up and down with your toothbrush in the teeth. Then right to left. And then you clean your toothbrush and you take your tongue out and brush your tongue. Then you clean your toothbrush and put it where you put it. Then you wash your mouth three times and that's how you clean it. Then you need to clean it because there's some germs after you eat. And those germs make your teeth ugly and when you talk to someone, you smell bad. Then you need to brush your teeth three times a day: in the morning, and after you eat, and at night. That's why you need to brush your teeth.

Example 4:

He should put it by putting together and then counting because it'll take a long time for you just to go like to put it, to take it off, then put it like that.

Suggested "Best Fit"

Example 1: Emerging
Sentence Structure Sophistication

- Simple sentences
- Compound sentences—coordinating conjunctions (e.g., *You put it in your mouth to spit it out and you're done*)

Example 2: No Evidence of
Sentence Structure Sophistication

- Sentence fragments—verbs not conjugated/tensed (e.g., *By counting . . . , Counting them . . .*)

Example 3: Controlled
Sentence Structure Sophistication

- Variety of complex clause structures—adverbial, relative, object complement (e.g., *put it where you put it*)

Example 4: Developing
Sentence Structure Sophistication

- Complex sentence—adverbial phrase (*because it'll take a long time for you just to go*)

*The big parts of a story should stick
together, but the small parts need some
stickum as well. When the big parts fit,
we call that good feeling coherence; when
sentences connect, we call it cohesion.*

—Roy Peter

*As we think and engage with the thoughts
of others through language, we construct
representations of ideas that are meaningful
to us and to others.*

—The College Board

CHAPTER 6

Discourse Features of the DLLP Approach

with Gabriela Cardenas

In this chapter, we focus on discourse, the last of the three levels of language covered by the Dynamic Language Learning Progression (DLLP) approach to language development teaching, learning, and formative assessment. Once students have to combine utterances and sentences for a specific purpose, they are in the realm of discourse (Nippold & Scott, 2010). Discourse involves the organization of spoken utterances or written sentences to formulate language in specific ways (e.g., conventions for spoken dialogue and narrative or expository texts). This organization requires ordering language and using linguistic devices so listeners or readers can make sense of what we are attempting to convey (e.g., Halliday & Martin, 1993; Heritage & Bailey, 2011; Owens, 2015; Schleppegrell, 2004).

There are four discourse features of the DLLP approach: coherence/cohesion, establishment of advanced relationships between ideas, stamina, and perspective-taking.

- *Coherence/cohesion* focuses on structuring and effectively organizing language for the listener both within and across sentences. By tracing the progression of coherence, teachers can become aware of how students are sequencing their oral discourse in temporal and logical ways. Tracing the progression of cohesion allows teachers to monitor how students are able to tie together the references they make in their explanations.

- *Establishment of advanced relationships between ideas* captures how students linguistically convey relationships between propositions (ideas) through the use of a range of different discourse connectors. This includes the use of such causal connectors as *because* and *so*, and contrastives, such as *however* and *on the other hand*.

- *Stamina* focuses on the mental model (representation of knowledge) students are working with and their understanding of the need to provide a complete, explicit explanation to a listener who may not share a common viewpoint or the same knowledge.

- *Perspective-taking* requires students to assume one perspective in their discourse (e.g., first-person perspective [*I*] or second-person perspective [*you*]) and maintain that so they do not confuse a listener or reader, or to overtly signal when they are appropriately changing perspectives within an ongoing conversation or text.

Various aspects of discourse play important roles in a range of English-language development or proficiency (ELD/P) standards, including connecting ideas, using logical structure, and providing details. These are all found in the English language development standards published by the California Department of Education (2012) and Council of Chief State School Officers (CCSSO, 2012). Discourse-level language is also called out in the Common Core State Standards for English language arts and mathematics (Common Core State Standards Initiative, 2010a, 2010b), among other academic standards, so students can use language to provide descriptions, explanations, arguments, and so forth, and do so in complete and intelligible ways in the classroom. Next Generation Science Standards (NGSS Lead States, 2013) require students to construct explanations, engage in argument, and communicate information (Lee, Quinn, & Valdés, 2013).

Examples of ELD/P Standards Related to Discourse Features

California: ELD Standards, Grade 4: Section 2: Elaboration on
Critical Principles for Developing Language and Cognition in Academic Contexts
Part II: Learning About How English Works. Bridging ELD Level

C. Connecting and Condensing Ideas 6. *Combine clauses in a wide variety of ways (e.g., creating compound and complex sentences) to make **connections between and join ideas**, for example, to **express cause/effect** (e.g., The deer ran because the mountain lion approached them), to make a concession (e.g., She studied all night even though she wasn't feeling well), or to **link two ideas** that happen at the same time (e.g., The cubs played while their mother hunted).*

CCSSO ELP Standards, Grade 6: Standard 9, Level 4

*Recount a more **detailed sequence of events or step**s in a process, with **a beginning, middle, and end**; introduce and develop an informational topic with facts and **details**; use a **variety of transitional words and phrases** to **connect events, ideas, and opinions** (e.g., however, on the other hand, from that moment on); provide a concluding section—with increasingly independent control.*

Examples of College- and Career-Ready Standards Related to Discourse Features

Common Core State Standards for ELA: Speaking and Listening, Kindergarten

Presentation of Knowledge K4: ***Describe*** *familiar people, places, things, and events and, with prompting and support, **provide additional detail**.*

Presentation of Knowledge K6: *Speak audibly and **express thoughts, feelings, and ideas clearly**.*

Common Core State Standards for Mathematics: Grade 3. Number & Operations-Fractions

Develop understanding of fractions as numbers A3: ***Explain*** *equivalence of fractions in special cases, and **compare** fractions by reasoning about their size.*

Sources: California Department of Education (2012); Council of Chief State School Officers (2012); National Governors Association Center for Best Practices, Council of Chief State School Officers (2010).

Subfeatures of Discourse

The discourse features can be broken down into further subfeatures. In our research study, we found that coherence in discourse is characteristic of well-crafted student oral explanations. Organization was a subfeature that contributed to the degree of overall coherence of each explanation. Coherent explanations were organized and demonstrated orderly control of information and ideas. That is, students presented information and/or ideas in a logical or accurate sequential (temporal) order, rather than "leapfrogging" around or providing a jumble of ideas that lacked meaningful ordering of clauses and sentences. Coherence was often signaled by use of coordinating conjunctions, such as *and, but*, and *so*, and overt transition words, such as *first, then, next*, and *before*. We found that cohesion was achieved through control of cohesive devices, such as accurate pronominal referential ties (e.g., *it, them* used to refer to *brush* and *cubes*) and use of word substitution (e.g., *blocks* used for *cubes* once *cubes* is introduced) within and across sentences. The degree of usage and the number of different types of cohesive devices varied across explanations (i.e., lack of or partial cohesion led to incomplete referential ties).

Establishment of advanced relationships between ideas captured how students linguistically conveyed relationships between propositions (ideas) through the use of additive, adversative (contrastive), causal, comparative, and conditional discourse connectors.

Sufficient stamina for the completion of an explanation was a salient feature of our sample students' oral discourse. Stamina required students to put into words what they had as the mental model for the procedure they were explaining. That is, they had to keep in mind how they completed the task they were explaining (i.e., cleaning their teeth or solving the mathematics problem) and select from memory what aspects of the procedure needed to be made salient so others might follow along successfully.

Perspective-taking, as it is expressed through the choice of different personal pronouns and any related nouns (*the girl/boy*) or proper nouns (*Dr. Stafford, my dentist*) for the actor or protagonist in the explanation, contributed to the discourse complexity. Specifically, first-person singular and plural pronouns *I* and *we*, second-person pronoun *you*, third-person singular pronouns *he/she*, and third-person plural pronoun *they* are the personal pronouns that can be chosen to reflect perspective in the explanations. We documented the degree of control of perspective-taking in students' explanations. For example, when a child moved back and forth between first-, second-, and third-person pronouns or between pronouns and any related nouns inappropriately (i.e., without

Key Terminology: Discourse Connectors

Additive (Conjunctive)

Used to conjoin or accumulate similar ideas (e.g., *also, moreover*, and *in addition*)

Adversative/Contrastive (Disjunctive)

Used to signal contrasting ideas (e.g., *whereas, but*, and *however*)

Causal

Used to signal causes and effects (e.g., *because, therefore*, and *so*)

Comparative

Used to make comparisons between ideas (e.g., *likewise, as*, and *similar to*)

Conditional

Used to signal reliance or contingency between ideas (e.g., *if, given*, and *since*)

signaling a meaningful change during production of an explanation), we documented these instances as inconsistent perspective-taking.

Most of the explanations in our DLLP cohort data produced by older students (both English proficient and English learners) showed that students were able to maintain perspective in their explanations. In contrast, the explanations of younger students sometimes still switched between perspectives without warning (e.g., *You put the cubes like this. Maddie [classmate] needs to add these. You do add it like this*), which could make their explanations difficult to comprehend. This feature is likely strongly tied to student cognitive development (i.e., an understanding that perspective-taking needs to be maintained or listeners and readers will lose sight of who is the actor or protagonist of the extended discourse). This cognitive development appears to be well established during the middle elementary years in our DLLP cohort data. We therefore recommend including this DLLP discourse feature in the formative assessment of explanations for students in kindergarten through third grade, unless an older student exhibits difficulties with managing perspective-taking in his or her explanations and will then also need monitoring and further assistance with this DLLP feature.

In this chapter, we show how focusing on discourse-level features of the DLLP approach allows teachers to follow the expansion of their students' language uses to convey a range of complex ideas, build on the organization of explanations, and provide sufficient detail and elaboration for the listener to make meaning. The chapter includes a number of examples that are tied to different content areas, grade levels, and language development levels. We show how teachers can generate actionable information to assist student progress on the four discourse features and conclude the chapter with ways self- and peer assessment can be supported toward this end.

In this chapter you will

- learn how discourse features convey meaning in student content learning,
- develop skills in identifying the different discourse features,
- gain an understanding of how discourse progresses along the DLLPs, and
- develop skills in analyzing language samples and finding the "best fit" on the DLLPs.

Coherence/Cohesion

Definition: Orderly flow of sentences and the varied and precise ways the text is tied together by cohesive devices	**Progression:** Limited attempts progressing to the use of temporal connectors and different cohesive devices

Coherence. Providing information in logically sequenced stretches of speech; shows that a student is taking account of the listener's needs to follow along as the student explains.

Coherence is established in the following ways:

1. Successful sequencing of propositions or statements using organizing discourse connectors, including the following:

   - *Coordinating conjunctions* include *for, and, nor, but, or, yet,* and *so* (FANBOYS).

   - *Transition words* include (but are not limited to) *first, next, after, once, finally, (and) then, while.*

2. The use of complete sentences, even if the sentences are not necessarily syntactically complex. Use of complete sentences for conveying the steps or process being explained aids in organization of discourse. In contrast, sentence fragments or disconnected phrases can lead to an overall lack of coherence.

Cohesion. Use of cohesive devices makes an explanation less repetitive and more efficient. Such devices include the following:

1. *Reference* to a full noun (that may or may not be accurately tied). References include (but are not limited to) the following words: *it, he, she, they,* and *them.*

Example [accurately tied reference]: *First I grab my toothbrush and I put the toothpaste on **it**.*

Unnecessary repetition with full nouns: *First I grab my toothbrush and I put the toothpaste on **my toothbrush**.*

Example [accurately tied references]: *And then I clean my brush and put it back where it was. After **that**, I rinse my mouth.*

Unnecessary repetition with full nouns: *And then I clean my brush and put my brush back where my brush was. After **I clean my brush and put my brush back where my brush was**, I rinse my mouth.*

Example [inaccurately tied reference]: *First I grab my toothbrush and I put the toothpaste on **them**.*

2. *Ellipsis* omits words that grammatically do not need to be repeated, such as a verb or noun appearing in a prior clause.

Example with ellipsis: *I clean my teeth by brushing, washing, and rinsing them.*

Without ellipsis: *I clean my teeth by brushing them, by washing them, and by rinsing them.*

Example with ellipsis: *I clean my tongue and the upper side and the other side.*

Without ellipsis: *I clean my tongue and I clean the upper side and I clean the other side.*

3. *Substitution* replaces a noun or pronoun with another word. This may include a generic term (e.g., *one, something*), a synonym, a superordinate category term (e.g., *animals, furniture*), and so forth.

Example: *There are many sections that I do.* **One** *is the molars here. The* **other one** *is the top teeth here.*

Unnecessary repetition without any substitution: *There are many sections that I do.* **A section** *is the molars here. The* **other section** *is the top teeth here.*

Development of Coherence/Cohesion

Table 6.1 shows how coherence/cohesion develops from the *Not Evident* to *Controlled* phases on the DLLPs for these discourse features combined. More sophisticated student explanations require little effort from a listener to understand the steps or process being explained.

Table 6.1   DLLP for Coherence/Cohesion

DLLP Not Evident	DLLP Emerging	DLLP Developing	DLLP Controlled
• **Coherence** ○ Lack of coherence in sequencing *any* propositions (statements) ○ Steps or process being explained is largely incomprehensible to the listener OR • **Cohesion** ○ No cohesive devices present	• **Coherence** ○ Some coherence by logically sequencing a few propositions using at least one coordinating conjunction (*and, but, so,* etc.) or one transition word (*then, next, first, finally,* etc.) to make the linkage ○ Explanations may require a lot of effort from a listener to understand the steps or process being explained AND • **Cohesion** ○ At least one instance of a	• **Coherence** ○ Logical sequencing of *most* propositions ○ Repertoire includes some different discourse connectors (should include both conjunctions and transition words) ○ Explanations may require some effort from a listener to understand the steps or process being explained AND • **Cohesion** ○ Some instances of cohesive	• **Coherence** ○ Logical sequencing of *all* propositions ○ Repertoire includes many different discourse connectors (should include both conjunctions and transition words) ○ Explanations require very little or no effort from a listener to understand the steps or process being explained AND • **Cohesion** ○ Several instances of cohesive devices (must be tied accurately)

DLLP Not Evident	DLLP Emerging	DLLP Developing	DLLP Controlled
	cohesive device (e.g., pronominal reference, ellipsis, or substitution) that may or may not accurately tie together two (or more) elements of the explanation (i.e., links backward or forward)	devices (may or may not be tied accurately)	

Examples of Student Explanations With "Best Fit" Placement on the Coherence/Cohesion DLLP

Below are some examples taken from the DLLP data corpus. The student's language status is included in parentheses. The bulleted text following each example explains the student's use of the language feature and provides a rationale for why we considered the explanation a "best fit" at that particular phase of the coherence/cohesion progression.

No Evidence of Coherence/Cohesion

[Researcher: Pretend you're talking to a friend who doesn't know how to clean her teeth. When you're ready, explain to her how to do it and why she should do it.]

*"You do like this. **And then** you put it inside on the other one **and** up there **and** up there more."*

[Researcher: And tell her why she should clean her teeth.]

*"Um um for you could go to sleep. **And then** you could go and hurry. **And** you could be first."* (English learner)

- Lacks coherence; actions in the propositions or statements out of order: *sleep* and then *go hurry*; repetitive use of coordinating conjunctions and transition words *and* and *and then*

- Inaccurate use of cohesive devices (reference with attempted pronominal tie [*it* does not refer to a previously introduced noun] and attempted substitution [*the other one* does not clearly refer to a previous noun])

[Researcher: Pretend you are talking to a classmate who has never done this activity. When you're ready, tell him how to use the cubes to find out how many there are and why using the cubes this way helps him.]

"Uh one, two, three, four, five, six."

[Researcher: And can you tell him why this way helps?]

"Because you have when you growed up, you have to count children." (English learner)

- Lacks evidence of coherence between utterances (no use of coordinating conjunctions and transition words)
- No use of cohesive devices to make a "best fit" placement

Emerging Coherence/Cohesion

*"She should do it because, because her teeth are going to get yellow and, and her **and** she's gonna smell bad with her teeth when she talks. **And** she may have a cavity. **And**, and, and, and she, she has to know also to brush her teeth like a circle. **Then** you brush it right here. You brush it on your right there. **Then** you, you brush it on your tongue for so your tongue can be clean too. **And** that's it."*

[Researcher: Anything else?]

"She has to do it because like when she's talking, like when she talks, like her when she talks, like she spit it out." (English learner)

- While there is sequencing of several statements, the logic of the connections is not always clear; repetitive use of *and* and *and then*
- Ambiguously tied cohesive devices (e.g., reference with attempted pronominal tie *it* may be referring to teeth, to the process, and/or to an implied toothbrush)

*"Well eh you're going, well a good strategy is just to start at fives **and then** do twos. That way you can count how many fives you have. **And then** count the twos."*

[Researcher: And can you tell her why this way helps?]

"Um I think, I think it will really help because um it's very easy to count by twos and fives." (English-only/proficient student)

- Initial sequencing of two actions, but the sequencing is repetitive of the same two actions; repertoire of coordinating conjunctions and transition words is limited to just repetitive *and then*
- One clear cohesive tie between *that way* and previously mentioned *strategy*. One ambiguous cohesive tie (*it* may also be referring to *strategy*)

Developing Coherence/Cohesion

*"I get the toothbrush **and** I wash <u>it</u> **first. Then** I put my toothpaste. **And then** I go side to side and [ellipsis] side to side. **And then** I clean my tongue **and** [ellipsis] the upper side **and** [ellipsis] my side teeth."*

[Researcher: Anything else?]

*"**And then** I just wash <u>it</u> with a glass of water."* (English learner)

- Logical sequencing of statements; small but expanding repertoire of coordinating conjunctions and transition words (*and, first, and then*)

- Uses two different cohesive devices (reference with attempted pronominal tie and ellipsis of omitted same verb for several conjoined sentences); ambiguous reference that implies inaccurate control of pronoun referent (i.e., uses *it* for *toothbrush* a second time after many other possible noun referents for *it*)

*"Um by putting <u>it</u> on a row and the same colors that <u>they</u> are. Um when you use green and you find more greens, you put <u>them</u> together. **And when** there's no more green, you find <u>another</u> color. **And then** you put them together. **And then** <u>the two</u> colors, you stick <u>them</u> together in a row bec-. <u>That</u> will be easy for her because if she splits <u>it</u> a lot um around, she'll be counting <u>them</u> **and then** she's not gonna know. She's gonna count <u>the same one</u>."*

[Researcher: Can you tell her why using the cubes this way helps her?]

*"Um because this is on a row and you, you could be counting <u>them</u>. **And** you know that **and when** you're done with this row, you're gonna know that this row you're not gonna count <u>it</u> anymore and count this row now. That's all."* (English learner)

- Logical sequencing of statements; small but expanding repertoire of coordinating conjunctions and transition words (*and, and when, and then*)

- Uses two different cohesive devices (reference with attempted pronominal ties and substitution [e.g., *the same one* for *same cube* or *same row*]; several ambiguous references that imply inaccurate control of pronoun referents *it* and *them* [e.g., could be referring to *cube(s)* or *row(s)*])

Controlled Coherence/Cohesion

*"The **first** thing I do when I clean my teeth is, I get my toothbrush **and** I put water on <u>it</u>. **And then** I put the paste on <u>it</u> **and** I start brushing my teeth. **And** on each side of my teeth, I take a good amount of time. **After** <u>that</u> I, I spit <u>some</u> out. **And then** clean my brush **and** put <u>it</u> back where <u>it</u> was. **After** <u>that</u>, I rinse my mouth and that's . . . **And then** I'm <u>done [= with it – omitted elliptically]</u>."* (English learner)

- Logical sequencing using a larger repertoire of coordinating conjunctions and transition words (*and, first, and then, after*)

- Several instances of correctly used cohesive devices (reference with several pronominal ties, substitution [e.g., *some* for *water/ paste*] and ellipsis)

*"So **first** he should put all the cubes. **First** he should pick a cube color. **Then** he should put <u>them</u> in, in or in, in order like blue. You can put blue in one sti- one s- <u>one of them</u> can be blue and then you can do it with all <u>the other colors</u>. **And then** he should, **and then after** he does that, he could find out what <u>each one</u> is. **Then** he could, he could know what the answer is. He should do <u>it this way</u> 'cause <u>this way</u> he can know how many cubes there are more easy because <u>they</u>'re all in one stick. **And** you know that if you don't know the answer for like this <u>yellow one</u>, **then** you could just see **and** you know that the white <u>one</u>'s ten. **And** it's <u>the same amount</u> so it's ten."* (English-only/ proficient student)

- Logical sequencing using a larger repertoire of coordinating conjunctions and transition words (*and, first, then, and then, after*). Note: *So* is not used as a true coordinating conjunction between two statements but rather is used as an attention getter at the start of a sentence

- Several instances of correctly used cohesive devices (reference with several pronominal ties and substitution [e.g., *one of them* for one color choice for cubes, *each one* for set of same color cubes])

In Appendix 6A, we have included several student explanations and invite you to read these, make note of the different sentences structures the students were using, and then attempt to place the explanations on the DLLP for coherence/cohesion. At the end of the appendix is an annotated version of each explanation giving what we think is the "best fit" on the DLLP for this feature and our rationale.

Mapping the Distribution of "Best Fit" Placement on the Coherence/Cohesion DLLP

Again, we provide a big-picture view of the distribution of students' explanations on the DLLPs for their development of coherence/cohesion (Figure 6.1). This includes students at all levels of English proficiency responding to the mathematics explanation task we gave them. The vast majority of explanations were at the *Emerging* phase, with the lowest proportion of explanations placed at the *Controlled* phase. A further 15% and 20% were placed at the *Not Evident* and *Developing* phases, respectively.

In the next section, we provide examples of how teachers have applied the coherence/cohesion DLLP to their day-to-day instruction and formative assessment routines.

Figure 6.1 Distribution of "Best Fit" Placement of Oral Explanations on the DLLP for Coherence/Cohesion

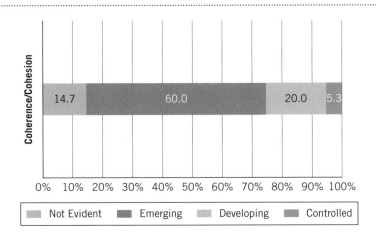

Using the Coherence/Cohesion DLLP to Generate Actionable Information to Assist Student Progress

In Ms. Garcia's combined first- and second-grade class, the students were focusing on the discourse feature coherence/cohesion in her mathematics lessons. Her students know that when they are explaining their ideas (a significant feature of their mathematics learning), using temporal discourse connectors and complete sentences will help others understand what they are saying.

In one particular lesson, the students were asked to solve a word problem. The formative assessment opportunities for language arose when students discussed the problem with their peers, along with possible strategies for solving it, and also during Ms. Garcia's regular one-on-one assessment conferences with students.

While Ms. Garcia listened to the discussions and students' explanations in her conferences, she paid specific attention to the logical sequencing of the explanations and the use of discourse connectors. As she listened, she noticed that many of her students' repertoires of transition words to link the steps they would take to solve the problem were mainly limited to *then*. We see this limited repertoire reflected in this student's written explanation (see Figure 6.2 on the next page):

> *First I wrote the 340 and the 226. I decomposed the 340 and the 226. Then I add the 300 and the 200 and I brought the 40 and the 20 together and they made 60. Then I brought the 0 and the 6 together. Then I put the 500 and 60 together and get 560 and then I brought the 560 and the 6 and got 566.*

Based on Ms. Garcia's evidence, she determined that this student was at the *Developing* level on the DLLP; he was using complete sentences

Figure 6.2 Student's Written Explanation in Response
to Mathematics Word Problem

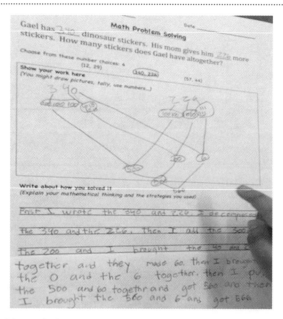

Source: Used with permission.

Figure 6.3 Student's Use of Transitions in Explanations
(Color-Coding Procedural Steps) Using Green,
Blue, Red, Purple, and Orange Sticky Notes

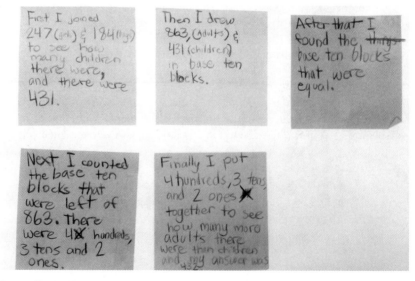

Source: Used with permission.

and showing evidence of a mental schema, but his discourse connectors were limited. She observed similar features in both the oral and written explanations of other students in her class. To support her students' development of discourse connectors, she suggested that they use colored sticky notes to visually show the steps taken to solve the mathematics problem and to encourage them to use different transition words as they explained across all sticky notes (see Figure 6.3; in this example, the student used green, blue, red, purple, and orange sticky notes). Another of her next steps was to explicitly model a wider range of these connectors in her own explanations, drawing students' attention to her usage. She also decided that she would use a written explanation she made up to discuss with the students what alternative discourse connectors could be used and how they would make clearer connections within the explanations.

The next example is from Ms. Navarro's third-grade science lesson. The students were engaged in a unit of study focused on the core disciplinary idea of structure and function and, in particular, the internal and external structure of plants that allow for growth and survival. At this point in the unit, the students were making observational drawings of the internal and external structures of desert plants, labeling the different characteristics of the plants, and then making predictions about the functions of the various characteristics. Toward the end of the lesson, the teacher asked one of the students, Nina, to share the work she had done that day with her classmates. This is what the student said:

> Some of my labels where I saw some bumps, and on top of the bumps were some thorns. And then I saw these light green spots, and so I had a question, and my question was "I wonder why there are light green spots?" And later I started writing this prediction, and then I went back to this question. And when I started reading that question again, it turned into a prediction, and my prediction was "This makes me think that the light green spots are there because it's dry." And that's it.

When the students share their ideas with each other or, as in this case, with the whole group, Ms. Navarro has formative assessment opportunities for both language and content. In this instance, she made a note that Nina had sequenced her statements effectively, using a number of different coordinating conjunctions and transition words in her explanation (then, later, so, when). She determined that Nina was somewhere between *Developing* and *Controlled* on the DLLP for coherence/cohesion. She decided that her next step with Nina would be to help her eliminate the repetitive and unnecessary use of *and* in front of the transition words, potentially through her one-on-one writing conferences with Nina, and lead her to a more unambiguous classification of *Controlled* on this DLLP feature.

We turn now to the second of the four discourse features of the DLLP approach.

Establishment of Advanced Relationships Between Ideas

Definition: Varied and precise use of discourse connectors (e.g., *moreover, because, when, since, although*) to establish relationships between propositions or ideas

Progression: Limited repertoire progressing to an expanded array through the use of additive, adversative, causal, comparative, and conditional discourse connectors

The establishment of advanced relationships between ideas discourse feature of the DLLP approach relates to the use of an expansive range of discourse connectors. In more complex explanations (i.e., beyond the simple chaining of additive relationships with use of *and*), children use more varied sorts of additive connectors (*in addition to, furthermore*), adversative connectors (*however, on the other hand*), causal connectors (*because, so*), comparative connectors (*like, as*), and conditional connectors (*if, whenever*) to establish more sophisticated relationships between ideas and processes.

For example, less sophisticated explanations tend to chain sentences, ideas, and steps together by using *and then* repeatedly throughout the explanation, but as a result, the nature of the relationship is not yet explicitly defined—they may not be causally linked at all. We know from research studies that students' discourse first conveys causality by using *and* to mean "I did this *and* (as a result) that happened" (Peterson & McCabe, 1987), and only later do students use discourse connectors to clearly establish causality (*because, as a consequence*) or a wider range of more nuanced connections between their ideas, such as comparison and conditional relationships.

We also found in the DLLP corpus data that several children, almost exclusively from Spanish-speaking backgrounds, used the English coordinating conjunction *for* as a causal discourse connector often in place of *so* used as a causal connector. This is presumably a direct transfer from the Spanish *para (for)*, which can be used in a causal fashion (e.g., "I use my brush **for** my teeth to not get dirty").

Below is an illustrative list of the most common connectors that establish advanced relationships. Appendix 6B has an extensive list of many different types of discourse connectors.

Additive: also, moreover, further, furthermore, what is more, in addition, additionally

Adversative/contrastive (disjunctive) connectors: but, or, otherwise, however, instead of, though, although, even though, even so, except, (and) while, otherwise, on the other hand, whereas, nevertheless, meanwhile

Note that *while* must have a contrastive connotation, otherwise it is treated as a temporal connector.

Causal connectors: because, so, since, therefore, as a result, as consequence, (in order) to, for, and

Note that *for* and *and* are nonconventional uses of a causal discourse connector.

Causal phrasing: That is why

Comparative connectors: like, as though/if, likewise, as + [adjective, e.g., *big, small*] + *as;* [comparative adjective, e.g., *bigger, smaller*] + *than; so* + [adjective, e.g., *big, small*] + *that*

Conditional connectors: when, if (. . . then), whenever (. . . then)
Note that *when* is considered a conditional discourse connector only when one proposition is dependent on the other (e.g., the child can only spit down the sink when [once] she has finished). If the propositions are just parallel temporal occurrences ("I clean my teeth when [at the same time] my mom is in the kitchen"), *when* is not considered conditional. As a rule, if you can replace *when* with *while,* then *when* is being used in a temporal fashion and should not be considered a conditional connector.

Development of Establishment of Advanced Relationships Between Ideas

Table 6.2 shows how establishment of advanced relationships between ideas develops from the DLLP *Not Evident* to DLLP *Controlled* phase.

Table 6.2 DLLP for Establishment of Advanced Relationships Between Ideas

DLLP Not Evident	DLLP Emerging	DLLP Developing	DLLP Controlled
• No discourse connectors between phrases and clauses to link advanced relationships between propositions, such as causal/conditional/comparative/contrastive (counterfactual), and so forth • No clarity in relationships between ideas	• Singular or repetitive use of one discourse connector to establish an advanced relationship • Possible use of inaccurate or illogical discourse connector within context of establishing distinct relationships between ideas	• Minimum of two different discourse connectors to establish an advanced relationship • Most often displays clarity in relationships between ideas	• At least three different discourse connectors to establish an advanced relationship AND • A minimum of two different connector words for the same type of relationship (e.g., causal, conditional) • Maintains clarity in relationships between ideas

Examples of Student Explanations With "Best Fit" Placement on the Establishment of Advanced Relationships Between Ideas DLLP

Following are some example teeth-cleaning and mathematics task explanations taken from the DLLP data corpus. The student's language status is included in parentheses. The bullets following the examples provide details of the use of the language feature and why we considered the explanation a "best fit" at that phase of the progression.

No Evidence of Establishment of Advanced Relationships Between Ideas

[Researcher: Now pretend you're talking to your friend and he does not know how to clean his teeth. When you're ready, tell how to do it and why he should do it.]

"And he do it right. It go get dirty."

[Researcher: And can you tell him how to do it, because he doesn't know how?]

"Slow." (English learner)

- Lack of advanced relationship discourse connectors

[Researcher: Pretend you are talking to a classmate who has never done this activity. When you're ready, tell him how to use the cubes to find out how many there are and why using the cubes this way helps her.]

"Uh. It helps her to be more efficient. Um uh, you would count by twos to get in each cube in a group of ten and put it off to the side. And then after you're done making groups of ten, you count all the groups of ten. And, and it's easier to count by tens." (English only)

- Lack of advanced relationship discourse connectors (Note: the transition words *and then after* are accounted for in the cohesion/coherence DLLP)

Emerging Establishment of Advanced Relationships Between Ideas

*"He does it like this. He has to get the pasta [= paste in Spanish], put it in the toothbrush, and brush. And then spit it out. And he should do that **for** his breath could smell good and his teeth to be white."* (English learner)

- Use of one causal connector, *for*
- Nonconventional use of *for* instead of *so*

*"Just help him? Um the smart way to do this would be um to first pair up all the colors like of one of one color. So then um, and then you pair up another one. Then pair up another color that's the same one. Then um **if** you see that they're like the same amount, um just check one more. Just check one more and then um. And then **if** you get the same ones, um you could count how many colors they are and then find the answer."* (English learner)

- Use of one causal connector, *if*
- *So* not used as a causal discourse connector (utterance was abandoned)

Developing Establishment of
Advanced Relationships Between Ideas

*"First you take either an electronic toothbrush or a regular toothbrush. You put it under the sink. You rinse it off. You put toothpaste on it, not too much, just a little. You rinse it back off, and then **if** you have an electronic toothbrush, press the button. And then first clean the top teeth, then the bottom teeth thoroughly. And **if** you have a regular toothbrush, make movements with the toothbrush to go up and down and then . . . for the top and then do the same for the bottom. [You should brush your teeth] **because** you don't want to get cavities, and you want your teeth to be healthy. And you don't want to get gum disease and you don't smell."* (English only)

- Use of two different discourse connectors: conditional (*if*) and causal (*because*)

- Clear relationships between ideas

*"Because five, five is a good number to use in counting because i- **because** um well it's friendly. You can use it in the counting really well **because** people know that it's two of them become ten. So it's useful in counting. And ten also. So you can do, **so** you should. But **if** you use other numbers like that, it will be pretty difficult to count. **Because if** you use threes, it'll be pretty difficult to count by threes. But I think this way is **better than** most ways."*

[Researcher: And can you tell him how to use the cubes?]

*"You can, you can, you can put, make a line with five cubes and then group them in one place. So that, so that's how you can use these cubes. And then you can a- do another of them and then connect them up and it will become ten. So it's useful **if** you like that."* (English only)

- Use of three different discourse connectors: causal (*because* and some uses of *so*), comparative (*better than*), and conditional (*if*)

- Relationships between ideas not always clearly expressed

Controlled Establishment of
Advanced Relationships Between Ideas

*"He should do it **because** it's something you just want to do. And you should **because** basically **if** you don't, your friends are going to not want to talk to you **because when** you talk, they aren't going to want to hear you or smell your breath. And they are going to think your teeth look weird. And how you brush your teeth is you get a toothbrush and put toothpaste on it. And then you can just move it around inside your mouth on your teeth. And you have to put it **so** that the bristles are facing your teeth **so** that they take the stuff that you ate off or the food that's left over off. And you should probably rinse out your mouth after with water."* (English-only/proficient)

- Use of different discourse connectors: causal (*because, so*), conditional (*if*)

- Clear relationships between ideas

> *"Well, first you have to s- make, you have to make a group of the cubes. You can do either five or ten or another group. But I did it, I did it in five **because** it w- it's, it's easier and it's **faster than** doing it by tens. But and **if** you did it in ones, it's okay. It's just that it might take a more whi-, it might take more, it might take a while **so** I would rather do in tens. And this way helps **because** it's, well, like I said, it was faster and easier."* (Former English learner)

- Use of different discourse connectors: causal (*because, so*), comparative (*faster than*), and conditional (*if*)
- Clear relationships between ideas

In Appendix 6C, we have included several student explanations and invite you to read these and then attempt to place the explanations on the DLLP for establishment of advanced relationships between ideas.

Mapping the Distribution of "Best Fit" Placement on the Establishment of Advanced Relationships Between Ideas DLLP

Again looking at the distribution of students' explanations on the DLLP for a mathematics task, but this time for their development of establishment of advanced relationships between ideas, we see that the majority of explanations were placed at the *Developing* phase (see Figure 6.4). A small number of student explanations were placed at the *Not Evident* phase. More than a quarter of the explanations were placed at the *Emerging* phase, and the remaining 22% were placed at *Controlled.*

Figure 6.4 Distribution of "Best Fit" Placement of Oral Explanations on the DLLP for Establishment of Advanced Relationships Between Ideas

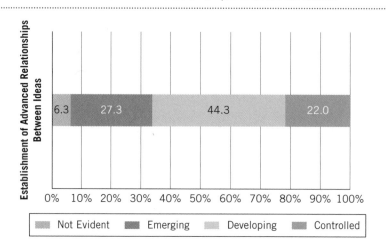

In the last couple of weeks, we have been talking a lot about conditional connectors. One of the reasons why it sort of shifted to conditional connectors, is I really felt as we were shifting to division and fractions and getting into geometry. I really felt this is it. This is a moment we can really introduce a couple of these conditional connectors and just see their application of them. . . . It was having them doing a lot of comparisons, having them look at shapes and comparing them. . . . And so as they were practicing that orally I wanted to see their application again in writing.

Using the Establishment of Advanced Relationships Between Ideas DLLP to Generate Actionable Information to Assist Student Progress

In the following excerpt, we return to Ms. Garcia's combined first- and second-grade mathematics class. She began this particular lesson with a "warm-up activity," engaging the students in a discussion about grouping eight beads of two different colors to make patterns for a necklace they could sell at the upcoming school fair. Such discussions provide Ms. Garcia with insights not only into her students' mathematical thinking but also into the language they use to convey their thinking. After one student proposed the pattern as "two yellow beads, four red, and two yellow," another student, Lisa, said, "And that makes eight." Ms. Garcia invited Lisa to explain to the group why there are eight beads in the necklace:

> Well that's two and then . . . well you have to add them up all together, because eight is an equal number and so you can do . . . but you can do this with a lot of numbers, but one thing it has is where maybe you have two groups and you can't do that with a seven because all the groups want the same amount. So you can't give three to one group and four to the other group, 'cause that wouldn't be fair. So you add, so it would have to add up to be four and four.

In terms of the mathematical content, Lisa was beginning to think about odd and even numbers; even though Lisa did not use those terms, Ms. Garcia also paid attention to her language usage, in particular the feature establishing advanced relationships. She noticed that Lisa was using the causal discourse connectors *because, so* and contrastive connectors *but, maybe.* Lisa was able to convey her idea in her explanation even though she did not express it very accurately. At the end of the discussion, while the students were moving to work on their tasks, Ms. Garcia made notes about Lisa's explanation and, with reference to the DLLP, determined that the "best fit" was the *Developing* phase. Her plan for advancing Lisa's ability with this language feature was to model explanations that establish advanced relationships—which would be beneficial for the whole class—and to paraphrase Lisa's explanations during their future one-on-one mathematics conferences.

As we saw earlier, during Ms. Navarro's third-grade science lesson, she was able to obtain evidence about the discourse feature coherence. In the same lesson, when she was discussing the predictions students were making, she heard two instances of the feature establishing advanced relationships. One student said:

> *I wonder why this cactus has flowers, because a lot of times I go to the desert I don't see cactus with flowers, I just see them with spikes.*

And another said:

> *I predict that when you cut a cactus open, there's water inside, in the lines, so they can drink water and not get dry.*

Although she was not listening specifically for this language feature, after extensive implementation of the DLLP approach, she was so attuned to the discourse features that she was able to identify the features relatively easily. She determined that both students were focusing on just one type of relationship causality, which put them at the *Emerging* phase in establishing advanced relationships between ideas on the DLLPs. However, she was pleased by what she heard, as the students' statements represented progress on their part. She made a note of her observation and planned to think about further opportunities she could provide in the science unit so students would need to express more than one relationship between ideas as they discussed science phenomena.

We turn now to stamina—how students stay engaged with their explanations long enough to reveal clearly what they have in mind so their audience can extract meaning from their words.

Stamina

Definition: The sustained attempt to produce a comprehensible explanation (i.e., enough detail but not too much)

Progression: No elaboration or lacks meaning progressing to a clear mental model with use of sufficient detail and elaboration for the listener to readily make meaning

Stamina is the notion that children have tenacity in giving sufficiently elaborated explanations. Students who have stamina may be very fluent throughout their production of an explanation, or they may even have some retracings and restarts initially but forge on to convey their explanations with sufficient detail for the listener to make meaning of what they are saying.

We extended stamina to language production from the reading realm. Our use of the term *stamina* is analogous to the notion of stamina in reading as children sustain attempts to decode and comprehend text without getting distracted by superfluous details or becoming too fatigued (e.g., Calkins, 2001; Hiebert, Wilson, & Trainin, 2010). However, for language production, the converse is necessary. Children need to sustain their attempts at an explanation to *encode* their thoughts in ways that are detailed and thorough and do not meander so far off task or topic that others will not be able to extract meaning from their words (Bailey & Heritage, 2014; Pitsoulakis Goral & Bailey, 2016, in press).

Development of Stamina

Table 6.3 shows how stamina develops from DLLP phase *Not Evident* to DLLP *Controlled*. Underlying stamina for language production is the notion of a mental model of the actions or processes students are explaining. Without having in mind exactly what they are explaining, students' explanations may omit important steps or details. The amount of detail must be just right, or meaning making may be impaired for the listener. An explanation that lacks stamina is one that is compromised or abandoned too soon, before the listener can extract all the necessary information to replicate a procedure, for example, or the student becomes stuck in one spot having to retrace or restart the explanation and does not ever recover the forward movement of the explanation before he or she runs out of stamina.

Table 6.3 DLLP for Stamina

DLLP Not Evident	DLLP Emerging	DLLP Developing	DLLP Controlled
• Response is short and incomplete in terms of expected content for the prompt. That is, the response does not convey that the child has a mental model of the processes being explained • Few to no details (lacking information on specifics of actions, events, thoughts, ideas, such as when, where, with what/whom, how, how often, etc.) • May abandon response (mid-sentence, mid-detail, mid-idea) • Response may contain restarts and retracings that are difficult to follow	• Response is short with some basic aspects of expected content. Mental model of the processes being explained is not fully discernible • May include some details (see *Not Evident* or *Controlled* columns) • Response may contain a number of retracings and restarts such that meaning making is disrupted in a few places	• Expanded response that conveys most but not all expected content for the specific prompt. Mental model of the processes being explained is more evident but not completely clear • Includes several expected details (see *Not Evident* or *Controlled* columns) • Response may contain a small number of retracings and restarts, but meaning making is not disrupted	• Sustained response giving all expected content for the specific prompt. Conveys that the child has a clear mental model of the processes being explained • Conveys actions, events, thoughts, and ideas in detail • Response may contain a small number of retracings and restarts but is fluent, and meaning making is not disrupted

Examples of Student Explanations With "Best Fit" Placement on the Stamina DLLP

Examples of explanations from the DLLP corpus data placed at the different phases of the stamina progression are given below. The student's language status is included in parentheses. Once again, the bulleted text following the examples provides details of the use of the language feature and our rationale for placing the explanations as a "best fit" at a particular phase of the progression.

No Evidence of Stamina

[Researcher: Now pretend you're talking to your friend and she does not know how to clean her teeth. When you're ready, tell how to do it and why she should do it.]

"Because it makes your teeth shiny and clean. You have to brush your teeth with a brush. That's all." (English only)

- Begins with a sentence fragment
- Lacks expected steps and detail
- Does not exhibit complete mental model

[Researcher: Pretend you are talking to a classmate who has never done this activity. When you're ready, tell her how to use the cubes to find out how many there are and why using the cubes this way helps her.]

"I could show her."

[Researcher: What would you tell her? Tell her how to do it?]

"Um counting."

[Researcher: Why does using the cubes this way help her?]

"So, so you could, could learn." (English learner)

- Lacks expected steps and detail
- Exhibits retracing
- Does not exhibit complete mental model

Emerging Stamina

"You first get the brush. You put some um something on it. And then you put it on your mouth. You brush your teeth. And then I say because it's to stay nice and clean. It's important to do, do your teeth and clean them. And then when you eat, when you eat in the morning and, and it's all night, you do it again. To clean your teeth." (English learner)

- Includes the most basic steps in the process

- Retracings impede comprehension

- Is not a clear mental model

"Okay. Um, why the c- the cubes help me how to count. Because it's easier and a little bit faster for me because um, because then if I had to do it another one, I'm not gonna do it. I'm gonna work at where I left and where I …"

[Researcher: And uh can you tell her how to use the cubes to find out how many there are?]

"Connecting thing, connecting them for." (English learner)

- Includes the most basic steps in the process

- Lacks detail to replicate the procedure

- Retracings impede comprehension

- Includes sentence fragments where thoughts were likely abandoned

- Is not a clear mental model

Developing Stamina

"You should clean your teeth because um if you don't, they'll get very bad. And they'll look bad and they get all yellow. And how you brush your teeth is you get a toothbrush and rinse it under water. And then you put toothpaste on it and then scrub it against your teeth for like a minute and a half, two minutes. And then don't swallow the toothpaste and you spit it out." (English-only/proficient student)

- Includes the required steps in the process

- Lacks some detail

- Ends abruptly

"Um so you like put, put the cubes in, in a group of—by their color. And then when they're all in the groups, you can count how many they're in, in all. Like, for example, they're all ten or just count them all up together."

[Researcher: Can you tell her why this way helps?]

"It helps this way because it's more organized or so you can, you can concentrate this way better. And like you would know what group this thing goes in if you lose one and then you put it back in its place." (English-only/proficient student)

- Includes the required steps in the process

- Lacks some detail

- Possibly includes unnecessary detail (losing/replacing a cube)

Controlled Stamina

"Well, how to brush your teeth is you grab a toothbrush and put the paste on it. And then you brush up or down first. It doesn't matter. And then you brush all the way at the back, and then all the way at the back on the other side and then next, the gums, and then on the top too. And then you just make sure you get every single tooth. And then when you're done, you just spit out the paste. And then you put some water in your mouth and you spit it out. Try to get all the paste. And then you wash your toothpaste, your brush. And then you put it away. And then you just floss in between your teeth and if you get some food in there, just like you could wash it with the water or you could just forget about it. And then take another, not take another piece, but if you were doing it on the left and took it out. And then I would try in the middle, and then right, then middle. Yeah."

[Researcher: Can you tell him why he should do it?]

"So you won't get bacterias in your teeth. And if you get one, it's not going to be simple." (English-only/proficient learner)

- Contains sufficient information and detail to possibly replicate the explained process

- Child possesses and conveys a mental model of teeth cleaning, without the addition of superfluous details

"Okay you should if you want to find out how many cu- how to find out how many cubes there are, and you want to do it the most efficient way, the way that I would do it would be that I would connect ten of them. And then I would just keep making um sticks of ten. And then at the end, I would count to see how many sticks of ten there would be. And then that would, then you would do that times ten, and then you would get your answer. And you should use that way 'cause it's an efficient way that you can do quickly." (English-only/proficient student)

- Contains sufficient information and detail to possibly replicate the explained process

- Child possesses and conveys a mental model of mathematical problem-solving procedure, without the addition of superfluous details

In Appendix 6D, we have included several student explanations and invite you to read these and then attempt to place the explanations on the DLLP for stamina.

Mapping the Distribution of "Best Fit" Placement on the Stamina DLLP

Staying with the explanations generated by the mathematics explanation task, we provide an overview of the distribution of students' explanations on the DLLP for stamina. As Figure 6.5 reveals, this discourse feature is very challenging for students in the DLLP corpus data across all levels of English language proficiency, including for English-only and proficient students. More than 50% of explanations were placed at the *Emerging* phase. Only 7% were at the *Controlled* level. A large proportion of the remaining explanations were at *Developing*, and just under 9% were placed at the *Not Evident* phase.

Figure 6.5 Distribution of "Best Fit" Placement of Oral Explanations on the DLLP for Stamina

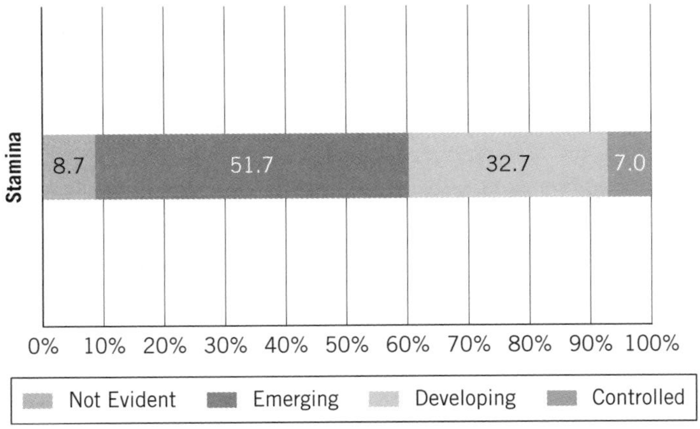

Using the Stamina DLLP to Generate Actionable Information to Assist Student Progress

This example of generating evidence of stamina is from a second-grade English language arts lesson. The students were working on a poetry unit, and in this lesson they were focusing on how poetic devices supply rhythm and meaning in a poem. During independent reading time, as students were individually reading poems, Ms. Bruner engaged in a formative assessment conversation with one of her students, José, to find out how well he was understanding poetic devices. After asking José to read the poem aloud and a brief discussion about the effect the author was trying to convey with the use of different typefaces, Ms. Bruner asked José why he thought it was important to the author that the poem be read in a certain way.

José responded:

> *Well . . . because it makes it sound better . . . and makes it . . . like . . .*
> *makes it sound better and makes it . . . um . . . make it sound . . . makes*
> *it sound like what the poem is describing.*

Ms. Bruner recognized that José was attempting to articulate a sophisticated idea (the use of the varying fonts and sizes to enhance the meaning of the poem about the movement of a bus), and he struggled to articulate his thinking. However, despite several retracings, he showed tenacity in forming his explanation, ultimately articulating the poet's intent. Ms. Bruner said to José:

I was listening carefully to what you were saying and I noticed that it was a bit challenging to explain your idea, but you did it! You kept going till you had said your thought and that is great!

José's explanation provided evidence for Ms. Bruner to add to the observations that she had made in recent weeks about his stamina. From this evidence, she determined the "best fit" for him on the DLLP was the *Emerging* phase. Her plan to move him forward was to keep providing opportunities to articulate explanations about challenging content.

A further example is also from a second-grade class. In this particular lesson, students were having a discussion about what helps them learn. The teacher, Ms. Cisneros, invited each of the students to share their ideas with their peers. When it was Brenda's turn, she said:

I like to collaborate with my research buddies. Then it really helps me. That's why I like to collaborate with people. So when I'm going to research lab sometimes, we go on the iPads and search up what we need if you don't have the answer. You search it up, and then sometimes it asks us a question and we don't know it. We each could take turns instead of just fighting over it.

Although Ms. Cisneros had not been particularly focusing on the language feature stamina, she recognized that Brenda's explanation was valuable evidence of her stamina; Brenda had given an expanded response to the question, and she had included a number of details to express her viewpoint. Ms. Cisneros made a note of this, putting Brenda's "best fit" at the *Developing* phase. She did not immediately make a pedagogical response, determining that she needed more evidence. Prior evidence had indicated an *Emerging* phase for stamina for Brenda, and Ms. Cisneros wanted to be sure that she had sufficient information about Brenda's current status to answer her question: "Is this a one-off or a real indication of progress?"

We move now to our fourth and final discourse-level feature of the DLLP approach.

Perspective-Taking

Definition: Taking account of the listeners' need to track referents so they can understand who is being talked about or what is taking place

Progression: Shift from inconsistent perspective-taking to maintaining or appropriately signaling shifts to maintain meaning making for the listener

In more sophisticated explanations, children display control of perspective-taking. That is, they are able to answer the prompt using the appropriate perspective of first, second, or third person (pronouns, nouns, and proper nouns referring to self and others). Also they are able to maintain the appropriate perspective throughout the explanation. For instance, the example below presents an explanation in which the child begins her response in third-person perspective when second-person perspective is more appropriate for the researcher's first prompt. Again, reminders of the researcher's prompts in full are provided in brackets below so the context can be fully understood.

[Researcher: Now, pretend you're talking to your friend and she does not know how to clean her teeth. When you're ready, tell how to do it and why she should do it.]

"The little girl has to do it, because her teeth will stay clean and they won't fall out and they won't turn like different colors and they won't fall out at the same time."

[Researcher: And can you tell her how she should clean her teeth?]

"You should brush on the bottom and then the top and then this part and then the back and in the back."

After the researcher's second prompt, the child switches to the appropriate perspective, presumably after having reheard linguistic cues from the researcher to address the friend directly (i.e., *tell her*).

Development of Perspective-Taking

Table 6.4 on the next page shows how perspective-taking develops from the DLLP *Not Evident* to DLLP *Controlled* phase. To progress from the early phases to the later phases of the progression, students must shift from the wrong or inconsistent perspectives (given the specific demands of a task prompt or a discourse context) to a consistent perspective or an appropriate switch. For example, if a student does switch perspective mid-explanation, that shift has to be explicitly signaled by the student (e.g., *I would then tell my friend, "You need to group the cubes."*), or it can be in the form of an appropriate response to an additional prompt or question from the conversational partner, who may redirect the perspective.

A key consideration for placement of an explanation on this DLLP feature is the length of an explanation. Explanations that are very short may not lend themselves to switching perspectives, by virtue of the fact they have fewer sentences or clauses for which a student needs to maintain or meaningfully switch perspectives. Eliciting additional explanations is recommended until at least four clauses are generated to make a determination that a student can control perspective-taking.

Examples of Student Explanations With "Best Fit" Placement on the Perspective-Taking DLLP

The bullets following the personal routine and mathematics example explanations below provide details of the use of the perspective-taking discourse feature, as well as our rationale for why we considered the explanation a "best fit" at a particular phase of the progression. The student's language status (either English learner or English-only/proficient) is included in parentheses.

Table 6.4 DLLP for Perspective-Taking

DLLP Not Evident	DLLP Emerging	DLLP Developing	DLLP Controlled
• Inconsistent perspective (i.e., spontaneously/ randomly switches back and forth between two or more perspectives that are inappropriate in the context), such that comprehension is difficult for the listener • If prompted, does not respond with requested perspective	• Inconsistent perspective (i.e., spontaneously/ randomly switches in a way that is inappropriate in the context), but comprehension is not severely impaired for the listener • If prompted, may or may not respond with requested perspective	• Switches perspective once (i.e., spontaneously/ randomly in a way that is inappropriate in the context) but is then able to maintain new perspective and/or, if prompted, responds with requested perspective OR • Consistent use of inappropriate perspective for context (e.g., consistent use of third person when second person is appropriate based on prompt expectations) AND/OR • Consistent in perspective but does not exceed three clauses (with overt subjects; i.e., insufficient evidence of control)	• Use of the appropriate perspective (given the prompt expectations) in a purposeful manner (i.e., introduces/ announces perspective switches that are appropriate, for example, in the context of reported speech) • Successfully manages switches in perspective (i.e., does not confuse the listener) if appropriate (i.e., when prompted for a different perspective by the researcher) AND • Must contain at least four clauses

No Evidence of Perspective-Taking

"Because, because you cannot uh **you** *can brush* **your** *teeth. That's all."*

[Researcher: Can you listen carefully? Pretend you're talking to your friend, and she does not know how to clean her teeth. When you're ready, tell how to do it, tell your friend how to do it and why your friend should do it. (Long pause) Tell your friend how to do it.]

"With **his** *hands."* (long pause)

[Researcher: And tell your friend why she should do it.]

"Because, because **they** *be, because* **her** *teeth is gonna be yellow."* (English learner)

- Switches perspective three times (*you → his → they → her*). Inconsistent: introduces third-person singular (masculine) pronoun having begun with second-person pronoun and then shifts to third-person plural briefly and then finally shifts to third-person singular (feminine) pronoun (possibly influenced by the researcher maintaining pronoun gender match to the student), all to refer to the same addressee

- Meaning making may be hard to follow
- Explanation is short, so establishing evidence for perspective-taking feature is not ideal; need additional language samples in additional contexts

[Researcher: Pretend you are talking to a classmate who has never done this activity. When you're ready, tell him how to use the cubes to find out how many there are and why using the cubes this way helps him.]

"Um how to count?"

[Researcher: I mean can you tell him how to do it? How to count?]

"Um with voice. Um."

[Researcher: Anything else?]

"No."

[Researcher: Okay. And can you tell him why this way helps?]

"Learn mou-, learn math." (English only)

- No overt perspective taken
- Explanation is short, so establishing evidence for perspective-taking feature is not ideal; need additional language samples in additional contexts

Emerging Perspective-Taking

*"So first **I** should tell, **we** should get a toothbrush and **we** should get toothpaste and spread it on the brush. And then **you** scrub it back and forth in **your** molars and **your** front teeth. Yeah, that's how."*

[Researcher: And can you tell her why she should do it?]

*"Oh, **she** should do it because **she**, so **she** won't have to go to the dentist and get cavities if **her** teeth turn yellow and get all dirty."*

[Researcher: Anything else?]

"No." (English-only/proficient student)

- Switches perspective three times ($I \rightarrow we \rightarrow you \rightarrow she$). Inconsistent: first switch from first-person singular to plural is appropriate to set up target addressee, but the second sudden shift to second person is not signaled. The third shift to third-person singular is possibly influenced by the researcher maintaining pronoun gender match to the student in the first prompt

- Meaning making may be hard to follow

*"Um this could help **him** because um, um when **he** forms the cubes and **he** sees that every single time in a line, there's an even number, um it, it's gonna be a even number. But when it's an odd number, it, it's gonna be a odd number. And, and then um it's easier to find the amount because once **you** put them in, in their order, like they, it's easier to count the amount that **you** have."*

[Researcher: And can you tell him how to do it?]

*"Um if there's a separate kind of colors, **he** can um like put them all together in, in one pile and then put the other colors, um uh uh put each color in one pile."* (Former English learner)

- Switches perspective twice (*he → you → he*). Inconsistent: first switch from third-person singular to second person is not signaled. The second shift back to third-person singular is possibly influenced by the researcher maintaining pronoun gender match to the student in the prompt
- Meaning making may be hard to follow

Developing Perspective-Taking

*"Um **I'd** put the pasta [= paste in Spanish] on it. **I** would like make circles in the back, front, sides and. Oh and **I** would um wash **my** tongue. I would also do it to my tongue. And then **I** would just rinse **my** mouth."*

[Researcher: And can you tell her why she should do it?]

*"**She** should do it because then **her** teeth are gonna get yellow. And like if **you** don't brush teeth, if **you** don't brush, someone's taking picture and **she** smiles, then **her** teeth are gonna look yellow. And yeah."* (Former English learner)

- Switches perspective three times (*I → she → you → she*). Inconsistent: first switch from first-person singular to third-person (feminine) singular possibly influenced by the researcher maintaining pronoun gender match to the student in the prompt. Second shift to second-person singular is sudden and not signaled before the return to third-person (feminine) singular
- Meaning making may be somewhat hard to follow

*"Okay so **you** had to all **you** have to do to find the cubes is what **I** did is **you–I** sorted them out by color. And **you** can tell that **you** can tell that that there's that the number of cubes there are because you're seeing them by color and they're in groups. And **I** think that's it."*

[Researcher: Can you tell her why this way helps?]

"Um because you can see them by color, and you can see them in different groups. And that's how you just tell that how much there are."

[Researcher: Anything else?]

"Um that's it." (English learner)

- Switches perspective twice (*you → I → you*). Consistent: first switch from second person is signaled by being related to actions of first-person singular referent. The second shift back to second-person singular is appropriate after the researcher's prompt; not unduly influenced by the researcher's mention of third person (*she*)

- Meaning making is straightforward

Controlled Perspective-Taking

"Okay. So you should put . . . you should get a toothbrush and get toothpaste. You take off the cap of the toothpaste and squeeze some toothpaste out of the tube onto your toothbrush. Then you turn on the sink and put a little bit of water on your toothbrush. And then you put the bristles in your mouth. And you move your hand back and forth so that you get the toothpaste all over your mouth. And then once you've done that for about two minutes, you spit the toothpaste out. And you get some water, rinse your mouth out and clean your toothbrush. And you should do that so that whenever you go to the dentist, you don't have cavities, and so that your teeth stay healthy." (English-only/proficient student)

- No switches in perspective: consistent use of second person to address hypothetical friend

- Meaning making straightforward

"You first have to find two, you first have to connect two cubes. Then put them in groups of colors, and then put them in a straight line. And then count by twos and your answer, you will have your answer."

[Researcher: And can you tell her why she should do it this way?]

"It's easier because it's counting by twos and you don't have to count by ones, um one, by ones. You don't have to count by ones." (English learner)

- No switches in perspective: consistent use of second person to address hypothetical classmate

- Meaning making straightforward

In Appendix 6E, we have included several student explanations and invite you to read these and then attempt to place the explanations on the DLLP for perspective-taking. At the end of the appendix there is an annotated version of each explanation that gives what we think is the "best fit" on the DLLP and our rationale.

Mapping the Distribution of "Best Fit" Placement on the Perspective-Taking DLLP

As mentioned at the start of this chapter, many students in the DLLP corpus data had control of perspective-taking in the first mathematics explanation task we gave them. This was true for both English learner students and English-only and proficient students. Figure 6.6 shows how perspective-taking is distributed across the DLLPs for students at all levels of English proficiency. The majority of explanations were placed at the *Controlled* phase. Less than 1% and 6% were placed at *Not Evident* and *Emerging*, respectively, and the remaining explanations were placed at the *Developing* phase.

Figure 6.6 Distribution of "Best Fit" Placement of Oral Explanations on the DLLP for Perspective-Taking

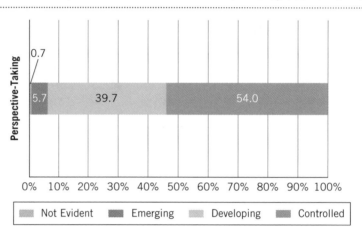

Given this distribution of performance on the DLLP for perspective-taking, we reiterate monitoring primarily for this DLLP language feature with kindergarten through third-grade students. Only on a case-by-case basis might formatively assessing perspective-taking be meaningful with older students (i.e., in cases where students' explanations seem esoterically difficult to follow in terms of reported addressee).

Using the Perspective-Taking DLLP to Generate Actionable Information to Assist Student Progress

As we noted in Chapter 2, teachers can use some of the tasks to get an anchor point for students' language learning early in the school year. This example is a case in point. A fifth-grade teacher, Mr. Daniels, worked one-on-one with his student Carlos, an English learner, to go through the mathematics explanation tasks. This was Carlos' response to the prompt to tell his friend how to find the number of cubes:

> *Okay, you, they should get the cubes and try to make them as long as possible. And then when he runs out and he has a little bit left, put them together and then count how many there are. So you will know.*

You should do it this way because if you don't, if you count them just spreaded out, you might get lost or confused and have to start all over.

As you can see, Carlos' use of pronouns was scattered. He used a range of pronouns: *you, they, he.* Because of Carlos' inconsistent use of pronouns, Mr. Daniels determined that his "best fit" on the DLLP was the *Emerging* phase. Mr. Daniels made an immediate pedagogical response, paraphrasing Carlos' explanation and modeling the accurate use of the pronoun:

Just so I understand your advice, what you are saying to your friend is, "You should get the cubes, put them together and then count how many there are. If you count them when they are spread out, then you might get lost." Did I get that right?

Carlos nodded and said: *"Yes, right."*

Mr. Daniels recognized that perspective-taking was a language feature he would need to pay particular attention to in order to ensure Carlos' development along the DLLP for perspective-taking. He planned to use the same task later in the year to gauge Carlos' progress, but he would also be listening for Carlos' use of this oral language feature in content-area lessons and making contingent pedagogical responses when appropriate.

Student Self- and Peer Assessment of the Discourse Features

When students understand that their own and their peers' explanations should be easy to follow and comprehend, they are able to listen to each other's explanations with that goal in mind. The more they understand what makes an explanation easy to follow, the better able they are to provide feedback, in any content area, about how easy or difficult it is to comprehend their peers' explanations and to point out why they feel that way.

To aid this process of feedback, teachers can provide short protocols for students to use, such as these:

- *My peer's explanation was easy to understand because _____.*

- *My peer's explanation was a little hard to understand because _____.*

- *One way my peer's explanation could be improved is _____.*

Students could be asked to focus on specific subfeatures or aspects of the explanation, for example, the use of different conditional connectors within the establishing advanced relationships between ideas discourse feature. They can articulate how clear the relationships between ideas are, as well as judge the adequacy of stamina, the clear description of their mental model, and "just right" amount of detail provided in the explanation.

Teachers across all disciplines can also pair students strategically so a student who is at an earlier phase on the progression on a particular feature can hear and read the explanations of a student who is ahead on that feature's progression. By assessing the peer and by being exposed to a model of more advanced discourse, the peer-assessment opportunity functions both to instruct and to monitor.

Students can also be encouraged to assess their own explanations with short prompts and other protocols. For example, the following is a brief set of prompts to self-evaluate:

- *When I was talking in my group today, I think my explanations were* _____. *This is because* _____.

- *My goal for tomorrow is to* _____.

Students can also review their own written work with reference to discourse features. For example, when the students have been focusing on contrastive connectors in a writing class, they might be asked to review their work for the use of specific words, such as *but, or, however*, and *instead of*, and make revisions if needed.

The following example of student self-assessment focuses on students' assessment of cohesion in their own explanations. The student was asked to tell his teacher which strategies he used to gain a better understanding of a geometry problem he had to solve. She wrote his response down verbatim on a card. Here is what she wrote as he dictated his strategy to her:

Whenever I try solving a word problem it helps to draw a picture to better understand the problem. Since a cylinder has two round faces and no square face, then it could not be the answer.

She asked him if the explanation of his strategy would make sense to another student if she were to make a collection of geometry problem strategies available for the whole class to use in the future. She left him to review how well his explanation communicated his strategy for other students wanting to use his approach. When she returned, the student told her that he should have used a different word for *problem* the second time he used it, because it repeated the same word without adding any new information. He suggested he change it to "what the question wants you to do." With this observation, he was showing an awareness of the need for cohesive devices, in this case substitution for a previous identical referent.

He also noticed that *it* in the second sentence could refer back to either *cylinder* or *square*, showing that he was aware of the ambiguity of the pronominal tie. He suggested a simple fix by spelling out *cylinder* once again. Note that the fix in this second sentence was actually his criticism of the first sentence, but the issue of avoiding ambiguity for the future reader of his strategy card was paramount and trumped repetitiveness in this instance.

Just as students who participated in the DLLP research project had been taught how to identify the "best fit" for their oral explanations on the sophistication of topic vocabulary DLLP, so too were other students in the project taught to place their explanations on the stamina DLLP. These students were taught to self-assess in the same manner as we describe for the students reported in Chapter 4 (Pitsoulakis Goral & Bailey, 2016, in press). The following third grader articulated what she did well in her explanation in terms of the level of detail a listener would need to replicate her mathematical procedure: *"I felt like it did a good job because I told people what I was sorting. And I didn't just say, 'Oh this goes here and this goes here.' And I told the answer and I told why I should do it and I told different ways to do it."* In her response to the self-assessment protocol, she clearly demonstrated her grasp of the stamina discourse feature; she drew attention to the fact that she told her listener exactly what she was doing with cubes in the task, and she highlighted the completeness of her explanation by pointing out that she included both how to do the task and why one should do the task her way.

In using the self-assessment protocol to identify areas for improvement, one sixth-grade student explained, *"I think I should improve on my clarity, and how that I explained it in the way when I was doing it. Add more detail in case someone's not there with me."* This self-critique shows how elementary students can successfully generate their own feedback through self-assessment (van Loon & Roebers, 2017). The intent is that through such experiences students can improve their language learning. As with the self-assessment of topic vocabulary in the explanations, we highly recommend that teachers adopt the scaffolded self-assessment process described in Chapter 4 so students can initially be supported in their discourse development as well. Furthermore, when a teacher takes the time to discuss with a student the feedback the student's self-assessment can generate, both teacher and student become more aware of the student's language use and possible ways to make progress. Through the use of self- and peer assessment, accountability for language use and learning can be heightened and students will be accountable to themselves and each other, as well as to the teacher. Self-assessment, especially, provides the students with agency in their own learning experiences, and this seems especially suited to English learner students who must learn language day in and day out (Bailey & Heritage, 2018), as well as to older elementary students who can more accurately evaluate their placements on the DLLPs.

What Students Say

[Self-assessment] showed me my strengths and my weaknesses, and it showed me what I need to work on and showed me what I didn't need to work on.

—Sixth-grade student

Writing-Specific Features of the DLLP Approach

The focus of this book has primarily been on the formative assessment of and support for the development of students' oral language explanations. However, the features can extend to students' written explanations. Furthermore, the DLLP project developed several DLLPs specific to features of written explanations, because some aspects of writing were not already covered by the eight existing DLLP features (Blackstock-Bernstein, Bailey, Woodbridge, Pitsoulakis, & Lee, 2016). Differences between oral and written explanations may be due to the greater cognitive demands and the planning that goes into writing, as well as language differences, such as greater diversity in vocabulary found in writing (e.g., De La Paz, 2007; Drieman, 1962; Marinellie, 2009). Past research has suggested that students begin to make purposeful distinctions between oral and written language only at sixth grade (Hildyard & Hidi, 1985). However, preliminary research with the DLLP corpus data suggests students can demonstrate an understanding of differences between oral and written explanations as early as first grade (Reynolds Kelly, Bailey, Blackstock-Bernstein, & Heritage, 2013). Specifically, even very young students in our corpus used contextualized language (e.g., references to the immediate context—the "here and now") more often in their oral explanations than in their written explanations.

The three additional DLLP features unique to the students' written explanations were as follows:

1. **Opening/closing statements:** Certain aspects of audience awareness—namely, making the context clear—were included in this feature.

2. **Decontextualization:** This feature combines subfeatures capturing appropriate elaboration and audience awareness in the explanations. Decontextualization helps provide the reader with sufficient explicit information to make meaning just from language alone and not from nonlinguistic clues found in a particular setting.

3. **Graphic representation supporting meaning making:** This feature captures all elements of the student's written representation (i.e., punctuation, spelling, handwriting, and illustration).

For completeness, the progressions for these features along with examples are provided in Appendix 6F; however, we do not expand on them here, given this book's primary focus on the development of oral explanations.

This chapter ends our detailed look at all the DLLP features. In the next chapter, we move to teacher implementation of the DLLP approach and consider lessons learned from our pilot implementation sites, as well as effective leadership for DLLP implementation and communities of practice for professional learning.

SUMMING UP

1. Discourse is the organization of spoken utterances or written sentences into stretches of language used for specific purposes (e.g., conversation, narration, creating expository texts).

2. There are four features of the discourse dimension in the DLLP approach: coherence/cohesion, establishment of advanced relationships between ideas, stamina, and perspective-taking.

3. Students use discourse conventions to participate in the classroom, where disciplinary practices in mathematics, science, and so forth require students

to construct explanations, engage in argumentation, and communicate information, for example.

4. The DLLP approach is designed to help teachers follow the expansion of their students' language uses to convey a range of complex ideas, build on the organization of explanations, and provide sufficient detail and elaboration for the listener to make meaning of their explanations.

5. Students can be supported to assess their own explanations in terms of discourse features and decide on their next steps in language development.

REFLECTION QUESTIONS FOR TEACHERS

1. How does what you have read about discourse usage and knowledge in this chapter square with your own thinking? What is the same? What is different?

2. How often do you plan for and intentionally teach discourse features during content instruction? Coherence and cohesion? Linguistic supports for relationships between ideas? Stamina? Perspective-taking?

3. How do you assess students' oral discourse formatively?

4. How do you assess students' written discourse formatively?

5. After reading this chapter, in what ways will you plan for discourse instruction and assessment?

REFERENCES

Bailey, A. L., & Heritage, M. (2014). The role of language learning progressions in improved instruction and assessment of English language learners. *TESOL Quarterly, 48*(3), 480–506.

Bailey, A. L., & Heritage, M. (2018). *Self-regulation in learning: The role of language and formative assessment.* Cambridge, MA: Harvard Education Press.

Blackstock-Bernstein, A., Bailey, A. L., Woodbridge, A., Pitsoulakis, D., & Lee, C. H.-Y. (2016). *Report of analyses with the Dynamic Language Learning Progressions written explanations including comparative analyses with oral explanations.* ASSETS Consortium (WCER) Project Deliverable, University of California, Los Angeles.

California Department of Education. (2012). *The California English language development standards.* Sacramento, CA: Author.

Calkins, L. M. (2001). *Guided reading and strategy lessons: The art of teaching reading.* New York, NY: Addison-Wesley Educational Publishers.

Common Core State Standards Initiative. (2010a). *Common Core State Standards for English language arts and literacy in history/social studies, science, and technical subjects.* Retrieved from http://www.corestandards.org/assets/CCSSI_ELA%20Standards.pdf

Common Core State Standards Initiative. (2010b). *Common Core State Standards for mathematics.* Retrieved from https://www.ccsso.org/sites/default/files/2017-10/MathStandards50805232017.pdf

Council of Chief State School Officers. (2012). *Framework for English language proficiency development standards corresponding to the Common Core State Standards and the Next Generation Science Standards.* Washington, DC: Author.

De La Paz, S. (2007). Managing cognitive demands for writing: Comparing the effects of instructional components in strategy instruction. *Reading & Writing Quarterly, 23*(3), 249–266.

Drieman, G. H. (1962). Differences between written and spoken language: An exploratory study. *Acta Psychologica, 20,* 78–100.

Halliday, M., & Martin, J. (Eds.). (1993). *Writing science: Literacy and discursive power.* Pittsburgh, PA: University of Pittsburgh Press.

Heritage, M., & Bailey, A. L. (2011). *English language proficiency assessment (ELPA) validity evaluation instrument: Protocol for analysis of language content in ELPA.* Enhanced Assessment Grant, US DOE, Evaluating the Validity of English Assessments (EVEA) Project Deliverable. Retrieved from http://www.eveaproject.com/doc/Analyses%20of%20Language%20Content%20Protocol%202009-26-11.pdf

Hiebert, E. H., Wilson, K. M., & Trainin, G. (2010). Are students really reading in independent reading contexts? An examination of comprehension-based silent reading rate. In E. H. Hiebert & D. Ray Reutzel (Eds.), *Revisiting silent reading: New directions for teachers and researchers* (pp. 151–167). Newark, DE: International Reading Association.

Hildyard, A., & Hidi, S. (1985). Oral-written differences in the production and recall of narratives. In D. R. Olson, N. Torrance, & A. Hildyard (Eds.), *Literacy, language, and learning: The nature and consequences of reading and writing* (pp. 285–306). Cambridge, UK: Cambridge University Press.

Lee, O., Quinn, H., & Valdés, G. (2013). Science and language for English language learners in relation to Next Generation Science Standards and with implications for Common Core State Standards for English language arts and mathematics. *Educational Researcher, 42*(4), 223–233.

Marinellie, S. A. (2009). The content of children's definitions: The oral-written distinction. *Child Language Teaching and Therapy, 25*(1), 89–102.

NGSS Lead States. (2013). *Next Generation Science Standards: For states, by states.* Washington, DC: National Academies Press.

Nippold, M. A., & Scott, C. M. (Eds.). (2010). *Expository discourse in children, adolescents, and adults: Development and disorders.* New York, NY: Taylor & Francis.

Owens, R. E., Jr. (2015). *Language development: An introduction.* Boston, MA: Allyn & Bacon.

Peterson, C., & McCabe, A. (1987). The connective 'and': Do older children use it less as they learn other connectives? *Journal of Child Language, 14*(2), 375–381.

Pitsoulakis, D., & Bailey, A. L. (2016, April). *Extending learning progressions to self-assessment: Students finding "best fit" for learning and instruction.* Paper presented at the annual meeting of the American Educational Research Association, Annual Conference, Washington, DC.

Pitsoulakis Goral, D., & Bailey, A. L. (in press). Student self-assessment of oral explanations: Use of language learning progressions. *Language Testing.*

Reynolds Kelly, K., Bailey, A. L., Blackstock-Bernstein, A. L., & Heritage, M. (2013, April). *Similarities, differences, and shifts in elementary-age children's use of social and academic registers in speech and writing.* Poster presented at the Biennial Conference of the Society for Research on Child Development, Seattle, WA.

Schleppegrell, M. J. (2004). *The language of schooling: A functional linguistic perspective.* Mahwah, NJ: Lawrence Erlbaum Associates.

van Loon, M. H., & Roebers, C. M. (2017). Effects of feedback on self-evaluations and self-regulation in elementary school. *Applied Cognitive Psychology, 31*(5), 508–519.

Appendix 6A

Practice Finding the "Best Fit" on Coherence/Cohesion

Read the following example explanations for K–6 English learners and attempt to place them on the DLLP (*Not Evident, Emerging, Developing*, or *Controlled*) for coherence/cohesion. Use the descriptors for the progression in Table 6.1 (page 138). Be sure to think of a rationale for each of your placements. For comparison, we have provided the four explanations again with coherence elements bolded and cohesion elements underlined. Our placements and rationale are revealed on the following page.

Example 1:

*Because his teeth need to be clean. **And** the bottom too, **and** his tongue. **And** he needs to clean in the sides. **And then** he needs to brush <u>them</u> every day. **Then** he has to clean the other side.*

Example 2:

***First** they need to count <u>it</u> **and then** they put <u>it</u> like. **And** they didn't put <u>it</u>. **And then** they put <u>it</u>. **First** they put <u>it</u> together. **Then** they count.*

[Tell her why using the cubes this way helps her.]

Because it's easy.

Example 3:

***First**, you need to turn on the water. **And then** you're gonna get your toothbrush and then put water on <u>it</u>. **And then** you get the toothpaste and put <u>it</u> on the brush. **Then** you water <u>it</u> a little bit. **And then** you brush your teeth in circles. **And then** you spit. And then **after** <u>that</u>, brush your bottom **and** up teeth. **And when** you're done with <u>that</u>, spit. **And** get some water, put <u>it</u> in your mouth **and** spit <u>it</u> out **and** you'll be done. **And** you should brush your teeth because you will be handsome, **and** your teeth will look clean, **and** your mouth will be fresh.*

Example 4:

*By counting **and** by your mind can count.*

[And why does using the cubes this way help her? Tell her that.]

For you can learn to count.

Suggested "Best Fit"

Example 1: Emerging Coherence/Cohesion

- Repertoire includes one **conjunction** (*and*) and one **transitional word** (*then*)

- Use of one <u>cohesive device</u> (pronominal referent)

Example 2: Developing Coherence/Cohesion

- Repertoire includes one **conjunction** (*and*) and two **transitional words** (*first, then*)

- Numerous instances of <u>cohesive devices</u> (pronominal referents; some ambiguous/inaccurate)

Example 3: Controlled Coherence/Cohesion

- Repertoire includes one **conjunction** (*and*) and four **transitional words** (*first, then, after, when*)

- Seven instances of <u>cohesive devices</u> (pronominal referents)

Example 4: No Evidence of Coherence/Cohesion

- Use of one **conjunction** (*and*)

- No use of <u>cohesive devices</u>

Appendix 6B

Discourse Connector Lists

Causal Discourse Connectors	Temporal Discourse Connectors
so	when
since	then
cause	after
because	before
if . . . then	while
in order to	now
whenever	once
therefore	after that
consequently	

Sequencing Discourse Connectors	Other Discourse Connectors
first	but
second	however
third	plus
next	instead of
finally	also
in the end	except
last	for
lastly	and
later	nor
subsequently	or
	yet

Appendix 6C

Practice Finding the "Best Fit" on Establishment of Advanced Relationships Between Ideas

Read the following example explanations for K–6 English learners and attempt to place them on the DLLP (*Not Evident, Emerging, Developing,* or *Controlled*) for establishment of advanced relationships between ideas. Use the descriptors for the progression in Table 6.2 (page 147). Be sure to think of a rationale for each of your placements. For comparison, we have provided the four explanations again with relational discourse connectors bolded. Our placements and rationale are revealed on the following page.

Example 1:

*You should clean your teeth **because if** you don't clean them, they will be yellow. And **whenever** you talk, your breath will smell bad. And people won't be able to talk. They won't want to talk to you **(be) cause** your teeth are yellow and your breath smells. And you should start with your toothbrush. Put water on it. Use your toothpaste. Don't put too much on it. Just put like a little bit. And then start brushing your teeth, the bottom. **But** don't brush it too hard or else you're gonna bleed. **Because** if you brush it too hard, it's like you're doing it too hard **for** it could start bleeding. And you should do it soft **but** not that soft. You should do it just normal. And **when** you finish, you should get your toothbrush and wash it. Then you can use one of the mouthwash or the dental floss.*

[Anything else?]

And clean them out.

Example 2:

*She should use the cubes **because** it's going to help her a lot. And she should use it this way **because if** you do it the other way, you might lose your place.*

[And can you tell her how to do it?]

Yes, put one by one in one by one, and you'll get the answer.

Example 3:

By learning and counting more easily.

[Can you tell him how to do it?]

Yes, I can show him how he could put them and how he could count. And how he could get to the numbers higher.

Example 4:

With a pasta [= paste in Spanish]. With the tooth-brush. With the water. Spit out the water.

[And can you tell her why she should do it?]

*She should do it **for** his teeth can be shiny always.*

Suggested "Best Fit"

Example 1: Controlled Establishment of Advanced Relationships Between Ideas

- Use of three conditional connectors (*if, whenever, when*)
- Use of two causal connectors (*because, for* [nonconventional usage])
- Use of one contrastive connector (*but*)

Example 2: Developing Establishment of Advanced Relationships Between Ideas

- Use of one causal connector (*because*)
- Use of one conditional connector (*if*)

Example 3: No Evidence of Establishment of Advanced Relationships Between Ideas

- Lack of discourse connectors to establish advanced relationships between ideas

Example 4: Emerging Establishment of Advanced Relationships Between Ideas

- Use of one causal connector (*for* [nonconventional usage])

Appendix 6D

Practice Finding the "Best Fit" on Stamina

Read the following example explanations for K–6 English learners and attempt to place them on the DLLP (*Not Evident, Emerging, Developing*, or *Controlled*) for stamina. Use the descriptors for the progression in Table 6.3 (page 153). Be sure to think of a rationale for each of your placements. For comparison, our placements and rationale are revealed on the following page.

Example 1:

So I like doing it this way because it's, it's very easy. And, and there are light and some are dark. I could do the light ones and then do the dark ones. And what was the other question?

[How do you find out how many cubes there are?]

I count them one by one and sometimes, sometimes I see like a pattern, like going by tens sometimes, and then I go by twos and sometimes by threes. And that's it.

Example 2:

Um she should do it like um she when, she um, when she wakes up and or she goes to bed, she has to clean her teeth. First putting the toothpaste on the toothbrush. Then brushing it sideways um circles and top and front and back. And then put a water and spit the um the toothpaste. Um um just spit it.

[Anything else?]

That's all.

[Okay. Did you tell her why she should do it?]

Oh. She, she should do it because um sh-when it's picture day, she, she'll have a nice um smile.

Example 3:

I could show her.

[What would you tell her? Tell her how to do it.]

Counting.

[Why does using the cubes this way help her?]

So so you could could learn.

Example 4:

You need to get your toothbrush, put some paste and put a little bit of water. And you go up and down with your toothbrush in the teeth. Then right to left. And then you clean your toothbrush and put it um oh you take your tongue out and brush your tongue. Then you put you clean your toothbrush and put it where you put it. Then then you wash your mouth three times and that's how you clean it. Then you, you need to clean it because there's some germs after you eat. And those germs um make your teeth ugly and, and when you talk to someone, you smell bad. Then you need you need to brush your teeth three times a day: in the morning, and after you eat, and at night. Um that's how, how why you need to brush your teeth.

Suggested "Best Fit"

Example 1: Emerging Stamina

- Lacks detail and content
- Mental model of the process being explained is not fully discernible

Example 2: Developing Stamina

- Lacks some detail in content
- Mental schema is more evident but not completely clear

Example 3: No Evidence of Stamina

- Lacks expected content (i.e., steps in process)
- Does not exhibit complete mental schema
- Required utterance-by-utterance prompting

Example 4: Controlled Stamina

- Elaboration of expected content and details
- Clear mental schema

Appendix 6E

Practice Finding the "Best Fit" on Perspective-Taking

Read the following example explanations for K–6 English learners and attempt to place them on the DLLP (*Not Evident, Emerging, Developing*, or *Controlled*) for perspective-taking. Use the descriptors for the progression in Table 6.4 (page 160). Be sure to think of a rationale for each of your placements. For comparison, our placements and rationale are revealed on the following page.

Example 1:

Okay. You should do them by ten because it's a lot more faster positive and and even quicker because, because it helps you get (be)cause the more you do stuff by tens, the more easy counting stuff will be for you.

[And can you tell him how to do it?]

You, you grab ten cubes then get another ten cubes. And then when there're no more cubes, and they're all grouped by ten, you count them out. And then you see that there is a hundred.

Example 2:

If I was talking to a friend, um I suppose, I tell her to, to wash her teeth 20 times left, right, down, and up. And, and count the ABCs two or three times. Then you count like rinse it off. Then count again 20 times left, right, up, down. Then sing the ABCs again. Then rinse it off and, and then done.

Example 3:

Well he can use the cubes this way or another way, like, like something, like a tower or something. But he can do it however he wants. Like, like, he can do sections or towers or something. And then, since I use sections, like, of nine, he can use sections of any different kinds, like sections of three, six, or something. So it will be easier since you can do multiplication with each section because if there's like random number, you don't really know how many there are. And that's it.

Example 4:

So it could. So she cou- could not go to the dentist.

[And can you tell her how to clean her teeth?]

With a toothbrush and some tu- uh I don't know how t- . . .

Suggested "Best Fit"

Example 1: Controlled Perspective-Taking

- Switches perspectives once (*you* → *they*)
- Perspective switches are appropriate; maintains reference to *you* for the friend being spoken to and then shifts to *they* and related pronouns for reference to cubes
- Meaning making for listener is not lost

Example 2: Developing Perspective-Taking

- Switches perspective once (*her* → *you*)
- Perspective shift is not appropriate; shift is made without adding a new referent (referring to same addressee)
- Meaning making for listener is not lost

Example 3: Emerging Perspective-Taking

- Switches perspective three times (*he* → *I* → *he* → *you*)
- First two shifts are appropriate; references his own mathematics strategy
- Second shift is not consistent; introduces second-person pronoun, having begun with third-person pronoun to refer to the same addressee
- Meaning making may be harder to follow

Example 4: No Evidence of Perspective-Taking

- Switches perspective (*it* → *she*) [possibly a false start and corrects perspective]
- Meaning making may be hard to follow
- Explanation is short, so establishing evidence for perspective-taking feature is not ideal; need additional language samples in additional contexts

Appendix 6F

Written Language Features
of the DLLP Approach

Opening and Closing Statements

DLLP Not Evident	DLLP Emerging	DLLP Developing	DLLP Controlled
No use of opening or closing statements: • Student launches into explanation without providing **content** (i.e., that the following text will contain an explanation/ instructions about a procedure) or **context** (cleaning teeth or using cubes with the goal of finding the total) • Student does not make closing statement that indicates explanation is over Note that the use of letter salutations (e.g., "Dear" or "Hi, [name]") or closings (e.g., "Sincerely" or "Bye") are not considered opening or closing statements.	Use of opening *or* closing statement, used in a minimal form: • Opening orients the reader by providing **content** OR **context** but not both • Closing indicates that explanation is over but does not refer to preceding information (includes statements like "the end" or "that's it") Starting the explanation with justification ("Why?" portion) may count as employing a minimal opening if one of two conditions is met: • Additional justification is provided elsewhere in the explanation OR • Following the justification, the student includes a minimal opening to initiate the procedural ("How?") component of the explanation	Opening used appropriately: • Occurs toward beginning of explanation • Announces both the **content** and the **context** of the explanation that follows (i.e., signals that the note contains an explanation about a specific procedure [teeth/mathematics activity]) . . . but closing is absent Starting the explanation with justification ("Why?" portion) may count as employing an appropriate opening if several conditions are met: • Justification announces context and content of explanation, *and* additional justification is provided elsewhere in the explanation	Opening used appropriately, and closing used appropriately or in a minimal form OR Closing used appropriately, and opening used appropriately or in a minimal form

DLLP Not Evident	DLLP Emerging	DLLP Developing	DLLP Controlled
	Opening or closing may contain extraneous information	OR • Following the justification, the student includes an appropriate opening to initiate the procedural ("How?") component of the explanation OR Closing used appropriately: • Occurs toward end of explanation • Refers back to content of explanation without adding new information • Is not the last step of the procedure . . . but opening is absent OR Both opening and closing are used in minimal form OR Two minimal openings are used (to introduce procedure and justification sections)	

Examples

DLLP Not Evident	DLLP Emerging	DLLP Developing	DLLP Controlled
frist you get your brush and you put it on your teeth brush brussh to sayt nice and clean why you should sayt nice and clean because that is going to make you best to eat and rest.	Ashley, using these cubes to find out how many they are you nead to put them in grups. You nead to put them in grups because it is esyer than caunting one by one. It is a helpful way than counting all of theme because you are going to get confised when you don't	Well, you need to count Is the first thing. Second If you want to go fast you need to know to times (? × ? = ?) third, If you want to go slow you need to count on ones. The point Is adding Is put one thing to another. It works like for example A farmer has 5 sheeps But his	First I will teach you how to clean your teeth. 1. Wet the tooth brush, 2. Put the tooth paste on the tooth brush, 3. Wet the tooth paste, 4. Brush your teeth 2 minutes, 5 your done spit the water, 6 rinse your mouth and wet your tooth

DLLP Not Evident	DLLP Emerging	DLLP Developing	DLLP Controlled
Examples			
<conventional> First you get your brush and you put it on your teeth brush brush to stay nice and clean because that is going to make you best to eat and rest. • Launches into explanation without orienting the reader • No closing	put theme in grups. It is a helpful way alse becase it is a faster way to count the cubes. *<conventional> Ashley, using these cubes to find out how many they are, you need to put them in groups. You need to put them in groups because it is easier than counting one by one. It is a helpful way than counting all of them because you are going to get confused when you don't put them in groups. It is a helpful way also because it is a faster way to count the cubes.* • Opening announces the full context, including the subject matter and end goal, but does not announce the content	cousin gave him four more. how much Does the famer have all together? So you put 5 sheeps next to four sheeps. And the farmer will have nine sheeps. And time tables I just like adding It just you add the number the times of the question example: I have 5 pencils but My friend gave 2×5 the pencil I have so what you do Is just like adding $5 + 5 = 5 \times 2$. That Is how you count, add, or times. *<conventional> Well, you need to count is the first thing. Second, if you want to go fast, you need to know to times. (? × ?= ?) Third, if you want to go slow, you need to count on ones. The point is: adding is put one thing to another. It works, like for example: a farmer has 5 sheeps but his cousin gave him four more. How much does the famer have all together? So you put 5 sheeps next to four sheeps. And the farmer will have nine sheeps. And time tables. I just like adding. It just you add the number the times of the question. Example: I have 5 pencils but my friend gave 2x5 the pencils I have. So what you do is just like adding $5 + 5 = 5 \times 2$. That is how you count, add, or times.* • Although student's explanation does not respond directly to the prompt, his closing summarizes the content of his explanation	brush. You have to clean your teeth because you don't want cavity, tooth pain or food in your teeth stuck. So it is important to brush your teeth to be clean. Brush your teeth every day. *<conventional> First I will teach you how to clean your teeth.* *1. Wet the toothbrush, 2. Put the toothpaste on the toothbrush, 3. Wet the toothpaste, 4. Brush your teeth 2 minutes, 5 you're done spit the water, 6 rinse your mouth and wet your toothbrush. You have to clean your teeth because you don't want cavity, tooth pain or food in your teeth stuck. So it is important to brush your teeth to be clean. Brush your teeth every day.* • Appropriate opening announces content and context • Appropriate closing restates the overall argument of the explanation

Decontextualization

DLLP Not Evident	DLLP Emerging	DLLP Developing	DLLP Controlled
Use of deictic language (i.e., relies on information about a specific aspect of student's here and now; verbal "pointing": *this, that, these, those, here, there*) that interferes with meaning making	No use of deictic language Ambiguously tied or omitted referents make it difficult for a naïve reader to follow the explanation	No use of deictic language Student unpacks the prompt with a full noun referent (e.g., *Group the cubes*)	No use of deictic language Student unpacks the prompt with a full noun referent (e.g., *Group the cubes*)
Note: Consider everything on the written page (including prompt/title on the top) when determining decontextualized language usage; if child is "pointing" or referring to information in the written prompt or title, this is pragmatically appropriate (they may assume the naïve reader will see this information as well and therefore not fully decontextualize their explanation)	For example, in the case of the mathematics task, the student may use pronominal forms to refer back to the spoken prompt rather than paraphrase the prompt in a lexicalized manner (e.g., *You should group them*, instead of *You should group the cubes*)	Use of appropriate co-reference within the text or to the written prompt/title on the page (e.g., *do it* [clean teeth] or *them* [teeth] for social task, *this activity* for mathematics)	Use of appropriate co-reference within the text or influenced by the written prompt/title on the page (i.e., *do it* [clean teeth] or *them* [teeth] for social task, *this activity* for mathematics)
	For example, the student may use quantified adjectives (*both, each, other, either, neither*) that have not previously been introduced	Naïve reader can understand the explanation based on what is on the written page (including prompt/title)	Naïve reader can understand the explanation based on what is on the written page (including prompt/title)
OR	Note: In the case of teeth-cleaning explanations, referents using pronouns that co-reference the written material prompt would be acceptable as long as they are not themselves ambiguous	Note: Cataphoric uses of *this* are acceptable (e.g., *You should count the cubes using this method [that I will be explaining in this paragraph]* as are existential uses of *it* (e.g., *It helps to . . .*)	Note: Cataphoric uses of *this* are acceptable (e.g., *You should count the cubes using this method [that I will be explaining in this paragraph]* as are existential uses of *it* (e.g., *It helps to . . .*)
Explanation does not contain enough content in the text to allow for decontextualization		BUT	
		Explanation does not exceed four clauses containing an overt or imperative subject (i.e., insufficient evidence of control)	

183

DLLP Not Evident	DLLP Emerging	DLLP Developing	DLLP Controlled
Examples			
You could use it by difrent ways as one dy one or by 2. I like doing it this way because it is more easy for me and if I get stuck from the cubes but I see how I already counted that cube. *<conventional> You could use it by different ways as one by one or by 2. I like doing it this way because it is more easy for me and if I get stuck from the cubes, but I see how I already counted that cube.* • Use of deictic referent (*that cube*) that points to the child's physical context • Use of *it* to refer to prompt • Use of *this way* in second sentence is not deictic (it is an anaphoric reference that is poorly tied to language in the explanation)	You should group it by 5 because it is a more ifishent way of counting things. It is also an easier way of counting. When you are done grouping them by fives you should count by fives. Each group is one five. *<conventional> You should group it by 5 because it is a more efficient way of counting things. It is also an easier way of counting. When you are done grouping them by fives you should count by fives. Each group is one five.* • Refers back to prompt using pronoun (*it*) with unclear referent	You scrub you teeth with the tooth Brush. You shud do it to not get carudeas. and to keep them clean. *<conventional> You scrub your teeth with the toothbrush. You should do it to not get cavities. And to keep them clean.* • Student avoids referring to prompt using pronominal forms • Use of *do it* is a decontextualized anaphoric reference to language in explanation (i.e., *scrub you teeth*) • However, explanation lacks sufficient length to provide evidence of control	In order to find how many cubes there are, you have to sort the cubes out in a certain way (in this case by color). If you find out how many cubes are in each group and multiply that by the amount of groups there is. This is the best way to do it because that way, you can just simply multiply instead of having to add a bunch of 1s together. *<conventional> In order to find how many cubes there are, you have to sort the cubes out in a certain way (in this case by color). If you find out how many cubes are in each group and multiply that by the amount of groups there is. This is the best way to do it because that way, you can just simply multiply instead of having to add a bunch of 1s together.* • Refers to prompt using full noun referents (e.g., *sort the cubes*)

Graphic Representation Supporting Meaning Making

DLLP Not Evident	DLLP Emerging	DLLP Developing	DLLP Controlled
No use of written language to convey meaning	Nonconventional use of punctuation, spelling, and graphic representation (handwriting, capitalization, etc.) severely interferes with meaning making for the reader	Some nonconventional use of punctuation, spelling, and graphic representation that partly interferes with meaning Student may compensate by making meaning for the reader in some other way (sequencing, formatting, organization of text, etc.)	Use of punctuation, spelling, and graphic representation (handwriting, capitalization, etc.) may or may not be conventional, but it is clear and easy for reader to make meaning. Occasional spelling or punctuation errors may occur, but they are minimal and do not interfere with meaning making

Examples

Examples would include illegible scribbling or drawing in lieu of writing	 You need to dith yor teth pecis you will get cadibs. And you shid dish yor teth on yor mlrs on yor noo teth and on yor tin.	 My mom doesn't now how to clean her teeth very well First you need to brush your teeth in circles then you need to clean your tung after you clean your top part at last you need to spit.	

185

DLLP Not Evident	DLLP Emerging	DLLP Developing	DLLP Controlled
Examples			
	<conventional> You need to brush your teeth because you will get cavities. And you should brush your teeth on your molars on your new teeth and on your tongue. • Invented spelling may well interfere with meaning making (e.g., *dith*)	*<conventional> My mom doesn't know how to clean her teeth very well. First you need to brush your teeth in circles. Then you need to clean your tongue after you clean your top part. At last you need to spit.* • Lack of punctuation partly interferes with meaning, but student compensates by capitalizing sentence initial words	First I will teach you how to clean your teeth. 1. Wet the tooth brush, 2. Put the tooth paste on the tooth brush, 3. Wet the tooth paste, 4. Brush your teeth 2 minutes, 5 your done spit the water, 6 rinse your mouth and wet your tooth brush. You have to clean your teeth because you don't want cavity, tooth pain or food in your teeth stuck. So it is important to brush your teeth to be clean. Brush your teeth every day. *<conventional> First I will teach you how to clean your teeth. 1. Wet the toothbrush, 2. Put the toothpaste on the toothbrush, 3. Wet the toothpaste, 4. Brush your teeth 2 minutes, 5 you're done spit the water, 6 rinse your mouth and wet your toothbrush. You have to clean your teeth because you don't want cavity, tooth pain or food in your teeth stuck. So it is important to brush your teeth to be clean. Brush your teeth every day.* • Minor spelling errors (e.g., *your* instead of *you're*) do not interfere with meaning • Missing punctuation does not interfere with meaning

Leading Language
and Content Learning

Part III draws from our experience of implementing the Dynamic Language Learning Progression (DLLP) approach in several school settings. For this section, we are joined by our colleagues Nancy Gerzon, Sandy Chang, and Eusebio Martinez. We focus on how school leadership plays a vital role in supporting the DLLP approach given its strong reliance on teacher time, investment in learning about the DLLP features, and focus on collaboration with colleagues. In addition, we provide a rationale for recommending communities of practice as the model of teacher professional learning for the DLLP approach. We conclude with detailed implementation suggestions and a practical appendix of meeting agendas for setting up and managing communities of practice in support of DLLP implementation.

*It's important for administrators to serve
in a role that is not easily quantified or
noted in the research: Encourager.*

—School leader

Leadership and Communities of Practice to Support DLLP Implementation

with Nancy Gerzon, Sandy Chang, and Eusebio Martinez

This chapter is in two sections. Recall that in Chapter 2 we provided several recommendations for teachers to implement the DLLP approach. Now, in Section 1 of this chapter, we turn to the role of leaders in supporting this implementation. We believe leadership is essential to any successful innovation or intervention by teachers in their classrooms. We share lessons learned from our DLLP implementations, as well as from the reports of professional learning leaders implementing the DLLP approach in several additional public school districts, about the ways leaders can support their teachers and students during implementation. Section 2 of this chapter focuses on teacher communities of practice (CoPs), which were so central to the DLLP implementation. We define CoPs and their attributes and provide suggestions for successful implementation that are drawn from the literature and our own experiences of the DLLP implementation.

Section 1: Lessons About Leadership

Leadership is critical in improving student learning. For example, a review of research on leadership commissioned by the Wallace Foundation noted that "leadership is second only to classroom instruction among all school-related factors that contribute to what students learn at school" (Leithwood, Louis, Anderson, & Wahlstrom, 2004, p. 5). During our pilot implementations of the DLLPs, we learned some important lessons about leadership that we share below.

Leadership to Empower Teachers in Implementing the DLLPs

A key role for leaders in our pilot schools and districts was to provide the conditions that would support teachers in the DLLP implementation. We found that the culture established by leaders was an important factor in teachers' implementation. Our implementation sites reflected a culture of inquiry in which teachers were supported to engage in action research to develop their practices at one site and to take part in a new professional learning opportunity at another. At no time did teachers feel they had to comply with leadership mandates in implementing the DLLP approach. Instead, they were encouraged to experiment and reflect on their practices in collaboration with one another to create buy-in for their DLLP implementation. For example, school leaders provided encouragement and modeling for interpreting students' responses during teacher meetings, in a sense learning alongside the teachers. As a result, teachers became more comfortable experimenting with the DLLP approach to build their own knowledge and skills about language and formative assessment.

What Teachers Say
(at the Start of DLLP Implementation)

Teacher A: [My students are] able to somewhat use time order when explaining the task, but they didn't really have a sense of listener's needs in explaining to someone the process, so I want to improve that.

Teacher B: When [my] students are trying to give an answer, they don't have the vocabulary to give the answer, so they're grasping and reaching for what they are going to say, and they're rambling on and on, using the definition instead of the actual words, and they get frustrated.

Teachers were initially tentative about finding the "best fit" on the DLLPs for their students. They were also concerned that they "got it right." Through encouragement from leaders to interpret the evidence they had obtained against the DLLPs and use their own judgment about the students' "best fit," they gradually became surer of themselves. They realized that if they determined a "best fit" one day but evidence the next day challenged their judgment, they could collect more evidence or change their instructional response. Elsewhere we have called this "day-to-day" stakes, with placements considered as "good enough for now," in contrast with high-stakes testing and decision making (Bailey, 2017). Contexts change. Students change. Placements on the DLLPs will change. Teachers need to feel confident in their use of the DLLP approach, rather than feel confident that they are spot-on for any given placement of student language on the DLLPs. If there is concern about uncertainty, more language can be sampled from a student, and colleagues can be consulted for their feedback.

Another way leaders provided the conditions for implementation was to give constructive feedback to teachers about their progress and how students were progressing during the project. The provision of feedback showed support for what teachers were doing and the leaders' commitment to their work and was an important factor in the DLLP implementation success.

Leaders also smoothed the way for teachers during potentially disruptive times for focusing on their implementation. For example, leadership support was particularly helpful during the California Assessment of Student Performance and Progress testing window, when teachers in Grades 3 through 5 needed to manage their testing schedules with DLLP implementation. In addition, leaders made sure to provide time for teachers to engage in DLLP work, from making video recordings of student discourse to preparing for CoP meetings.

Throughout the implementation, it was apparent that teachers did not need to be "told" what to do. With their school administrators' support, they were able to develop their expertise in ways that worked for them as individual teachers, ultimately making the DLLP implementation their own.

Sustained Commitment Is Necessary

In addition to showing commitment to the DLLP implementation, another condition for success was important for leaders to sustain that commitment over time. While teachers reported that they had increased their knowledge and skills and had seen developments in students' language, they also indicated that they would have liked longer on the project to further develop their knowledge and skills, in part because increased time would also have allowed for students to develop their use of particular DLLP language features. For example, a first-grade teacher said that she spent the year focusing on one feature because *"it takes time to see those large gains"* with first graders. This teacher chose sophistication of sentence structure as the feature to work on with her students. As the teacher noted, first-grade teachers are *"responsible for reading foundational skills, and that includes comprehension and writing,"* and she wanted to focus on *"one thing and making sure that one thing gets really good in first grade."* This teacher felt that she could pass her first graders, with their gains in sentence sophistication, on to the next teacher, *"where second grade can take that and [the students] can write those expanded sentences and stick with that one topic even though there's only three sentences."* Second-grade teachers *"can help [students] turn that into multi-paragraphs, but [students] have to be very good at expanding those sentences first."*

This lesson of sustained commitment was underscored by the demonstration school teachers who, at the end of one year, decided to continue their DLLP work for another school year. While these teachers felt they had gained in confidence after a full school year of meeting and focusing on language development and formative assessment, they believed that their expertise could be exponentially increased if they capitalized on another year of working together in their CoP. The school's leadership valued the commitment the teachers were willing to make and supported the teachers' continued focus, paying attention to how their practice was progressing and how students' language development was moving forward.

District Leadership Support Matters

District leadership was also instrumental in the success of DLLP implementation in the public schools. The initial meetings between school leadership and DLLP researchers were coordinated by the district. Everything from the DLLP implementation calendar to coming up with creative ways to support professional learning and compensating teachers was district-driven.

A pivotal piece of district leadership was determining, with school leadership, which teachers would be approached to participate in the DLLP pilot implementation. These invitations were issued based on those teachers who the district and school leadership thought would follow the DLLP implementation through its full course, from obtaining the necessary professional learning to recording student data and scheduling to participate in DLLP CoP meetings.

Once teachers were selected, the district set up a time to meet with the teachers and brief them on the details of the work they would be embarking on. The district leaders scheduled and participated in professional learning meetings for the teachers with DLLP project personnel and compensated teachers for their attendance.

As a result of district leadership actions, from the outset of the project, it was clear to both school leaders and teachers that the DLLP implementation mattered to the district. The leadership from the district completed the important alignment in commitment from the district to the school to the classroom. Teachers were left in no doubt about the support for their work in trying out new practices and learning from their DLLP implementation, and we believe that it was a motivating factor in teachers' willingness to develop new knowledge and skills, even though they found the work challenging at times.

At the culmination of the DLLP project, the district coordinated a gathering of DLLP personnel and county, district, and school leadership. The meeting was held to discuss the DLLP project experience, impressions of the results, and future considerations for research and practice.

Intermediate Agencies Have a Role

During the DLLP project, the role of the local intermediate agency—in this case a County Office of Education (CoE)—was to ensure the entire project was conducted effectively and with sufficient support. To these ends, the CoE sent two of its instructional leaders to support the DLLP implementation by observing classrooms, assisting teachers in their initial recordings of student oral language, and maintaining direct communication with DLLP personnel. Additionally, CoE leadership was present at the monthly DLLP CoP meetings to provide support toward the public school pilot implementation. CoE leaders helped facilitate the meetings and shared notes and impressions with DLLP personnel. The CoE maintained a vested interest in the project and how its outcomes related to other English learner students in its jurisdiction.

Overall, the successful planning, implementation, and outcomes of the DLLP approach to language development and formative assessment were the result of a concerted effort by myriad individuals. From the CoE through the different levels of district and school leadership and the teachers and students involved, every consideration was made about how to best use resources in conducting a successful implementation. Open communication, sustained support, and teamwork all played pivotal roles in making the DLLP approach a success.

In Section 2, we turn to the CoP model that we adopted for the DLLP implementation. The goal of this section is to provide background about the collaborative professional learning structure that will support teachers' DLLP implementation.

Section 2: Engaging in a CoP

Defining CoPs

People have always worked collaboratively. Collaborative groups are formed to pool knowledge, share skill sets, more equitably divide tasks, and create solutions that would not be possible for individuals working alone. Educators experience a multitude of collaborative groups that are organized in many ways.

The term *community of practice* is usually attributed to Jean Lave and Etienne Wenger. They argued that individuals learn in social contexts with other members of their communities who share common goals (Lave & Wenger, 1991). A CoP can occur in any context and is a group of people who share information, insights, tools, and experiences about a common interest or subject (Wenger, 1998). Within a CoP, group members interact regularly to learn from one another. A CoP is focused on knowledge exchange and growth (Wenger, McDermott, & Snyder, 2002), rather than the completion of work products or tasks.

In a CoP, learning is situated within the group's context, members' personal experiences, and their relationships (Lave & Wenger, 1991). In the case of teachers, learning is situated in schools and classrooms, is developed through relationships with other teachers, and is focused on the specific experiences that take place with students and colleagues.

CoPs Support Effective Professional Learning

Implementation of the CoP model for teacher professional learning has been well-documented (Buysse, Sparkman, & Wesley, 2003; Wesley & Buysse, 2001) and adopted by key educational and research organizations (e.g., *Up Close: Redesign PD Community of Practice*, 2016) as an effective structure for school-based teacher professional learning. CoPs also align with Learning Forward's *Standards for Professional Learning* (Killion & Crow, 2011), which describe key characteristics of effective professional learning as ongoing, connected to practice, aligned with school and district goals, and collaborative.

The use of a CoP as a professional learning model also reflects a key idea emerging in the professional development literature: teacher agency, as noted in a recent report from Learning Forward and the National Council for Teaching and America's Future (Calvert, 2016):

> In the context of professional learning, teacher agency is the capacity of teachers to act purposefully and constructively to direct their professional growth and contribute to the growth of their colleagues. . . . Teachers who have agency are aware of their part in their professional growth and make learning choices to achieve those goals. (p. 4)

This perspective resonates with our earlier recommendations about teacher choice in the language features they focus on (see Chapter 2) and also the kind of leadership support for teacher learning described in Section 1 of this chapter.

The CoP approach is one of many professional learning models that can be effectively applied in school settings. Teachers may be familiar with similar models, such as inquiry teams, professional learning communities or teams, lesson-study groups, student study teams, or Looking at Student Work groups. When implemented well, the CoP approach has similarities with many of these professional learning models. However, what sets the

CoP apart from other approaches, and why we selected it, is that it provides a learning experience for adults through participating with others in joint activity for the purpose of increasing knowledge and skills in teaching. Just as students learn from interacting with others, so, too, do adults. The CoP model promotes discourse; allows all teachers to participate equitably, based on their current levels of expertise; and supports educators in inquiry, reflection, and refinement of classroom practice.

Guiding Principles of the DLLP CoP Model

Essential features of the DLLP CoP model are informed by findings from the DLLP implementations and support teacher learning and agency in the following ways.

Establishing a Specific Focus for Learning

Teachers establish a specific focus for learning that guides their application of key DLLP practices and is based on each teacher's context and students' needs. This focus changes over time as teachers gain expertise.

Creating Shared Capacity to Support English Learners

Teachers focus their activity on the language needs of EL students, with the goal of advancing language learning through daily instructional actions to move language learning forward. Teachers learn to use learning progressions that can help them identify appropriate next steps in instruction for EL students at any point on the DLLPs.

Using Evidence of Student Learning

Teachers share, build on, and generate new knowledge about effective language development using evidence of student learning from their own classrooms. Student evidence grounds teacher dialogue and the use of pedagogical responses that enhance students' language development.

Thinking Together

DLLP implementation agendas are designed to support teachers to think together, a collaborative process through which teachers focus on not just understanding an issue but thinking it through from different perspectives to develop new knowledge and new ways to approach future classroom practices related to language development. Research points to thinking together as a critical element of a CoP implementation and sustainability (Pyrko, Dörfler, & Eden, 2015), or what brings a CoP to life.

Using Learning Routines and Meeting Protocols

DLLP implementation agendas are grounded in the use of learning routines and meeting protocols, which provide guiding questions and structures to examine new conceptions of teaching and learning. These routines are revisited over time as teachers gain expertise and confidence to use the DLLPs across multiple features. The learning routines support equitable learning, a focus on inquiry, and deeper analysis of key concepts.

Formatively Assessing Students' Language Development

Teachers co-construct opportunities to formatively assess students' language development and consider pedagogical action, including feedback to students, to take next steps in learning. Exploring pedagogical responses that best support students' next steps in learning along the DLLPs and to develop strategies and approaches for effective feedback is a central learning activity within the CoP.

Sharing Ownership of the Team Process

The CoP requires shared ownership of the team process, with a particular focus on equitable learning for all group members. It is critical that all group members have equal opportunities to advance their DLLP practices, such that more expert teachers provide guidance and ideas about practice to less expert peers, and less expert teachers bring new perspectives into the community. If more expertise is needed on a specific topic, group members can decide to bring in an outside member on an as-needed basis (e.g., a middle school mathematics teacher can be invited to talk about content language expectations that elementary school teachers should be working toward).

Ensuring Structures and Time for Implementation

Significant shifts in how teachers and students learn take time, and systems must ensure adequate structures and time for DLLP CoP implementation. Meetings are scheduled for a minimum of 60 minutes once per month, and learning routines contribute to efficient use of meeting time.

Vertical Team Structure

CoPs thrive when there are multiple perspectives at the table. As we saw in our DLLP implementations, vertical team structures offer varied perspectives of language learning as language develops across multiple grade levels.

Supporting Teacher Learning During the First Year of Implementation

As a result of observations during implementation of the DLLPs, we anticipate that in the first year of implementation, CoP meetings will shift over time to become more

- specific to the individual learning needs of teachers and students,
- driven by teacher inquiry, and
- focused on teacher feedback to refine new and emerging practices.

To support these anticipated shifts during implementation of the DLLPs, we provide three CoP agendas in Appendix 7A. Each agenda follows a similar outline, uses dialogue routines, and promotes teacher inquiry and goal setting. The agendas are structured to meet teachers' needs as they develop knowledge in use of the DLLPs and in practices that support collaborative teacher learning. The three agendas are samples only. Since a goal of the CoP is to encourage teachers to consider and apply what will work most effectively for their own learning, we encourage teachers to revise these agendas in ways that will be most useful in their contexts.

The Use of Meeting Protocols

Meeting protocols are structured processes designed to promote efficient and meaningful communication and learning. Their use ensures that all voices in a group are heard and that there are multiple opportunities for listening, reflection, and feedback. Using protocols appropriately helps teachers build the culture and skills for productive collaborative work. The protocols used in the CoP agendas are "timed"; they involve having a specific time limit in which to speak and asking that listeners do not speak at certain times. While this can feel awkward at first, teacher members and/or facilitators are encouraged to keep to the protocols whenever possible. The benefit is that the DLLP CoP meeting protocols

- promote equitable participation by all group members,

- create an environment of trust where participants are encouraged to ask questions and give and receive feedback,

- ensure adequate time to consider evidence of learning as it applies to the DLLPs,

- explore different perspectives and ideas about language learning, and

- provide opportunities for teacher reflection and analysis of next steps in their own learning.

The Use of Inquiry Questions

Inquiry is at the heart of CoP meetings. Using inquiry questions to structure the meetings supports teachers to fully explore one another's learning and draw connections between what they are learning about the DLLP approach to supporting language development through formative assessment, and how they will apply this new knowledge and these new skills in the content classroom. Each agenda item includes a starter set of inquiry questions, which can be posted and shared during the meeting. Facilitators or teachers leading the meetings can use these questions, write their own, or have participants identify areas of inquiry to guide their own learning. The opportunity to practice using inquiry to guide learning provides another mechanism for teachers to intentionally practice new ways of learning together.

Launching the DLLP CoP

Leaders found it helpful to meet with all participating DLLP teachers prior to implementation to outline key goals and expectations for the project and to define roles and responsibilities. Leaders should be able to tell teachers what the goals of this initiative are and how the initiative aligns with current school improvement work. Teachers will want to have an understanding of the CoP model, when they will meet, and how those meetings will be structured. And they will also want to know what supports they may receive throughout the project as they are learning new skills and knowledge—in particular, how school leaders and/or academic coaches will be involved and will support them as they work to rethink how language learning takes place in their classrooms.

We now turn to the role of leaders in the CoPs.

Leading the CoP

It is very difficult to shift norms of professional learning in schools. Teachers' experiences of professional learning are generally poor. A recent survey of 1,600 teachers indicated that the majority of teachers characterize professional development as irrelevant, ineffective, and not connected to their core work of helping students learn (Bill & Melinda Gates Foundation, 2014). Moving toward a system in which teachers set directions and guide their own professional learning requires significant leadership support. The DLLP pilot implementations, along with research on professional learning implementation, point to the following leadership strategies to support teachers as they develop knowledge and skills to participate in their DLLP CoP.

Focus CoPs on Instruction

Schools are busy places, and there are many noninstructional issues that require discussion and review. Ensure CoP meetings stay focused on instruction and student learning. Leaders can support this by attending CoP meetings, encouraging teachers to use the agendas effectively, and offering reminders that this is a time set aside for teacher learning and a focus on student learning.

> ## What Leaders Say
>
> The proof is in the process! The DLLP began at [our school district] with a few teachers uncertain of how to move forward. However, the structure of the project, with its priority on consistent communication, and assurance that teachers are meant to plan their instruction as intended without influence from the project, created authentic opportunities to see growth. And growth was evident! The expressed excitement of our teachers as they realized the growth of their students was encouraging and well worth the effort.

Provide Clear Expectations That Describe the Value of Enhanced Teacher Collaboration and Teacher Inquiry

In effective teacher collaboration, teachers seek to learn what they do not yet know, ask questions to inform their learning, and use evidence of student understandings to guide deeper thinking about their own instructional practices (Slavit, Nelson, & Deuel, 2013). Leaders should clearly articulate the expectations of collaborative learning, model the effective use of inquiry, and note when teams are using these skills in ways that promote teacher and student learning.

Support Teachers to Take Risks
and Experiment With New Practices

During DLLP implementation, teachers benefited from sharing and receiving feedback on emerging practices in an environment where it was safe to take risks and share both what worked well and where they needed to further refine their practices. A significant way to ensure that this trust is in place is for leaders to consistently express interest in the CoPs and what teachers are learning, to engage in discussions regarding implementation of new instructional and assessment practices, and to celebrate in ways that honor teachers' emerging understandings about language development and formative assessment during content lessons.

Promote Teacher
Choice and Goal Setting

As mentioned in Chapter 2, pilot implementation found that early DLLP implementation benefited from teachers having a choice as to which DLLP features they considered most important in their classrooms. Similarly, it helped teachers to start small and focus on one language feature at a time. Leaders can offer teachers options as to how to manage their own learning by laying out long-term implementation goals and allowing teachers a choice in how they best meet those goals in their own classrooms and contexts.

What Leaders Say

After three sessions focused on the DLLP with Middletown (NY) teachers, we are starting to see a developing understanding of how these tools can support individualized instruction with English learners. Allowing teachers to work together and assess the work of their own students has been key. For example, an ESL and a reading intervention teacher independently arrived at the same insight for one of their common students—they needed to closely focus on teaching the transitional words that connect ideas. This was a powerful learning moment for the teachers that would not have happened without focused collaboration.

Honor the Complexity of This Work

There is no checklist a teacher can tick off to say that the DLLP approach has been implemented correctly. When leaders hear teachers ask "Am I doing it right?" that is a signal that teachers may need support to understand that this work is complex and that doing it right will look different in each classroom. Teachers need to be encouraged to develop their own routines, data collection tools, and feedback practices to implement the DLLP approach and to deepen practices over time.

Support Teachers'
Individual Classroom
Learning Outside of the CoP

While inquiry and reflection are hallmarks of CoP meetings, teachers require leadership support to address new learning practices within their classrooms. Leaders can support teachers' individual learning by touching base informally with teachers about emerging practices, providing additional academic supports (such as coaching support) to discuss emerging practices, and identifying resources for teachers to use as they explore DLLP implementation.

Clarify and Communicate the Context in Which This Will Be Implemented

DLLP CoPs happen within the context of schools where there are often multiple professional learning initiatives under way. Leaders need to clarify how the DLLP and CoP work aligns with school goals and also with other current and past improvement initiatives.

SUMMING UP

1. Leaders play a critical role in the success of DLLP implementation.

2. Leaders create a professional culture in which teachers feel safe to experiment and take risks.

3. Through encouragement, providing feedback on classroom practice, and participating and modeling in CoPs, leaders show their support for teachers in developing their knowledge and skills.

4. There are major benefits to DLLP implementation when all levels of leadership are aligned in support of it.

5. A CoP is an effective model for professional learning that brings teachers together to engage in inquiry and develop new knowledge and skills.

6. A CoP supports teacher agency, providing opportunities for teachers to decide what they want to focus on and to develop and reflect on their practice in collaboration with peers.

7. There are several guiding principles that ground CoPs and make them effective.

8. Leaders can play a supportive role for CoPs.

REFLECTION QUESTIONS FOR TEACHERS

1. What key affordances (e.g., like-minded colleagues, supportive school leadership, existing professional learning practices consistent with a CoP model) exist in your context for supporting the implementation of the DLLP approach in your school/classroom?

2. Conversely, what major obstacles for implementation of the DLLP approach lie in your path? How might these obstacles be addressed?

3. Have you participated in a CoP for professional learning? What have you found beneficial or less beneficial? Why?

4. What are you looking forward to learning about the DLLP approach to language development and formative assessment in content lessons with your colleagues?

As we stated at the beginning of this book, our purpose in writing it is to increase teachers' knowledge of language development—specifically, explanation skills—so they can better support language learning day by day in their classrooms en route to college and career readiness. We end the book by expressing our hope that the stories we have told, the information we have provided, and our recommendations and lessons learned will inspire teachers to try implementing the DLLPs in their classrooms not simply to *inform* their instruction but to *transform* it. We know from our experience that the investment of time and effort in this new learning will have significant payoff for those the teachers care about most—their students.

REFERENCES

Bailey, A. L. (2017). Progressions of a new language: Characterizing explanation development for assessment with young language learners. *Annual Review of Applied Linguistics, 37,* 241–263.

Bill & Melinda Gates Foundation. (2014, December). *Teachers know best: Teachers' views on professional development.* Retrieved from http://k12education.gatesfoundation.org/wp-content/uploads/2015/04/Gates-PDMarketResearch-Dec5.pdf

Buysse, V., Sparkman, K. L., & Wesley, P. W. (2003). Communities of practice: Connecting what we know with what we do. *Exceptional Children, 69*(3), 263–277.

Calvert, L. (2016). *Moving from compliance to agency: What teachers need to make professional learning work.* Oxford, OH: Learning Forward and NCTAF.

Killion, J., & Crow, T. L. (2011). *Standards for professional learning.* Oxford, OH: Learning Forward.

Lave, J., & Wenger, E. (1991). *Situated learning: Legitimate peripheral participation.* New York, NY: Cambridge University Press.

Leithwood, K., Louis, K. S., Anderson, S., & Wahlstrom, K. (2004). *How leadership influences student learning.* New York, NY: Wallace Foundation.

Pyrko, I., Dörfler, V., & Eden, C. (2015, January). Thinking together: Making communities of practice work. *Academy of Management Proceedings.* Briarcliff Manor, NY: Academy of Management.

Slavit, D., Nelson, T. H., & Deuel, A. (2013). Teacher groups' conceptions and uses of student-learning data. *Journal of Teacher Education, 64*(1), 8–21.

Up close: Redesign PD community of practice; A report from the field. (2016). *JSD, 37*(6), 8–9.

Wenger, E. (1998). *Communities of practice: Learning, meaning and identity.* Cambridge, UK: Cambridge University Press.

Wenger, E., McDermott, R. A., & Snyder, W. (2002). *Cultivating communities of practice: A guide to managing knowledge.* Cambridge, MA: Harvard Business Press.

Wesley, P. W., & Buysse, V. (2001). Communities of practice: Expanding professional roles to promote reflection and shared inquiry. *Topics in Early Childhood Special Education, 21*(2), 114–123.

Appendix 7A

Agendas for Communities of Practice

Agenda A: Initial Learning and Implementation of the DLLP Approach— A Focus on Language Features

Lessons From Pilot Implementation: Rationale for Agenda A

In early stages of implementation, teachers are focused on understanding the DLLP approach: high-leverage language features, language progressions, and formative assessment. First, the focus is on what the language features sound (or look) like in the classroom and how to collect evidence of student learning to document the "best fit." During this stage, teachers are encouraged to start small and choose one language feature to address each month, or for longer if they wish.

Teachers are still exploring the specific elements of the DLLP approach to language development and formative assessment and may need time to focus more on "what this is" than "how to apply this." This early stage is enhanced by teachers having a choice in what they will learn and an opportunity to reflect on the DLLP approach. This agenda focuses specifically on teachers' understanding and use of language features and does not yet focus deeply on the language progressions and formative assessment. These will be covered in more detail in later-stage agendas. In addition, this meeting agenda includes more structure and fewer inquiry questions than the later-stage ones.

Learning Outcomes

- Explore individual and team learning about the DLLP approach.
- Use student evidence to explore DLLP language features.
- Explore next steps for your own learning and use of the DLLP approach.

Agenda A: Typical time frame for initial learning is 3 to 4 months and would be used for the first three or four monthly meetings.

Time Frame	Activity	Purpose	Activity Structure	Inquiry Questions
5 minutes	Review meeting agenda	Identify participant learning expectations	Step 1: Review agenda and meeting goals. Step 2: Participants write and post what they want to address today to support their learning. This can be in the form of questions or statements.	• What content do you want to cover today to support your learning? • What questions do you want to make sure are raised at this CoP meeting?
10 minutes	Identify each participant's learning focus (DLLP element)	Identify DLLP language features focused on in the past month Establish small groups for next activity	Step 1: Participants name the DLLP language feature they would like to focus on/focused on this past month. This information is posted by the facilitator. Step 2: Select small groups of three to four teachers for activity below. As much as possible, group teachers together who will work on/worked on the same DLLP language feature.	• Which language feature(s) did you select to work on this month? • In what contexts (e.g., content area, oral/written language, activities, participant structures) did you observe this language use?
20 minutes	Small-group discussion on language learning by participant learning focus	Share key learnings from work done this past month Develop shared understanding about DLLP language features and the types of evidence to collect from students for specific language features	Step 1: Identify a timekeeper. Step 2 (3 minutes): Participants write down three to four learnings they had this past month. Step 2 (12 minutes): In round-robin fashion, each person has a few minutes to share two to three key learnings about the DLLP language feature he or she focused on in the past month. Teachers may wish to share student evidence they have collected during their turn to share. If participants have questions or observations, they jot them down to ask later.	• What did you learn about student language learning? • How did you think about evidence collection to inform student placement in this language feature? What evidence did you collect that was most useful?

Time Frame	Activity	Purpose	Activity Structure	Inquiry Questions
			Step 3 (8 minutes): The small group has a discussion about what was shared, noting interesting points, similarities, and differences in teacher responses. If questions arose in Step 2, those should be asked during this step. Step 4 (7 minutes): The small group identifies three to four key ideas to share about the DLLP language feature, evidence collection, and interpretation, and writes one per sticky note to post in the next activity.	• What did you learn about your own students' language learning this past month using evidence (student work/ discourse) and the DLLPs?
15 minutes	Large-group discussion on DLLP approach elements	Deepen the group's emerging understandings about the DLLP language features	Step 1: Post the DLLPs of the language features. Step 2 (6 minutes): Each small group briefly reports its findings from the small-group activity, and posts the information on the DLLP language feature it discussed. Step 3 (8 minutes): The CoP has a large group discussion to highlight what members notice about their group's emerging understandings about the specific language features of the DLLP approach.	
15 minutes	Explore "best fit" and next steps for student language learning	Review evidence of student language learning and consider best fit and next steps for their learning	Step 1 (4 minutes): Teachers review the evidence they gathered and brought to the meeting. Teachers write what they have been thinking about "best fit" and note any questions they have about how to collect evidence to identify "best fit."	• What did you learn about student language learning? • Based on this information, what are next steps for student language learning?

(Continued)

(Continued)

Time Frame	Activity	Purpose	Activity Structure	Inquiry Questions
			Step 2 (8 minutes): Working with a partner, review the evidence you brought with you and discuss how you are thinking about "best fit." Discuss, based on this information, what are next steps for student language learning. **Step 3 (3 minutes):** Each team member shares a highlight about what's next for a student based on evidence collected.	
10 minutes	Capture key learnings, set focus areas for the next month	Identify a focus area for the coming month	**Step 1:** Teachers write notes to capture their reflections from the meeting. **Step 2:** Each teacher identifies a focus area for his or her learning in the coming month.	• What were the most challenging aspects? • How can we best support teachers?

Agenda B: Deepening Focus on Language Progressions, Linking to Content Instruction

Lessons From Pilot Implementation: Rationale for Agenda B

As teachers develop familiarity with the specific language features, and how to collect evidence of the language features in the classroom, they will naturally move to deepen their learning in other aspects of the DLLP approach. During the pilot implementations, this second phase of learning included a desire to better understand the language learning progressions and also how the specific language features are integrated with each other and learning academic content. In addition, teachers will begin at this stage to figure out how they'll streamline content and language instruction. These three critical areas may take shape at different times for different teachers. The agenda addresses all three issues simultaneously, though teachers can focus on one or another of these topics with only slight changes to the agenda.

During this stage, the activities are designed so teachers bring student artifacts to the meetings, including audio recordings, written work, and examples of how they are documenting evidence collection. These artifacts are meant to engage teachers in dialogue about how the DLLP approach is being applied in classroom practice.

Teachers may also wish to invite others to the meeting, to share their expertise on specific aspects of this work. Examples of those whose expertise might be solicited for meetings are special education directors, English-language coordinators, ESL teachers, heads of content-area departments (e.g., mathematics, science, history), and vice principals or instructional leaders who should be keeping up to date on how the teachers' professional learning is progressing and what further supports they may need.

Learning Outcomes

- Understand each learning progression for the DLLP language features.

- Develop instructional and assessment strategies to support language learning in the content areas.

- Explore ways colleagues collect and use evidence of language learning in the classroom, and use this information to develop or deepen strategies in your own classroom.

Agenda B: Typical time frame for deepening focus and linking to content instruction is about 3 to 4 months and would be used for the next three to four monthly meetings.

Time Frame	Activity	Purpose	Activity Structure	Inquiry Questions
5 minutes	Review meeting agenda	Identify participant learning expectations	**Step 1:** Review agenda and meeting goals. **Step 2:** Participants write and post what they want to address today to support their learning. This can be in the form of questions or statements.	• What content do you want to cover today to support your learning? • What questions do you want to make sure are raised at this CoP meeting?
25 minutes	Explore what teachers are learning about language learning progressions	"Think together" about how language develops for one of the language features	**Step 1 (5 minutes):** Select one language feature to explore deeply in the next 20 minutes. (This should be a language feature that all the participants have focused on individually in the past few months.) **Step 2 (5 minutes):** Identify key findings that teachers in each grade level have had regarding how language develops for this language feature. Post these findings, by grade level and/or English language development level, to show different types of vertical progression. **Step 3 (10 minutes):** Discuss, in the whole group, what you observe about these progressions. Each teacher may wish to consider how this discussion, which includes teachers from all grades, informs his or her own understanding of development of that language feature. **Step 4 (5 minutes):** In round-robin fashion (and without discussion), teachers identify one thing they will do as a result of this "thinking together."	• How does student understanding of language develop in each of the language features? • What information about early stages of language development do you need to know to support your students? • What information about later stages of language development do you need to know to support your students? • How do you use information about the developmental progression in each of the language features to support student learning? • In what ways do students show awareness of their developmental progress in language learning?

Time Frame	Activity	Purpose	Activity Structure	Inquiry Questions
25 minutes	Explore strategies to increase dual focus on language and content	Develop new strategies to streamline learning and formative assessment of both language learning and content learning	For this activity, teachers will share artifacts of student learning. Artifacts might include audiotapes, examples of student work, planning tools (such as document collection strategies), and/or examples of contingent pedagogy. Teachers will have deeper discussions if they work in groups of three to four for this activity. Complete the following steps for each teacher who presents an artifact. This should take about 12 minutes per teacher. Step 1: Teacher presents artifact, highlights the context for this artifact, and responds to these guiding questions. • Where did I place the student on the DLLPs? • What does this artifact represent in terms of content learning? • What did I do in response to this artifact? Step 2: • Discussion prompt for teacher and colleagues: • What does this artifact raise in terms of how to streamline student evidence about language learning and content learning? • What may be some next steps for this student regarding both language development and the content learning goal? Repeat review for all small-group members.	• How feasible is it for you to attend to this language usage during content instruction? • What strategies would be most useful to you for supporting language learning in the content areas? • How can you streamline your instruction to attend to both language learning and content at the same time? • What are you noticing about how language features develop, alone and/or in concert with other language features?

(Continued)

(Continued)

Time Frame	Activity	Purpose	Activity Structure	Inquiry Questions
15 minutes	Identify areas of growth and next steps in practice	Develop shared understanding of what teachers are learning and where they can be supported to take next steps	Step 1: Have teachers state (without discussion) one language feature where they have seen growth in their students and name one reason they believe this growth has taken place. Step 2: Have teachers state one aspect of the DLLP approach they wish to focus on in the next month and one takeaway from this meeting they will apply in their own classrooms to meet that focus area. Step 3: Go around one more time and have teachers identify one way they can support a colleague's learning focus in the coming month. (This should be specific and targeted to one colleague.)	• What did you learn about your own students' language learning this past month, in particular in areas where there has been growth? • To what do you attribute that growth? • What can you build on to deepen the area of growth you've identified?
10 minutes	Capture key learnings, set focus areas for the next month	Identify a focus area for the coming month	Step 1: Teachers write notes to capture their reflections from the meeting and identify a strategy they can use to support a colleague, as defined above. Step 2: Discuss goals and focus for next meeting.	• What were the most challenging aspects? • How can we best support teachers?

Agenda C: Refining and Deepening DLLP Practices, Integrating Contingent Pedagogy

Lessons From Pilot Implementation: Rationale for Agenda C

As teachers gain knowledge of the high-leverage language features and the DLLP approach, they will be ready to engage more fully with the use of formative assessment to guide contingent pedagogical responses to students during learning. As teachers develop skills in this area, they more directly involve students in formative assessment so students begin to have a role in understanding how to take their own next steps in learning.

In these final stages of learning the DLLP approach, teachers will also deepen connections to how the language features are integrated and support one another. As we saw in the pilot implementations, teachers may begin to explore connections, synergies, and integration, both in terms of how they are supporting the development of language features in the classroom and how they are collecting evidence.

There is no one right way to implement the DLLP approach. Teachers should be encouraged to figure out ways that work best for them, with their own students and in their own classrooms. Sharing examples in meetings at this time should spark new ideas and support refinement of existing practices. Teachers in this stage of learning may realize for the first time that it's just fine to do it their own way and also see why that is necessary. As teachers adopt the DLLP approach for use in new subject areas, exploration and revisions to existing tools and templates will be a key part of implementation.

Learning Outcomes

- Refine instructional and assessment strategies to support language learning in content areas.

- Learn strategies to respond contingently to evidence of learning.

- Identify strategies for students to use evidence of learning to take next steps in their own learning.

Agenda C: Recommended monthly meetings for refining and deepening DLLP practices (unlimited number of meetings, as desired).

Time Frame	Activity	Purpose	Activity Structure	Inquiry Questions
10 minutes	Meeting introduction and review of goals	Identify participant learning expectations Consider ways to support colleagues in their learning	**Step 1:** Each teacher shares a response to the prompt: "With regard to the DLLP approach, something I am wondering about is . . ." **Step 2:** After teachers share what they are wondering about, they each write a brief note about one way they can support a colleague's "wondering" during the meeting. **Step 3:** Review meeting agenda and ensure alignment with ideas that came out during this intro.	• What topics or concepts are on people's minds as the meeting begins? • How might we support one another to explore the ideas that were raised?
15 minutes	Explore two teachers' strategies for evidence collection	Focus on streamlining evidence collection for both content and language learning Focus on refining tools and templates for each teacher's classroom context	During this meeting, two teachers will share examples of how they are collecting evidence of language and content learning. **Step 1:** Two teachers take turns presenting a strategy they have used to collect evidence. During sharing, the teacher reflects on why the tool is structured the way it is and how it has been working to support evidence collection and evidence use. **Step 2:** Colleagues discuss the tools that have been shared, with an eye toward what they can learn from their use. Topics that may come up are • how the tool helped the teacher quickly and efficiently *use* evidence with students, • how the tool was used with students to share evidence of learning, • how the tool supported both language learning and content learning, and • how the tool might be refined or used in other ways.	• What strategies are your colleagues using to document language learning and content learning? How are they streamlining this work? • How do you best document evidence you are collecting about student language learning? How are you able to document student growth in language learning? • What can you do to create DLLP resources or tools that will work well in your own classroom?

Time Frame	Activity	Purpose	Activity Structure	Inquiry Questions
40 minutes	Artifact review, responding contingently to evidence of learning	Explore strategies to respond contingently to evidence of learning during daily instruction	Teachers will work in groups of three to four for this activity. Each teacher turn takes 8 to 10 minutes. Step 1: Each teacher takes a turn to share and discuss an artifact of student work. As the artifact is shared, the teacher will highlight a. evidence of student language development, b. evidence of student content knowledge, c. how the teacher interpreted that evidence, d. what the teacher did as a result of that evidence, and e. how the student used the evidence. Each presentation will be followed by a brief discussion about what this artifact shows. As teachers develop expertise in using evidence contingently, the focus of this discussion will shift from a focus on what teachers do with evidence to a focus on what students do with evidence and, further, how students support one another to learn.	• What strategies do you regularly employ to respond contingently to evidence of learning? • What evidence do you have that these strategies are supporting students to take next steps in their learning? • How have students used the evidence about their learning? • In what ways do students show awareness of their progress in language learning/ their placement on the DLLPs? • How do you use discourse in your classroom? In what ways do you structure discourse for peers to support one another's language learning? Content learning?
10 minutes	Closing reflections and next steps	Focus on identifying next steps and preparing for the subsequent meeting	Step 1: Teachers return to what they wondered about at the beginning of the meeting and identify what they are now thinking about those issues. Step 2: Each teacher identifies an inquiry question for the next monthly meeting, which the facilitator will use to guide planning. Step 3: Teachers identify their own next steps in learning that they will be focused on in the coming month.	• What do you want to focus on next? • What are key next steps in your own learning? • How do you best support the learning of your colleagues?

Launch Activities: An Implementation Checklist

Stage/Timeline	Implementation Tasks
Getting ready	Coordinate with district office and prepare the following: ☐ Write the learning expectations for teachers engaged with the DLLP approach. ☐ Identify teachers to participate in the DLLP implementation (ideal team size is six to eight teachers). ☐ Clarify inclusion of different grade levels for vertical teams. ☐ Outline additional supports available for participating teachers (stipends, release time, English language development or literacy coaching, etc.). ☐ Identify CoP facilitators (teacher leaders, academic coaches, principals). ☐ Define roles and responsibilities for district and school leaders and participating teachers. ☐ Clarify the differences between types of teacher meetings, and define how the CoP is different from other meetings teachers attend.
Launch activities	☐ Invite and finalize participation and team structure. ☐ Establish a schedule for CoP meetings throughout the year. ☐ Communicate the learning expectations for teachers, the importance of collaborative learning, and the CoP structure. ☐ Provide planning opportunities for CoP facilitators.
Launch meeting	☐ Communicate the outcomes and expectations for the work. ☐ Explore the DLLP approach (visit DLLP.org and projectexcel.net/pages/learning-resources-2/). ☐ Identify the importance of "starting small," and have teachers select manageable goals to begin implementation. ☐ Brainstorm and come to agreement on strategies for bringing evidence of student learning to the CoP meeting (audio examples, written examples, use of target students). ☐ Introduce DLLP web resources and tools—"Quick Tool: Description of Target Language Features" (visit DLLP.org/resources). ☐ Develop an understanding among team members that this work takes time and they will be supported throughout the time it takes to learn how to implement the DLLP approach. ☐ Discuss and review CoP ground rules.
Ongoing meetings/early implementation	☐ Introduce additional DLLP resources and tools—"Tools for Documenting Language Features in the Classroom for Formative Purposes" (see Appendix 2B, page 52; also visit DLLP.org/resources). ☐ Use Agendas A, B, and C as guidelines throughout the year and beyond.

Index

A SAGE Publishing Company

Helping educators make the greatest impact

CORWIN HAS ONE MISSION: to enhance education through intentional professional learning.

We build long-term relationships with our authors, educators, clients, and associations who partner with us to develop and continuously improve the best evidence-based practices that establish and support lifelong learning.

Solutions you want. Experts you trust. Results you need.